# ULTIMATE
# MARINE AQUARIUMS

# ULTIMATE
# MARINE AQUARIUMS

## SALTWATER DREAM SYSTEMS
### AND HOW THEY ARE CREATED

## MICHAEL S. PALETTA

MICROCOSM

t.f.h.

PROFESSIONAL
SERIES™

**T.F.H. Publications**
One T.F.H. Plaza
Third and Union Avenues
Neptune City, NJ 07753
www.tfh.com

This book has been published with the intent to provide accurate and authoritative information
in regard to the subject matter within. While every precaution has been taken
in preparation of this book, the publisher and author assume no responsibility for
errors or omissions. Neither is any liability assumed for damages resulting
from the use of the information herein.

ISBN 1-890087-74-2

Printed and bound in China

**Library of Congress Cataloging-in-Publication Data**

Paletta, Michael S.
    Ultimate marine aquariums: saltwater dream systems and how they
        are created / Michael S. Paletta.
        p. cm.
    ISBN 1-890087-74-2
    1. Marine Aquariums. II. Title.

SF457.1.P359 2003
639.34'2—dc21                                                    2003041004


Designed by Eugenie Seidenberg Delaney

Co-published by
Microcosm Ltd.
P.O. Box 550
Charlotte, VT 05445
www.microcosm-books.com

*To my loving wife and children for their patience
and understanding*

*to my parents for their love and unquestioned support*

*and especially to my fellow hobbyists, without whose willingness to
let me into their homes and share their passions and secrets,
this book would not have been possible.*

# Contents

*The author's 550-gallon reef in his home near Pittsburgh, Pennsylvania. Dramatic advances in the state of marine aquarium keeping in the past decade have come about, he says, because many aquarists—including those whose systems are profiled in these pages—have freely shared their discoveries and husbandry "secrets" in books, magazine articles, aquarium society gatherings, and online exchanges.*

# Acknowledgments

I AM MOST GRATEFUL FOR THE ENTHUSIASTIC COOPERATION and support of many individuals throughout the marine aquarium world who have freely shared their experiences and suggestions with me.

My sincere thanks go to: Parker Adams, Tip Airey, Sam Angil, Vince Apauron, Adam Atassi, Ed Bauman, Eric Borneman, Don Burdick, John Burleson, Tony Calfo, Herm and Annabelle Canil, Dr. Bruce Carlson, Ted Chua of All Seas Marine, Eric Cohen of Sea Dwelling Creatures, Ron Coleman, Gregg Cook, Chris Cortese, Jamie Cross, Charles Delbeek, Dustin Dorton, Svein Fosså, Dale Fox, Bob Goemans, Ray Greco, Dirk Griffith, LeRoy and Sally Jo Headlee, Bob Hecht, Dave Herr, Dr. Rob Hildreth, Greg Hiller, Richard Hoffman, Linda Hoffmeister, Ron Hunsiker, Bob James, Salty Dave Jancetic, Kelly Jedlicki, Sanjay Joshi, Dave Kearney, Stuart Keefer, Doug Kevis, Deanna King, Millie Klevens, Daniel Knop, Irwin Korzin, Steve Kubrick, Jack Lentz, Dr. Peter Linden, Matt Littleton, Kurt Loos, Jeff Macaré, Bob Mankin, Joy and Gary Meadows, Greg Meeker, Scott Michael, Rob Miller of ERI, Martin A. Moe, Jr., Patrick Monaghan, Edmund Mowka, Gary Myers, Jim Newman, Alf Jacob Nilsen, Des Ong, Beth Paletta, Teresa Elaine Pallone, Burton Patrick, Bill Pauley, Dick Perrin, Marcus Resch, Dana Riddle, Brad Rosen, Greg Sachs, Jerrold Savaard, Greg Schiemer, Mark Scott, Wayne Shang, Terry Siegel, Greg Smith, Bob Stark, Howard Swimmer, Leng Sy, Sam Tabora, Ed and Brian Taimuty of Wet Pets Pet Shop, Petra Talley, Pablo Tepoot, Perry Tishgart, Sue Truett, Frank Tosto, Jeff Turner, Steve Tyree, Tony Vargas, Jeff Voet, Jim Walters, Bob Wilkens, Dave Wodecki, and Joe Yaiullo.

Many other associates played a role in assembling this book, and I wish to thank Alesia Depot, Eugenie Seidenberg Delaney, Alice Lawrence, James Lawrence, and everyone at Microcosm for making this book a reality.

# Introduction

*Scarcely imagined even a decade ago, home reef aquariums, such as this outstanding 700-gallon system created by Wayne Shang of Fremont, California, are now filled with living, growing, thriving stony corals and other marine organisms once thought impossible to keep in captivity. (Profile, page 128.)*

ONE NEED NOT GO VERY FAR BACK into the history of marine aquariums to uncover a painful secret: however startling in color, rarity, and price, saltwater fishes and invertebrates seldom survived long in captivity. Not for nothing was this considered a hobby requiring deep pockets and a willingness to attempt the impossible. Early marine aquarists stubbornly replaced specimens that died, even while searching for ways and means to keep their animals alive and well.

During the last 15 years, advances made in marine aquarium husbandry have been nothing less than breathtaking. Many corals and fishes that were once widely thought impossible to keep are now not only surviving in our captive systems, but are in many cases reproducing on their own or being propagated by amateur aquarists.

These achievements have come, for the most part, as the result of trial and error by tinkerers, experimenters, and small-scale entrepreneurs. Many lessons have also been borrowed from marine biologists, as the natural processes and conditions that exist on the world's coral reefs have come to be better understood. Early marine tanks did little more than borrow equipment from the freshwater world—airstones and floss filters, feeble lights more appropriate to a dimly lit jungle stream than shallow reef waters in blazing tropical sun.

Step by step, aquarists unraveled the mysteries of biological filtration, discovered the importance of vigorous water circulation, learned that lights brighter than anything ever used over freshwater aquariums made important differences. Anecdotal reports of what did and did not work—shared in magazines and by word-of-mouth and a few books—played a significant role in guiding the evolution of the hobby.

In science, one of the means for proving that something works is by having others replicate it. Unfortunately, much time and effort has been expended trying to replicate one ballyhooed methodology after another, many of them ultimately yielding inadequate results or poor prospects when implemented over the long term. Even today, wildly divergent techniques are being used by many home aquarists, often with mixed results.

While communication today is much improved—via the Internet, better books, marine aquarium societies, and conferences—the designs and parameters of a significant number of successful marine systems have not been pooled in one place to demonstrate what does and does not work. With corals particularly, the factors that are crucial to optimize growth rates, coloration, polyp extension, and other measures of health have not been closely examined to see what is working over a representative sampling of successful systems.

The genesis for this book came out of my own travels around the United States, Canada, and Europe, where I have been fortunate enough to see many outstanding marine aquariums, including those in this book. While viewing these tanks, I found many methods and surprises, but there was one factor in common: these owners were conscientious about their systems and their animals. Many could be described as showing almost fanatical attention to detail, and all were able to describe the equipment used, the livestock in the tank, and the parameters of the water without having to look at the log.

There is a saying that "nothing good ever happens fast in a marine tank," and for the most part, the level of success achieved in these tanks was not accomplished overnight, but rather through trial and error over time. In many cases, the owners had gone through a series of ever-larger tanks, improving their equipment configurations, choices of fishes and corals, and husbandry techniques along the way. By sharing their techniques, they may well help many others find success more quickly and avoid unnecessary mistakes.

These hobbyists range from doctors, dentists, and lawyers to professional aquarists. There are nuclear engineers and chemists and a college student. They range in age from their mid 20s to their mid 50s. Only a few systems represented are owned or cared for by women. Once virtually an all-male hobby, marine aquarium keeping is just beginning to attract more women, and I hope that future editions of this book will include more of their setups.

Despite the busy lives and careers of the hobbyists whose tanks are shown here, they all have a genuine passion for what they are doing, and all spend time with their tanks on a daily basis. In interviewing them, I found their intimate knowledge about their systems and livestock quite startling. They know when things do not look quite right as well as where everything is supposed to be. As a result, they often are able to head off a problem before it becomes too serious or shift a coral being attacked by another before it is seriously damaged.

In addition to their beauty, each of the tanks chosen for this book had something unique or instructive going on. I looked for, and found, a wide

*"Step by step, we unraveled the mysteries of biological filtration, discovered the importance of vigorous water circulation, learned that lights brighter than anything ever used over freshwater aquariums made important differences."*

range of filtration approaches, lighting systems, and water circulation systems. Some stood out for their choices of corals or fishes. One of the intangibles of a marine aquarium is its ability to hold a visitor's attention. The health of the fishes and corals as well as the aquascaping plan are crucial, but some tanks just have the ability to captivate viewers. Most are simply wonderful to watch, full of interesting livestock and with something new to notice on each visit.

During the compilation of this book, I was able to collect data and background information from 50 very successful marine aquariums. The photographs of each tank, along with the descriptions of the equipment and methodologies used, should provide capable aquarists with the ability to replicate these systems. Water parameter data can be used to track the effectiveness of the equipment and the scheduled maintenance activities. I hope that these photographs also demonstrate the level of success now achievable using various standard reefkeeping approaches. This should help put to rest some of the theoretical explanations so commonly espoused as to what factors are necessary for a successful marine aquarium.

## ANALYSIS OF PARAMETERS

Initially this book was meant to be a photo compilation, but the data collected from the system owners seemed too valuable to leave unexamined. Having analyzed the accumulated information, I was able to discover which factors were truly critical for success—and which were not. Some of these finding are straightforward and a good confirmation of things we've known or suspected for some time. Others are a little startling.

The display aquariums range in **size** from 40 gallons to more than 20,000 gallons. Ignoring the largest and smallest, the average size is 260 gallons. While this is larger than the tanks of most hobbyists, bigger systems are definitely becoming much more common than was the case as little as 10 years ago. At the time of data collection, the newest of the tanks was slightly over a year old, while the oldest systems had been up and running for more than 12 years. Many of these tanks are newer and bigger editions of earlier tanks. This is due to a number of factors including the fishes and corals outgrowing the previous tanks, consolidation of several smaller tanks, or the tank's owners moving into more spacious homes or workspaces. By the same token, it should also be noted that a number of these tanks are no longer set up in the configurations shown in these images. This is a consequence of various factors, including hurricanes, changes in personal circumstances, or job relocations. Lives changes, and so do the aquariums that accompany them.

An analysis of the **livestock** showed that 56% of the tanks house small-polyped stony (SPS) corals predominantly, while 20% are dominated by soft corals and large-polyped stony (LPS) corals. Twenty-two percent have a relatively equal number of soft and SPS corals. One tank houses live rock and fishes only.

In terms of **filtration** or general methodology, almost 85% of the tanks use a protein skimmer as their primary means of filtration and would be classified as "Berlin" in their general approach. Interestingly, 40% of these tanks also utilize a refugium of some type as part of the system—either in their sump or as a separate unit. This is not part of the classic Berlin formula and is a dramatic change in philosophy that has developed over the past few years.

Algae or some other "natural"—rather than equipment-driven—approach for filtration is used in 8 (16%) of the tanks. This appears to be a move toward

*"Interestingly, 40% of these tanks also utilize a refugium of some type as part of the system—either in their sump or as a separate unit. This is not part of the classic Berlin formula and is a dramatic change in philosophy that has developed over the past few years."*

more natural methodologies, as evidenced by the low number of bare-bottomed tanks. Only 10% of the tanks use no substrate, which further illustrates the move to natural means for nutrient export though the use of bacteria and microfauna in beds of calcium carbonate substrate, usually coral sand or gravel.

As for **filtration adjuncts**, three-quarters of the systems utilize activated carbon to some extent to remove excess nutrients through adsorption. In some cases, carbon is employed continuously; in others, it is used periodically for a number of days each month. The rationale for using activated carbon is to remove dissolved organic wastes and thus provide maximum light penetration. Carbon is being used in both Berlin and natural-style systems.

A large majority—92%—of the tanks are given regular **water changes** for the export of nutrients. The percentage of water changed in these tanks ranged from 1 to 57% each month, with the average being 17% monthly. The high percentage of water changes differs from the well-publicized anecdotal reports of some hobbyists never doing water changes. It appears that there is a strong correlation between the regular performance of water changes and being successful with a marine aquarium. Curiously, the average amount of water changed is not as great as might have been expected. This may be due to the meticulous care given to the tanks (e.g., not overfeeding, using efficient nutrient-control systems), making large monthly water changes unnecessary.

Although higher-tech **control and monitoring systems** are now available, the equipment employed on these tanks varies greatly. Several systems use multiple monitors and computers to track and control aquarium conditions, but these are far from the norm. Most systems are largely owner-controlled,

*Considered by many to be one of the most spectacular home aquariums in the world, David Saxby's 1,500-gallon reef aquarium in London, England, displays the current state of the art in keeping marine fishes and corals. (Profile, page 184.)*

*Proof that coral reef organisms can grow and thrive for years in well-kept home aquariums, Professor Terry Siegel's Provincetown, MA, reef is filled with fishes and corals that have lived under his care for up to 15 years. Note the exceptional colony of Turbinaria, or scroll coral, at center. (Profile, page 27.)*

with simple appliance timers used to switch lights on and off. One system is so balanced that the only technology devices to be found are a powerhead and lighting timers—no skimmer, overflow, or sump is employed—making a statement of elegant simplicity.

The optimum artificial **lighting** for a reef tank—in terms of spectrum, total wattage or intensity, duration of the photoperiod, etc.—is the subject of ongoing debate within the marine aquarium community. It is fascinating to see what is actually working in this sampling of outstanding systems. Of the 42 tanks housing SPS corals, about 20% (8) tanks are using metal halide lamps exclusively. The color spectrum of the bulbs clearly tends toward a whiter or more bluish light, although there is no single formula for success. One system uses 6,500 K bulbs exclusively, 2 tanks use 10 K bulbs exclusively, and 1 tank uses 20 K bulbs exclusively, with the remainder using mixed metal halide combinations. It is also interesting to note how few tanks use 6,500 K bulbs, which cast a yellowish light, exclusively for lighting, despite reports that these bulbs produce maximum photosynthetically active radiation (PAR) and accentuate growth in SPS corals. Just 12% (5) of the systems profiled employ only fluorescent lamps. These systems demonstrate that corals will thrive without metal halide lighting, but it should be noted that the tanks lit by fluorescent lamps are running with more than 5 watts per gallon, on average, which may help to account for their success.

The remaining majority, almost 70% of the tanks, use a combination of metal halide lamps and fluorescents for illumination. Of these, 14 use 6,500 K lamps with actinics, 12 use 10 K lamps with actinics, and 2 use 20 K lamps with either actinics or daylight tubes. In addition, 1 tank uses a combination of different metal halides along with fluorescent lamps.

A more surprising result from this survey was how much light some of these tanks have over them. The conventional wisdom is that 4 to 5 watts of light per gallon will produce optimum coral coloration and growth. Some of these aquariums have 8 or even 10 watts of light per gallon of artificial illumination, which is significantly more light than traditionally recommended. Disregarding the 20,000-gallon mixed tank that has only 0.9 watts of light per gallon, the average amount of light on the SPS tanks is 6.45 watts per gallon. The amount of light ranges from 1.9 to 21 watts of light per gallon. The higher than expected average shows that more light is probably better. Once slowly acclimated to this lighting regimen, corals seem to respond with significant growth rates and bright coloration.

One other aspect of the lighting that should not be overlooked is the photoperiod. The full dawn-to-dusk daylength in the Tropics, where our livestock originates, is 12 hours, with several hours of very intense light at midday. The total photoperiods in these captive systems ranges from 8 to 14 hours, with an average of 9.8 hours. The maximum intensity photoperiod, during which all lights are on, ranges from 1.5 to 10 hours. Considerable experimentation is still being done with photoperiod manipulation, with no hard-and-fast rules yet established.

While lighting is a major consideration in the planning of a new marine aquarium system, **water movement** is often an afterthought or completely neglected. It shouldn't be. If one thing distinguishes the systems in this book from the tanks of "average" marine hobbyists, it is water circulation. The total volume of water moved per hour within many of these tanks is much greater than that seen in many other systems of comparable size. To establish a measurement method that would work for aquariums with a tremendous range of volumes, I added the total manufacturers' rated flows through all pumps, powerheads, surge devices, etc., in a given system (in gallons per hour) and divided it by the display tank's volume to provide a value I called "total turnover." This is, admittedly, a rather crude measure of water movement as it does not take into account factors such as head (height of water discharge above the pump's level), direction, or randomness of the water movement. These factors are certainly important to the effectiveness of the actual flow throughout the tank, but the total turnover value does provide some relative sense of the water movement. Among all tanks surveyed here, turnover ranged from 4 times per hour to 65 times per hour, with an overall average of more than 17 times per hour. This is significantly higher than normally recommended in most reefkeeping guides. Strong water movement appears to play a significant role in maintaining the health of fishes, corals, and other invertebrates in these captive systems.

Many of these aquarists incorporated wavemaking devices, rotating water returns, and other techniques to create chaotic or random water flows, while reducing the straight, laminar flow seen in basic systems. As increased water movement is less expensive to create and power than more intense lighting, I hope that hobbyists may be inspired by these systems to enhance the currents in their own tanks.

*"The conventional wisdom is that 4 to 5 watts of light per gallon will produce optimum coral coloration and growth. Some of these aquariums have 8 or even 10 watts of light per gallon of artificial illumination, which is significantly more light than traditionally recommended."*

Coral reefs in the wild have exceptionally clear, clean water, and the low **levels of nutrients** measured in these tanks is a hallmark of successful captive reefkeepers. Thirty-six of the 50 tanks (72%) register 0.00 or undetectable levels of phosphate, and those with measurable phosphate have levels averaging 0.036 ppm. These measurements were undoubtedly of inorganic phosphate. It would be interesting to see measurements of organic phosphate, which is more difficult to detect but just as problematic in terms of nourishing algae and inhibiting calcification.

In addition, 26 of the 50 tanks (52%) had undetectable levels of nitrate. Of the tanks that did measure either of these compounds, the range was only 0.1 to 0.2 ppm for nitrate and 0.01 to 0.1 for phosphate. While there are valid questions as to the accuracy, particularly at low levels, of most commercial/hobby test kits, the lack of microalgae and health of the inhabitants in these systems suggests that the measurements reported are probably not far off.

Measurements of numerous **other chemical and physical parameters** were also collected in the survey. These included temperature, specific gravity, pH, calcium and alkalinity. When averaged across all 50 tanks, they provide a standard that any tank can be compared against. The temperature for these tanks ranged from 76 to 82 degrees F, with an average of 78.5 degrees. The specific gravity levels ranged from 1.022 to 1.027, with an average of 1.025. The pH ranged from 7.95 to 8.4, with an average of 8.2. The calcium levels ranged from 300 to 500 ppm, with an average of 410 ppm. The alkalinity levels ranged from 6.5 to 15 dKH, with an average of 9.8. Measurements of other elements, such as iodine, strontium, oxygen, magnesium, etc., were reported from only a small number of tanks, so that optimal or average numbers are not reported here. Beginners may take heart in knowing that most of the experts do not bother to measure these minor and trace elements.

Finally, one of the nonquantifiable observations I've made in visiting these systems involves **coral pigmentation**. Just a very few years ago, displays of live corals exhibiting intense colors were virtually unknown in the aquarium world—including the systems of the world's leading coral biologists. Once aquarists had figured out how to keep stony corals alive in captivity, they were confronted with the fact that most corals took on a brownish coloration. Too often, the only real color in an SPS tank was the purple coralline algae on the rocks.

As the images here show, reefkeeping arts have evolved dramatically, with aquarium corals now beginning to rival the beauty of their wild counterparts. Now not only are the growth tips showing pigments (often the only colored portion of these corals in the past), but now entire colonies are brightly colored. This may be due to better selectivity when the corals are being collected, but improvements in lighting, waste removal, calcium supplementation and improved coral nutrition must be credited.

It is interesting to note that many of the owners of these tanks trade and give away fragments of these corals as a necessity of having to regularly trim specimens that are threatening to overgrow the space allotted to them. Robust growth creates certain new problems, but it has also helped distribute especially beautiful corals around the country—even around the world. Some aquarists consider this insurance of sorts: should something happen to the mother colony, a daughter colony in someone else's tank can return a fragment or two so that the coral can be re-established.

The keeping of coral reef organisms has truly made phenomenal strides in the past decade or so. It is my hope that the images and and descriptions of the many beautiful and successful tanks in this book, along with the data on key parameters, will provide blueprints for others to follow.

For those just starting on a path to having an "ultimate" aquarium, here is an opportunity that pioneering reefkeepers never had. The methodologies followed by the successful aquarists in this book vary widely, but a conscientious approach to providing a high level of care for their marine animals is a common theme. At least in part to help others keep their fishes, corals, and other livestock healthy and thriving, the owners of these systems have freely shared their secrets of success. The equipment and methods are all here, ready to be replicated. The determination to do it right and to be the best marine aquarium steward possible is up to you.

—*Michael Paletta*
*Pittsburgh, Pennsylvania*

*Closer to the appearance of a wild reef than previously thought possible, this 400-gallon reef designed by Robert Dalton of Dublin, California, may signal the next major captive aquascaping advance: giving corals the room to display their natural growth forms and the conditions to bring out their most vibrant colors. (Profile, page 79.)*

# Bulletproof Reef

*A kaleidoscopic mass of corals packed into a rejuvenated 55-gallon aquarium is living proof that a low-tech approach can work.*

## AQUARIUM PROFILE

**OWNERS:** Sally Jo and LeRoy Headlee, Boise, ID. Geothermal Aquaculture Research Foundation (www.garf.org).

**DESIGNER:** Sally Jo Headlee (her first attempt).

**ESTABLISHED:** February 1996 (empty, used 55-gallon tank, Valentine's Day gift).

**PHOTOGRAPHED:** September 2001 and January 2002.

### TANK

**DISPLAY TANK:** 55 gallons, glass.

**DIMENSIONS:** 48" x 12" x 18".

**LOCATION:** Office. This room features all four bulletproof reef systems and several coral tanks for coral cuttings.

**CABINETRY/ARCHITECTURAL DETAILS:** Oak stand and hood. The hood was custom made to hold six lights with two computer muffin fans at each end to extract heat. The hood is divided in half so when the lid is lifted three lights are raised and three remain down on the tank. "I love the design of this hood. It makes the tank a lot easier for me to work with," says Sally Jo.

**SUMP:** 8 gallons (connected to "glug-glug box," holding 2.5 gallons of makeup water).

I T STARTED AS A VALENTINE'S DAY GIFT from husband to wife in 1996, a humble 55-gallon glass tank from an enthusiastic reefkeeper to a spouse with no experience in setting up or maintaining a marine aquarium. The equipment was unsophisticated—inexpensive powerhead pumps, a toy-like skimmer, and none of the state-of-the-art gear favored by so many advanced aquarists. No metal halide lights, no Kalkwasser dosing system, no electronic controllers.

Today the tank is widely regarded as one of the most remarkable in the reefkeeping world. Virtually none of the rock substrate is visible, having been overgrown with hundreds of stony coral colonies interspersed with zoanthid polyps, pulsing *Xenia*, and mushroom anemones. The diversity and coloration of the corals is astonishing, if not outright flamboyant. The animals are healthy and vividly pigmented with polyps fully extended. Visitors invariably go away astounded, and vowing to "borrow" some of the tricks they have just seen.

Located in the office of Sally Jo Headlee in a Victorian home that is the headquarters of the Geothermal Aquaculture Research Foundation (GARF) in a historic district of Boise, Idaho, the 55-gallon reef is noteworthy in a number of ways. It was built on a foundation of man-made rock and has been stocked with captive-propagated coral fragments, rather than wild-collected colonies. While blazing with color, the reef has no large "show" specimens—a curiosity explained by the fact that this system is constantly pruned to yield coral fragments and cuttings to be passed along to other hobbyists.

"I was extremely afraid of my first tank," says Sally Jo, who now calls her

*A base of handmade, artificial rock lies almost completely hidden in a collection of some 200 different growing corals.*

*Serving as a fragment farm, this reef is constantly pruned to supply cuttings for propagation and sale to other aquarists.*

*Lush growths of pulsing Xenia and various zoanthids fill the spaces between stony corals.*

*Remarkably, this intensely colorful and productive system is illuminated with fluorescent lighting only.*

## CIRCULATION

**MAIN SYSTEM PUMP(S):** This tank began with 3 Maxi-Jet 1000's however over the years she has added three more powerheads in the main tank to provide necessary water movement as the tank animals grow and mature. Aquarium Systems manufactures these powerheads, now labeled Maxi-Jet 1200.

**ADDITIONAL PUMPS:** 6 Maxi-Jet 1200 power-heads.

**WAVEMAKING DEVICES:** None.

## CONTROLLERS:

**TEMPERATURE CONTROLS:** None.

**FANS:** The hood was custom made to house two small computer fans with an additional 4-inch fan over the sump and one in the back of the hood. Sally Jo has two room air conditioners in her office, which she operates on the same timer as the lighting system. "We have found from our years of research that keeping the temperature as stable as possible is critical. A difficult task in Idaho where the temperature fluctuates not only from summer to winter but in any given day can change 40°. I am constantly adding or removing a fan to keep the temperature at a steady 78°F."

**HEATERS:** Submersible heater placed directly in the sump.

**CHILLER:** None.

## FILTRATION:

Eco Sand Plenum, GARF grunge (cultured live sand).

**SKIMMER:** Original Sea Swirl skimmer replaced with CPR Bak-Pak hang-on-tank unit. "I do not place a skimmer on my tanks at the beginning stages. Since I use all man-made rock and seed the tank with our grunge, it is important not to skim out any of the beneficial organisms needed to seed the rock and age the tank. With my bulletproof reef tanks I place the skimmer on the tank at about the 6-month stage, paying close attention to the animals and the water parameters. Once I place a skimmer on the tank, I never turn it off or shut it down."

**MECHANICAL FILTER:** None.

**UV STERILIZER:** "I placed this device on the unit when the tank was about 1 year old. (I won it at a tradeshow raffle.) I now firmly believe that a UV sterilizer is a tremendous asset to the overall health and balance of any closed system. Most noticeably, it seems to maintain healthy SPS corals, keeping them disease-free. At GARF we have over 40 separate systems, which gives us the flexibility to test many products, and have found that the tanks with UV sterilizers are able to maintain even the most delicate SPS and LPS coral colonies."

**CARBON:** Never used.

**LIVE ROCK IN DISPLAY TANK:** 90 lbs. Aragocrete (man-made rock) designed and created by Edward Postma.

system a bonsai reef. "LeRoy made me roll up my sleeves and get my hands into that first tank." With the guidance of her husband, Sally Jo has become an accomplished reefkeeper, coral propagator, and aquarium photographer. At least part of the reason why this tank is so successful is the meticulous care that she takes in keeping it picture-perfect for almost daily shooting sessions with a digital camera.

The Headlees used man-made live rock to form the initial base structure. No live rock of any kind was ever placed in the tank. This was done in an attempt to see if a reef tank could be set up using only a live rock substitute made from a simple recipe of concrete and aragonite. By avoiding live rock, the Headlees believe that unwanted algal species as well as coral predators and pathogens were kept to a minimum.

Once this reef structure was in place it was inoculated with LeRoy's trademark "grunge," which is live sand taken from the older, long-established tanks at GARF. This material contains beneficial bacteria, algal spores, microfauna, aragonite rubble, snail shells, and other detritus. After inoculation, the tank was allowed to establish itself without a skimmer for 6 months. This was done so that nutrients were not removed but made available to allow microfauna to proliferate and to let the tank reach a kind of equilibrium.

At the 6-month mark, a small, hang-on-the-tank skimmer was introduced to remove unwanted waste that had accumulated. The only other filtration for this system is provided by a sand bed that has deepened over time from 4 to 6 inches. A UV sterilizer is employed to stop diseases from gaining a foothold.

During the first 6 months, the lighting was kept relatively low, with the blue spectrum being favored. Only three 40-watt fluorescent bulbs were used in a 2:1 ratio of blue bulbs to daylight tubes. This was done to maximize the growth of coralline algae that favor blue light and also to keep microalgae growth to a minimum. At approximately 6 months, the regular fluorescent lamps were gradually replaced with 6 110-watt VHO fluorescent lamps. The tank is now lit with 660-watts of VHO fluorescent light or approximately 11 watts per gallon for this 55-gallon tank. The bulbs used are either daylight (full-spectrum) or actinics, in a ratio of 1:1.

The corals selected for this tank were all taken from cuttings either from other hobbyists or from the GARF broodstock. No wild colonies have ever been added, only fragments. The corals were chosen for their brilliant coloration, to see if over time they would keep their colors, even without metal halide lighting. In the relatively shallow confines of this reef, fluorescent lighting has proved more than sufficient.

To maximize the growth and color of these corals, Sally Jo and LeRoy have attempted to optimize the water conditions as well. The calcium and alkalinity levels are kept at slightly higher levels than normal seawater to promote growth. In addition, the nutrient levels, such as nitrate and phosphate, are kept low. Sally Jo is able to do this by keeping only six fish in this tank and by doing a 10% water change every month. This, coupled with her daily additions of calcium and buffer additives, greatly contributes to the tank's success.

The patience with which this tank was established and the attention to detail in maximizing the conditions for coral growth have paid off. The corals introduced as fragments have had a survival rate of over 90%.

Befitting GARF's nonprofit status, the Headlees readily share the lessons they have learned with the public through the foundation's website, workshops, and speaking appearances. Unabashed promoters of reefkeeping, the methods

*Although it requires regular pruning to prevent territorial battles between different coral species, this reef is an inspiration for aquarists with a limited budget.*

they have learned, and the products they have developed, the Headlees have dubbed these techniques "the bulletproof reef system," and believe it is a simple route for newcomers entering the marine aquarium hobby. They preach a message of using man-made rock and captive-grown livestock both to lessen the pressures on wild reefs and to give aquarists hardy animals that are already adapted to aquarium conditions.

While the number of tanks in her office now numbers six and all call for daily care, for Sally Jo it is a labor of love that has resulted in a tank that only gets more spectacular over time.

**SAND/SUBSTRATE IN DISPLAY:** 40 lbs. GARF grunge (cultured live sand). Started as 4 inches over the plenum and now in places is 6 inches. Much of the addition is empty shells, which provide homes for miniature starfish, copepods, etc.

**SAND/SUBSTRATE IN SUMP/REFUGIUM:** None. "I place all of my supplements, makeup water, and equipment such as heater, UV, and skimmer in the sump or overflow device."

**PLENUM:** Eco Sand Plenum custom made by Corals and Clams. ("We now consider a plenum to be optional under a deep sand bed.")

### LIGHTING:

"I treat each one of my reef tanks as a living, growing organism. As the tank matures, the needs of all the animals increase. I start off my new tanks with low lighting as well as more blue lighting. The focus is to seed my man-made rock with organisms found in our live sand. Coralline algae seems to love low light as well as blue light. With this 55-gallon tank, I started out with three 40-watt bulbs, two blues, one white. My favorite 40-watt bulbs are the Blue Moons and Tritons. They keep their color spectrum until they burn out. A timer allows the bulbs to remain on for about 12 hours. After I notice good coralline algae growth, usually about at the 2-month stage, I add another Triton.

"After the tank has matured and stabilized, I upgrade the lighting. My favorite bulb on the market today is the VHO. The tank that is featured here has six 110-watt Super Actinic VHO bulbs over it. I began adding the 110-watt bulbs to the unit at about 1 year. I slowly increase the lighting, making certain that I do not shock any of the animals. I do this by removing two of the 40-watt bulbs, replacing them with two 110-watt bulbs. I add one 50/50 and one actinic white. In about 2 weeks, I remove the remaining two 40-watt bulbs, place the next two 110-watt bulbs, and adjust the amount of time the lights are on. In about 2 months, I add the next two 110-watt bulbs. For the past 5 years, this tank has had six 110-watt VHO bulbs over it, one white one blue, from back to front. Every 2 weeks, I clean the salt splashes off the bulbs. I change the bulbs every 6 months, making certain to maintain the true spectrum. I change two at a time, waiting about 2 weeks before removing the next two. I mark the date on the bulb so as not to forget when the next bulbs need to be changed. We use the old bulbs on tanks that are being upgraded to VHOs."

**PHOTOPERIOD:** 12 hours.

**NATURAL LIGHT:** "I try to avoid this."

**LIGHTING CONTROLLER(S):** Appliance timer. "Half of my lights come on about a half hour before the others. The same happens at night where half of them go off about a half hour before the remaining three follow course."

*A much-coveted colony of encrusting Montipora with bright green polyps is surrounded by beautiful, featherlike polyps of Anthelia sp., or waving hand coral.*

## SYSTEM PARAMETERS & CHEMISTRY

**WATER TEMPERATURE:** "I keep all of my tanks as close to 78°F as possible at all times. All of the animals seem to do well at this temperature and the *Xenia*s simply cannot thrive at higher temperature."

**SPECIFIC GRAVITY:** 1.023-1.025.

**PH:** 8.2 "I pay a great deal more attention to the animals than to the test kits and have to admit that I rarely use a test kit."

**ALKALINITY:** 4.5 meq.

**CALCIUM:** 500+ "I find that the SPS corals grow much faster and some of the snails reproduce better with the higher calcium levels."

**NITRATE:** Zero or not enough to register a reading.

**PHOSPHATE:** Zero.

**RESINS OR DEVICES USED TO REDUCE NITRATE OR PHOSPHATE:** None.

**WATER SOURCE:** Boise's tapwater.

**SALT:** Aquarium Systems Instant Ocean.

**WATER CHANGE SCHEDULE:** At least 10% every month, or after cutting corals for propagation.

**ADDITIVES OR SUPPLEMENTS USED:** Twice each week: 2 tsp. Seachem Reef Calcium, 2 tsp. Seachem Reef Plus, 2 tsp. Seachem Reef Complete. "My dosing is for a 55-gallon unit, so you will need to either increase it or decrease it depending on the size of your system. The Seachem Reef Plus needs to be kept in the refrigerator. If the tank has a skimmer, I add the Reef Plus first and wait until the skimmer has slowed, down then add the remaining two supplements."

**MAKE UP WATER:** 1 tbsp. (heaping) Seachem Reef Advantage Calcium per gallon, 1 tbsp. (heaping) Seachem Reef Builder per gal. "I use the Seachem Reef Advantage Calcium for 1 week, every day. The next week I use the same measurements and the same daily addition, however I use the Seachem Reef Builder. I repeat this back and forth every week."

**MAINTENANCE SCHEDULE:** "I work with my tanks every day. I average at least 5 hours a day on the six tanks in my office. When we travel, I give my tanks a good haircut (pruning) before leaving as well as make certain that all the corals are securely glued in place. The older the tank becomes, the more each animal matures and thus propagation and placement becomes a daily battle. I also watch closely that each animal is not fighting for placement and has room to grow."

## LIVESTOCK

**FISHES:** 11.

**STONY CORALS:** More than 120 different types.

**SOFT CORALS:** More than 80 different types.

**OTHER LIVESTOCK:** "I like to keep at least 75 hermits and 75 snails to add to the biodiversity and to act as the janitors of the tank. They get into the cracks and crevices I can't reach."

**SPAWNING EVENTS:** Damselfish, hermit crabs, and snails have been observed spawning, and a *Pocillopora* sp. colony has spawned on at least two separate occasions.

## FEEDING

**REGIMEN FOR FISHES:** Fishes get *Spirulina* flake food twice a day ("a big pinch") with occasional feedings of frozen brine shrimp as well as some macroalgae.

## NOTES

**PROBLEMS WITH THIS SYSTEM:**
1. Overflow box and siphon have occasionally been clogged by algae or a snail, causing the tank to overflow onto the floor.
2. "Next time I would start with a brand-new tank, for this one was given with great love but many scratches.
3. "The tank became too full, too fast, and now I have no more room to add new animals."

**THINGS OWNER LIKES BEST ABOUT THIS SYSTEM:** Everything!

**SUCCESSES:** "I have taken over 160,000 pictures and honestly do not feel that any one of them reflects the incredible beauty, color, or movement these animals exhibit daily."

**GUEST COMMENTS:**
1. "You ruined my trip to Belize. When scuba diving I saw nothing like what you have displayed in your closed system in Boise."
2. "How can you ever get any work done with this beautiful tank sitting in your office?"
3. One child sat in front of my tank, looked up at her father, and informed him she never wanted to go back home.

# Species Galore

*The fantastic biodiversity of the coral realm is captured in a modest footprint in this 120-gallon home reef in Los Angeles.*

DIVERSITY OF SPECIES IS A PRIMARY GOAL of many reef hobbyists—a reflection of the mind-boggling assemblage of different organisms on coral reefs in the wild. Unfortunately, accomplishing this in a captive system demands an understanding of the animals' needs as well as a sense of what is aesthetically pleasing. Many reef tanks end up with species incompatibilities that prevent these systems from achieving their full potential.

One look at the 120-gallon reef tank of Leonard Ho, with some 50 species of stony corals and 20 species of soft corals, and it is immediately apparent that a diverse and visually appealing reef can be housed in a relatively modest footprint. The present tank has been established for more than 6 years, and many of the corals and fishes have been in Leonard's systems for more than 15 years. His experience with previous systems allowed Leonard to design a tank that maximizes diversity yet provides a perfect environment for an amazing array of inhabitants.

To maintain this many healthy animals in a tank of this size, Leonard uses the latest and best equipment available, including a large Euro-Reef skimmer. Using 8 to 12 ounces of activated carbon for two weeks of every month, Leonard does only two 30-gallon water changes per year. Even with this below-average schedule of water changes, the nutrient levels have remained low; nitrate is less than 2 ppm and phosphate undetectable. This may in part be the

## AQUARIUM PROFILE

**OWNER:** Leonard Ho
   www.reefscapes.net.
**LOCATION:** Los Angeles, CA.
**DATE ESTABLISHED:** August 1996.
**DATE PHOTOGRAPHED:** November 2001.

### TANK
**CONFIGURATION:** Rectangular.
**DISPLAY TANK VOLUME:** 120 gallons.
**DISPLAY TANK DIMENSIONS:** 48" X 24" X 24".
**DISPLAY TANK MATERIAL:** Glass.
**SUMP VOLUME:** 30 gallons.
**LOCATION:** Living room.
**CABINETRY:** 30 inch DIY pine stand, 15 inch pine canopy.

### CIRCULATION
**MAIN SYSTEM PUMP(S):** Iwaki 30 RLXT (~1,000 gph) and Iwaki 30 RLT (~500 gph).
**WATER RETURNS:** Iwaki 30 RLXT to Sea Swirl. Iwaki 30 RLT through chiller to flared output.
**ADDITIONAL PUMPS:** Tunze 2002.

*Not particularly easy to keep is this delicate hard-tube featherduster worm (Protula bispiralis) (1) a filter-feeder.*

*A favorite fish is this Peppermint Hog (Bodianus masudai), one of several rare species in this aquarium.*

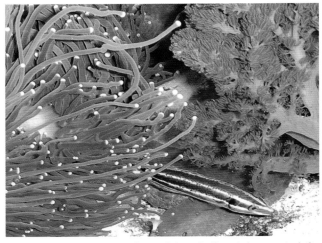

*A large, bright green torch coral (Euphyllia glabrescens), left, resembles an anemone with its long tentacles.*

*Another unusual specimen is a relatively recent discovery, the "Mystery Wrasse" (Pseudocheilinus ocellatus).*

*Contrasting colors and shapes give this tank visual complexity and biodiversity—the goal of many reefkeepers.*

*A much-coveted color morph of the lobed brain coral (Lobophyllia sp.) is an eye-catching specimen.*

*Responding to excellent captive conditions, Leonard Ho's collection of stony and soft corals have put on annual fall mass-spawning displays in recent years.*

result of there being just five fishes in the tank with very limited waste. In addition, eight clams are housed in this tank, and these may assist in scavenging nitrogenous compounds out of the water column.

The tank is lit with more than 10 watts per gallon of artificial light (800-watts of metal halide light and 440-watts of fluorescent light). The corals have responded with incredibly vivid colors and very high growth rates. Calcium is supplied via a Kalkwasser reactor as well as a calcium reactor. Even with all of this supplementation, the calcium is still slightly low, at approximately 370 ppm with an alkalinity at 9 to 10 dKH. These levels are no doubt due to the rapid growth of the corals and their consumption of calcium and carbonate. The levels are stable, however, possibly due to the calcium-based substrate that Leonard uses to cover the bottom of the tank. Water motion is supplied via two external pumps and a powerhead that move approximately 2,000 gallons of water through the tank every hour. This oscillating water movement is created by the use of a Sea Swirl rotating water return from one pump.

There is nothing particularly radical about any of his methodology, but Leonard's attention to detail seems to make this system so successful. His impressive collection of stony corals showcases numerous colonies of brightly colored *Acropora*, *Montipora*, and *Pocillopora* and includes a huge colony of *Montipora capricornis* that was grown from a small fragment and a colony of *Acropora yongei* that has been in Leonard's tanks for over 10 years. A testament to the optimum conditions is the mass spawning in the tank every September by many of the soft and stony corals.

**WAVEMAKING DEVICES:** 1-inch Sea Swirl oscillator.

## CONTROLLERS
**TEMPERATURE CONTROLS:** Neptune. Aquacontroller 2.
**FANS:** Two 4 inch ball-bearing fans.
**HEATERS:** 300-watt submersible.
**CHILLER:** 1/3 hp Aqualogic Delta Star (inline).

## FILTRATION
**SKIMMER:** Euro-Reef CS6-2.
**CARBON:** 8-12 ounces, two weeks per month (fresh each month).
**LIVE ROCK IN DISPLAY TANK:** ~150 lbs. Pacific live rock (mostly Fiji).
**SAND/SUBSTRATE IN DISPLAY:** 200 lbs. Aragonite: 50% CaribSea Seaflor and 50% CaribSea Oolitic.
**AVERAGE DEPTH:** 3 inches; ranging 2-5 inches.

## LIGHTING
**FLUORESCENT BULBS:** Four 110-watt URI VHO Super Actinics powered by IceCap 660.
**PHOTOPERIOD:** 13 hours on average—varies according to AquaController program.
**HOW OFTEN REPLACED:** Every 6 months.
**METAL HALIDE BULBS:** Two 400-watt Ushio 10,000 K metal halides powered by magnetic ballasts.
**PHOTOPERIOD:** 9 hours on average—varies according to AquaController program.
**HOW OFTEN REPLACED:** Every 12 months.
**HEIGHT OF LIGHTS ABOVE WATER SURFACE:** Metal halide: 10 inches. VHO: 8 inches.
**NATURAL LIGHT:** Indirect and minimal.
**LIGHTING CONTROLLER(S):** Neptune AquaController 2.

## SYSTEM PARAMETERS & CHEMISTRY
**WATER TEMPERATURE:** Winter 77 to 79°F, summer 79 to 81°F.
**SPECIFIC GRAVITY:** 1.026.
**PH:** 7.8-8.4.
**ALKALINITY:** 9-10 dKH.
**CALCIUM:** ~370 ppm.
**NITRATE:** <2 ppm.
**PHOSPHATE:** Undetectable.
**MUNICIPAL WATER SUPPLY:** Yes.
**NATURAL SEA WATER:** Yes (Catalina).
**REVERSE OSMOSIS:** Yes.
**DEIONIZATION:** Yes.
**SALT USED:** Instant Ocean, Reef Crystals.
**WATER CHANGE SCHEDULE:** About 30 gallons, twice per year.
**ADDITIVES OR SUPPLEMENTS USED:** Kalkwasser via kalkreactor. Calcium reactor. No others used.
**MONITORING EQUIPMENT:** AquaController 2 for pH.
**DOSING EQUIPMENT USED:** SpectraPure LiterMeter.

## LIVESTOCK
**FISHES:** 5.
**STONY CORALS:** About 50 species.
**SOFT CORALS:** About 20 species (counting polyps and corallimorpharians).

**OTHER LIVESTOCK:** 8 *Tridacna* clams (2 *Tridacna crocea*, 6 *T. maxima*). Various serpulid tubeworms, gorgonians, et al.

**NOTEWORTHY SPECIMENS:** *Bodianus masudai, Amphiprion leucokranos, Pseudocheilinus ocellatus, Zebrasoma rostratum* (10 years old). Many corals well over 10 years old. *Acropora yongei* was among the first imported from Bali.

**SPAWNING EVENTS:** Annually, around September.

## FEEDING

**REGIMEN FOR FISHES:** Mixed diet: Ocean Nutrition Prime Reef (frozen), Selcon soaked *Artemia*, fresh microalgae (harvested from overflow), homemade seafood blend. Fed 1-2 times daily (about 0.75 ounces).

**REGIMEN FOR CORALS/INVERTS:** None.

## NOTES

**PROBLEMS OVERCOME WITH THIS SYSTEM:** I was able to create a successful reef, capable of sustaining a rich diversity of inverts and vertebrates with minimal care required.

**THINGS THE OWNER WOULD LIKE TO CHANGE:**
1. I should have started with a slightly wider and deeper tank. Because of the location (between two "pillars") I am only able to have a 48-inch tank. But I should have gotten a 30 inch wide 28 inch deep tank.
2. I would have designed the tank to be more impervious to water damage and earthquakes (i.e., coating the stand's interior with marine sealant).

**THINGS OWNER LIKES BEST ABOUT THIS SYSTEM:** The diversity of life housed within this small, self-contained ecosystem gives me the opportunity to study and appreciate an exotic and complex interactive community.

**SPECIAL ABOUT THIS SYSTEM:**
1. The successful incorporation of a broad range of species.
2. Rare and unusual species (mostly fishes).

**FAVORITE COMMENTS BY OTHERS ABOUT THIS AQUARIUM:**
1. "Your system is so natural."
2. "I like your aquascaping."
3. Nice comments about coral health and appearance from peers.

**OVERALL POSITIVES:**
1. Species diversity (both "display" and cryptic species); mixture of SPS, LPS, soft, clams, worms, sponges, etc.
2. Inhabitant's health, as exemplified by annual spawning event of multiple species and corals' growth and pigmentation.
3. Ease of care/low maintenance.

**OVERALL NEGATIVES:**
1. Need larger tank size (too small for greater species diversification and housing certain fish species).
2. I would have chosen more aesthetically pleasing cabinetry.
3. I wouldn't have packed some SPS in as tightly.

*Heavy skimming and regular use of activated carbon to remove dissolved wastes and coral toxins is one tactic used to alleviate the pressures of a crowded reef.*

The fishes that Leonard has placed in his tank are well thought out also, each selected for its beauty and rarity. His Black Longnosed Tang *(Zebrasoma rostratum)* has been in his tanks for more than 10 years. In addition to being an unusual sight in North American aquariums, this fish's jet black color appears striking against the brightly colored corals that dominate the tank. In a contrary manner, the rare *Bodianus masudai*, with its long red-and-white-striped body, blends in with the corals, as does the pastel-colored *Pseudocheilinus ocellatus*. Even the clownfish that Leonard has chosen, *Amphiprion leucokranos*, are much coveted by those who appreciate rare fish.

Leonard has been able to create an aquascape that is both pleasing to look at and natural in appearance. The mix of stony corals, soft corals, clams, worms, sponges, and uncommon fishes give this tank the look of a small section of a reef that is sought by many reefkeepers, yet is rarely achieved. Just as impressive is Leonard's claim is that this level of success is possible with very low maintenance. That further supports what is possible if careful planning and the biological requirements of the animals are taken into account when a system is initially set up.

# Godfatherly Reef

*Prof. Terry Siegel's 486-gallon reef is stocked with a number corals and fishes that have been in his care for 10 to 15 years.*

AS ONE OF THE GODFATHERS OF MARINE AQUARIUM KEEPING in the United States, Professor Terry Siegel has been successfully keeping marine fishes and invertebrates longer than most saltwater hobbyists have been driving. Fortunately for all the newcomers, Terry has been more than willing to share his experience and hard-earned expertise both by writing an ongoing stream of magazine articles and by acting as the editor of *The Marine Aquarist* and currently *Aquarium Frontiers* and *Advanced Aquarist's Online Magazine*. In these cutting-edge magazines, Terry provides relevant information for advanced aquarists and helps increase the likelihood of success for even the most inexperienced hobbyist.

Like all of the most highly regarded writers in the marine field, Terry speaks from the hands-on experience of maintaining his own home reefs. When he retired from his active professorship at New York's Pratt Institute of Technology to move to Provincetown, he decided to take the risky step of moving his three well-established, successful tanks and combine them into one larger 486-gallon tank in a new home.

Moves tend to be traumatic for both owners and marine livestock. Only by being well prepared was Terry able to make this 10-hour move without losing any of his charges—many of them having been in his care long enough to considered part of the family.

The new tank has provided a more spacious and beautiful setting for his reef, and it is unique in a number of ways. Unlike most reef tanks, this one utilizes very little live rock. The thinking behind this is simple: the corals are so large that it was not really necessary to mount them on live rock to add to the basic structure of the tank.

## AQUARIUM PROFILE

**OWNER:** Terry Siegel.
**LOCATION:** Provincetown, MA.
**DATE ESTABLISHED:** 1999 (contents from 3 old reef tanks placed into new tank after move from NYC to Provincetown).
**DATE PHOTOGRAPHED:** June 2001.

### TANK
**CONFIGURATION:** Rectangular.
**DISPLAY TANK VOLUME:** 486 gallons.
**DISPLAY TANK DIMENSIONS:** 10' X 26" X 30".
**DISPLAY TANK MATERIAL:** Glass.
**SUMP VOLUME:** 340 gallons.
**CABINETRY:** The tank is set into a wall; the sump is in a room behind the wall.

### CIRCULATION
**MAIN SYSTEM PUMP(S):** Jacuzzi 3/4 hp. About 4,000 gph.
**WATER RETURNS:** Three double-ended returns from Jacuzzi, each splitting into a "Y" in the tank.
**ADDITIONAL PUMPS:** One Gemini, about 1,000 gph.
**WAVEMAKING DEVICES:** Two in 40-gallon refugium.

### CONTROLLERS
**FANS:** Very large fan that turns on with metal halide lamps, but used only in the summer.

## FILTRATION

**SKIMMER:** Marine Technical Concept's HSA 1000.
**CARBON:** 2 lbs., change every two months.
**BIOLOGICAL FILTER:** One.
**REFUGIUM:** 40 gallons, 3 fishes, numerous coral fragments, 2 *Dendronephthya*, 1 tiger tail cuke, 2 green emerald crabs (*Mithrax sculptus*), numerous snails.
**LIVE ROCK IN DISPLAY TANK:** Very little.
**SAND/SUBSTRATE IN DISPLAY:** Aragonite, 3-inch depth.
**SAND/SUBSTRATE IN SUMP/REFUGIUM:** 4-inch oolitic sand bed.

## LIGHTING

**FLUORESCENT BULBS:** Twelve 23-watt power compacts.
**PHOTOPERIOD:** 14 hours.
**HOW OFTEN REPLACED:** Once per year
**METAL HALIDE BULBS:** Six 260-watt 6,500 K Iwasakis.
**PHOTOPERIOD:** 12 hours.
**HOW OFTEN REPLACED:** Once per year.
**OTHER BULBS:** Six compact prism pendants (CustomSea Life).
**NATURAL LIGHT:** None.
**LIGHTING CONTROLLER(S):** Outdoor timers.

## SYSTEM PARAMETERS & CHEMISTRY

**WATER TEMPERATURE:** 75 to 82°F depending on time of year.
**SPECIFIC GRAVITY:** 25.
**PH:** 8-8.3.
**ALKALINITY:** 10 dKH.
**CALCIUM:** 400.
**NITRATE:** Unmeasurable.
**PHOSPHATE:** 0.02 ppm.
**RESINS OR DEVICES USED TO REDUCE NITRATE OR PHOSPHATE:** None.
**WELL WATER:** Yes.
**REVERSE OSMOSIS:** Yes
**DEIONIZATION:** Yes
**SALT USED:** Instant Ocean
**WATER CHANGE SCHEDULE:** 20% every 3 months.
**ADDITIVES OR SUPPLEMENTS USED:** Strontium and Lugol's iodine, every month.
**MONITORING EQUIPMENT:** pH meter.
**DOSING EQUIPMENT USED:** Spectra Pure.
**MAINTENANCE SCHEDULE:** Scrape coralline algae off the glass.

## LIVESTOCK

**FISHES:** 12 large fishes.
**STONY CORALS:** 25 very large corals.
**SOFT CORALS:** 5.
**NOTEWORTHY SPECIMENS:** Average age of fishes is 10 years; average age of corals is 15 years.

## FEEDING

**REGIMEN FOR FISHES:** Heavy flake feeding every day: OSI Marine *Spirulina* Flakes, nori.
**REGIMEN FOR CORALS/INVERTS:** Daily feeding, first into the refugium, which then enters the whole system: ESV's Spray-Dried Marine Phytoplankton, Golden Pearls.

*An intensely colored Achilles Surgeonfish (Acanthurus achilles) swims over the open mantle of a giant clam (Tridacna squamosa).*

One aspect of this tank that is rarely seen elsewhere is the longevity of the specimens: these corals and fishes have all been kept for a relatively long time in captive aquarium conditions. Most of the fishes average at least 10 years of age and most of the corals 15 years. Another unique feature is that it houses fishes that generally are not considered appropriate for a reef system. These include a mix of seven surgeonfishes, a Niger Triggerfish, a Harlequin Tuskfish, and a Navarchus Angelfish. Even with these fishes, the invertebrates are thriving, as demonstrated by the size and health of the *Tridacna squamosa* and *T. derasa* clams, the huge heads of *Echinopora* and *Euphyllia* and the dinner-plate-sized colony of *Turbinaria*. In addition to having much more open space than most reef tanks, this system also has a sump that, at 340 gallons, is almost as big as the display tank itself. The total volume of water no doubt helps to keep the system stable, with low nutrient levels that certainly contribute to the health of the corals and clams.

Unlike most hobbyists, Terry has not been constantly adding or replacing fishes and corals over the years. Instead, he has allowed his specimens the time and space to grow and live to their natural sizes. As a result, his corals look much more like the colonies pictured in books and magazines documenting wild reefs. While most of us think of a 6-inch colony of a stony coral as quite large, this is but a fragment on the natural reef or in Terry's tank, where the beauty of larger, more mature coral colonies can finally be realized. Fifteen-year-old captive colonies are dramatically different in appearance than small colonies and provide a template of what captive raised corals can look like.

Curiously, the usual aggressiveness of the tangs toward each other in smaller tanks is not a major problem in Terry's tank. Their color and health,

*Stony corals the size of this scroll coral (Turbinaria sp.) are rarely seen in home aquariums, requiring both ample room to grow and years of consistently good conditions. The Niger Triggerfish (Odonus niger), right, is uncommon in reef tanks.*

particularly in the Sohal and Achilles Tangs, are as brilliant as any seen on a reef. The large size of the tank and the numerous nooks and crannies provided by the corals may help diffuse the hostility between specimens. Even typically aggressive fishes like the Harlequin Tuskfish and the Niger Triggerfish behave themselves and do not bother their tankmates. The large heads of coral coupled with the large brightly colored fishes give the tank a majestic appearance that is quite unlike that of newer tanks containing multiple small heads of coral. Visitors are prone to being transfixed by the aquatic tableau which has been described as "a living work of art."

**NOTES**

**PROBLEMS OVERCOME WITH THIS SYSTEM:** Moving everything, and aggression among seven surgeonfishes.

**THINGS THE OWNER WOULD LIKE TO CHANGE:** Lower electrical consumption.

**THINGS OWNER LIKES BEST ABOUT THIS SYSTEM:** Very long term success with corals and fishes.

**OVERALL POSITIVES:** Marriage of art and science.

# Hybrid System Reef

*A thousand watts of blue-white light provide a realistic and pleasing underwater look for Jon Kick's 150-gallon display tank.*

## AQUARIUM PROFILE

**OWNER:** Jon Kick
  www.thereptileaddict.com.
**LOCATION:** Pets Plus in Lockport, NY.
**DATE ESTABLISHED:** 1995.
**DATE PHOTOGRAPHED:** August 2001.

### TANK
**CONFIGURATION:** Rectangular.
**DISPLAY TANK VOLUME:** 150 gallons.
**DISPLAY TANK DIMENSIONS:** 48" X 24" X 30".
**DISPLAY TANK MATERIAL:** Glass.
**SUMP VOLUME:** 30 gallons.
**LOCATION:** Fish room of pet store.
**CABINETRY/ARCHITECTURAL DETAILS:** Pine stand and hood.

### CIRCULATION
**MAIN SYSTEM PUMP(S):** Two Rio 2500s.
**WATER RETURNS:** CPR overflow box.
**ADDITIONAL PUMPS:** Two Rio 1500s, two Maxi-Jets.

### CONTROLLERS
**FANS:** Paddle fans in hood.
**HEATERS:** None.
**CHILLER:** In line.

### FILTRATION
**SKIMMER:** EPX 300.

DURING THE PAST DECADE, numerous methodologies have been developed to make reefkeeping easier. Jon Kick of Pets Plus in Lockport, New York, has taken three of these approaches and hybridized them to create an outstandingly successful system. In John's 150-gallon tank, a Jaubert-style plenum is combined with a 6-inch deep sand bed as well as a protein skimmer from the Berlin method. The result is a thriving aquarium that has low nutrient levels despite containing a large number of corals and fishes.

Jon says that the plenum, coupled with the deep sand bed, has allowed him to cover a significant portion of the bottom of the tank with live rock. This cannot usually be done with a classic Jaubert design, which calls for a shallow substrate to be placed over the plenum so that too much live rock does not compact the substrate and allow anaerobic conditions to develop. By having a deep sand bed over the plenum, compacting is avoided and few anaerobic pockets have resulted. This allows the tank to be filled with live rock and corals, in contrast to true Jaubert systems that are sparsely stocked. The use of a protein skimmer and carbon have also kept the yellowing of the water to a minimum, avoiding a commonly seen shortcoming of the plenum system when it is overstocked or when inadequate free space is present above the plenum. The plenum and deep sand bed have kept the calcium and alkalinity levels at normal levels without there being a need for additional supplementation. It should be noted that a monthly 20% water change schedule also helps maintain these levels.

*Once dominated by soft corals, this tank is now home to more than 30 colonies of stony corals blanketing some 200 pounds of Fiji Islands live rock.*

This system initially started out as a soft coral tank, with Jon still uncertain about how successful the use of these combined methods would be. However, once the tank got through an initial break-in period that included a battle with hair and bubble algae, Jon became more ambitious and today large- and small-polyped-stony corals predominate in the system. There are still several brightly colored soft corals in the tank, including a beautiful lime green *Sinularia* that was grown from a cutting.

The tank makes an instant impression on first-time visitors, with the vivid coloration of the corals immediately catching one's eye. The hot pinks of the *Seriatopora hystrix* and the *Pocillopora eydouxi* stand out and contrast beautifully with the green coloration that is so apparent in other species. The luminescent quality of the corals is likely due to the combination of lighting that Jon has chosen. The tank is lit with two 400-watt 10,000 K metal halide lamps as well as two VHO actinic tubes and four 50/50 power compact lights. This combination produces a very clean, blue-white light that makes the tank pleasing to view and seems to intensify the hues of the corals. Jon uses activated carbon, changed monthly, to keep any yellowing from preventing maximum light penetration of the water. The lights are 12 inches above the water's surface, and several of the corals have grown right up to the surface to receive the maximum benefit from this lighting system.

Jon reports that this tank still has occasional bouts of hair algae, but these have been sporadic and self-limiting and are probably traceable to nutrients in the otherwise low-nutrient tapwater he uses. This algae has not hampered the growth of the corals or the overall health of the tank when it has died off. The fish population has also thrived in this system, even though it is only fed twice per week. The fishes are able to feed on a large population of organisms that now reside in the deep sand bed as well as the live rock. Several difficult-to-keep species, including Sunburst or Fathead Anthias (*Serranocirrhitus latus*) and Green Mandarinfish (*Synchiropus splendidus*) are thriving on this microfauna population.

In many instances, hybridizing systems and methodologies has not proved successful for other aquarists. However, as can be seen by the health and vitality of both the fishes and corals in this system, it is possible when done with care and expertise. In this case, it appears to have made a tank that is easier to maintain than most, with fewer supplements and less maintenance.

**MECHANICAL FILTER:** HOT Magnum in sump.
**UV STERILIZER:** 20-watt Emperor Aquatics.
**CARBON:** 1 lb., continuous use, changed monthly.
**BIOLOGICAL FILTER:** 200 lbs. live rock
**LIVE ROCK IN DISPLAY TANK:** 200 lbs. Fiji ultra.
**SAND/SUBSTRATE IN DISPLAY:** 6 inches Florida live sand.
**JAUBERT PLENUM:** Yes.

## LIGHTING
**FLUORESCENT BULBS:** Two 48-inch actinic VHO, four 96-watt 50/50 power compacts.
**PHOTOPERIOD:** 11 hours, replaced every 6 months.
**METAL HALIDE BULBS:** Two 400-watt German 10,000 K.
**PHOTOPERIOD:** 8 hours., replaced every 12 months.
**HEIGHT OF LIGHTS ABOVE SURFACE:** 12 inches.
**LIGHTING CONTROLLER(S):** 2 timers.

## SYSTEM PARAMETERS & CHEMISTRY
**WATER TEMPERATURE:** 78 to 80°F.
**SPECIFIC GRAVITY:** 1.025.
**PH:** 8.3.
**CALCIUM:** 350-450.
**NITRATE:** 0.
**PHOSPHATE:** 0.
**RESINS OR DEVICES USED TO REDUCE NITRATE OR PHOSPHATE:** Poly Bio Filter pads.
**MUNICIPAL WATER SUPPLY:** Yes.
**REVERSE OSMOSIS:** Deionization: Poly-Filtered water.
**SALT USED:** Coralife.
**WATER CHANGE SCHEDULE:** 20% per month.

## LIVESTOCK
**FISHES:** 12.
**STONY CORALS:** 30.
**SOFT CORALS:** 20.
**NOTEWORTHY SPECIMENS:** Orange *Ricordea*, green *Nephthea*.

## FEEDING
**REGIMEN FOR FISHES:** Fed 2 times per week, frozen food or flakes.
**REGIMEN FOR CORALS/INVERTS:** Fresh-hatched brine shrimp, 2 to 3 times per week.

## NOTES
**PROBLEMS OVERCOME WITH THIS SYSTEM:** Hair algae and bubble algae.
**THINGS THE OWNER WOULD LIKE TO CHANGE:** Go to a larger tank.
**FAVORITE COMMENTS BY OTHERS ABOUT THIS AQUARIUM:**
1. "Is that alive?"
2. "It looks like when I went diving in the ocean."
**OVERALL NEGATIVES (OR THINGS TO DO DIFFERENTLY NEXT TIME):**
1. More circulation.
2. Tank not big enough.
3. Next time use a drilled tank.

# Marc's Reef

*A magnificent reef built into a spacious Florida family room, this Jeff Turner-designed system is more than a decade old.*

## AQUARIUM PROFILE

**OWNER:** Marc Silverman.
**DESIGNER:** Jeffrey A. Turner, Reef Aquaria Design, Inc. reefaquariainc@aol.com.
**LOCATION:** Pine Crest, FL.
**DATE ESTABLISHED:** March 1993.
**DATE PHOTOGRAPHED:** December 2001.

### TANK
**DISPLAY TANK VOLUME:** 235 gallons.
**TANK DIMENSIONS:** 84" X 24" X 27".
**TANK MATERIAL:** Plate glass with 8 through hole fittings in bottom.
**SUMP VOLUME:** Two 60-gallon sumps with 1-inch pipe joining the reservoirs.
**LOCATION:** Family room adjacent to kitchen.
**CABINETRY/ARCHITECTURAL DETAILS:** Behind sit-down bar area on 28 foot custom wall unit.

### CIRCULATION
**MAIN SYSTEM PUMP(S):** Two 40 RLXT Iwaki.
**WATER RETURNS:** At surface on right and left sides.
**ADDITIONAL PUMPS:** 70 RLT Iwaki, intakes above sand to remote chiller outside of house.
**WAVEMAKING DEVICES:** Two Intermatic digital timers, alternating each pump from left to right every 6 hours each to mimic tidal action.

BUILD A LARGE AQUARIUM INTO THE WALL of a showcase, architect-designed home, and there is more than a little pressure to ensure that it is well planned and set up properly, lest it lose some of its luster or, in the worst case, become an algae farm in a sumptuous setting. When Marc Silverman commissioned Jeff Turner to design and install a 235-gallon reef tank in his family home in the Miami suburb of Pine Crest, he did so with the understanding that this was going to be a long-term project. After running for almost 10 years, this tank has only gotten better—both in the size and health of the livestock and in the ease with which the system is maintained.

Having installed scores of large reef aquariums for demanding and prominent clients, Jeff acknowledged the ever-changing world of reefkeeping technology and made allowances for the equipment to be changed or upgraded as improvements were desired. While the display tank, dominating a spacious open family area behind a curved marble bar, appears much as it did when first installed, the underlying methodology and gear running the system have changed significantly over the years.

Originally, the approach was standard Berlin Method, with filtration provided by large countercurrent skimmers and moderate current provided by an external pump. However, when a newer, more-efficient recirculating venturi skimmer became available, the countercurrent skimmers were replaced. The extra space that then opened up allowed for two refugiums using a mud substrate to be added. These refugiums increased nutrient export from the system and also gave the added benefit of producing significant quantities of

*Access to skimmer and tank paraphernalia is tucked into a cabinet between the tank and a fastidiously kept bar area.*

*Various stony corals such as this beautiful purple Acropora secale have reached sizes that require occasional pruning.*

*Under-tank space houses the main system pump, center, and two dedicated circulation pumps, as well as a pair of Caulerpa-filled Ecosystem refugiums, each with a 20-pound mud bed and 24-hour lighting. UV sterilizers help with disease control.*

*Aggressive water circulation, with alternating water flow directions, comes via water returns strategically hidden in the reef.*

## CONTROLLERS

pH controller for new calcium reactor.

**TEMPERATURE CONTROLS:** Two thermostats in series on chiller: digital primary controller with mechanical pen set to override if system becomes too cold.

**FANS:** Three 70 cmf fans move air through cabinetry and exhaust to tall ceiling.

**CHILLER:** 1-ton (hp) custom chiller-titanium exchanger commercial unit.

## FILTRATION

**SKIMMER:** Euro-Reef G-3.

**MECHANICAL FILTER:** Magnum filter used occasionally to polish water.

**UV STERILIZER:** Two 25-watt Aquanetics-Quartz sleeves.

**CARBON:** 2 units Chemi-pure once in a while.

**BIOLOGICAL FILTER:** 3 gallons Bio-Balls used mainly to soften noise in overflows.

**REFUGIUM:** EcoSystem Miracle Mud, 20 lbs. each sump with *Caulerpa,* 24-hour lighting.

**LIVE ROCK IN DISPLAY TANK:** 350 lbs. Florida branch live rock, 1993.

**SAND/SUBSTRATE IN DISPLAY:** 2-3 inches Florida Keys live sand.

**OTHER:** Pro-Cal calcium reactor by MTC.

## LIGHTING

PFO-6 foot fixture with reflector/fans and tempered-glass lenses.

microfauna to feed the fishes and invertebrates. In similar fashion, when the chiller needed to be replaced, a more energy-efficient custom heat exchanger was used. This required adding a water pump, but this addition increased the water motion within the tank. Jeff's design was unusual and quite impressive in mimicking tidal action, using digital timers to switch pumps on and off at 6-hour intervals to simulate tides flowing across a reef.

The lighting is intense and is meant to replicate the quality of light striking a reef. More than 1,600 watts of light, both metal halide and VHO fluorescent, are used to illuminate the tank. The "on" cycles are staggered so that the maximum light intensity only strikes the tank for a relatively short period just as occurs on a natural reef in the midday hours.

Seeing the growth and health of the corals in Marc's well-established reef, it is easy to verify that this system works. Coral growth became so robust that calcium supplementation had to be augmented—from just a Kalkwasser reactor to the addition of a calcium reactor and then the weekly addition of a two-part calcium/buffer supplement. This keeps calcium and alkalinity levels equal to those found in natural seawater. Maintenance is made easier because all water changes are carried out with fresh seawater—a service available to Miami-area aquarists—every 3 months. Jeff stops by to ensure that everything is humming properly, but Marc does the day-to-day feeding and monitoring, and he reports that there is very little general maintenance required other than cleaning the glass and harvesting the *Caulerpa* from the refugium. The low nutrient levels recorded are quite different from many older tanks where

*Bright green branching frogspawn coral (Euphyllia divisa) adds a spot of vivid color and tentacles that sway in the ever-shifting currents.*

nutrients can accumulate over time and cause algae to become a constant problem.

This system is also living proof that jamming as many corals as possible into a new tank to make it look full is not necessary—or advisable. This tank was modestly stocked with choice animals, and they have been given room to grow. Even after a decade, there is still space for the corals to expand, and burning and competition among the various colonies is minimal. It seems that when corals are given enough space initially, they will grow away from each other and minimize confrontation in order to use their energy for growth and reproduction rather than aggression. The absence of obvious turf battles defies the usual rule that stony and soft corals cannot prosper in the same aquarium. This tank is also well stocked with more than 40 fishes, and several of them have even spawned in the tank, including the anthias.

It would not be fair to discuss the beauty of this tank without also mentioning the cabinetry and aquascaping that work together to set this tank apart. By designing the tank to rest behind the wall in a very active area, Jeff was able to hide all of the necessary equipment. The live rock structure appears massive, but is quite open with ample places for the fishes to swim and hide—in, under, through, and behind the rock and corals. This serves to keep the interest level in the tank high, as not all of the fishes are visible at any one time, and seems to enhance the illusion of the tank being a window on a vast reef world. By creating this system with a long-term perspective, Jeff Turner and Marc Silverman have been able to produce a reef tank that is the focal point of an incredible home and that seems to grow more handsome each year.

**FLUORESCENT BULBS:** Four 160-watt 72 inch URI actinics with IceCap ballast.
**PHOTOPERIOD:** 9 hours.
**HOW OFTEN REPLACED:** Yearly.
**METAL HALIDE BULBS:** Four 250-watt German 10,000 K with HQI ballasts.
**PHOTOPERIOD:** Two 8 hours; two 6 hours.
**HOW OFTEN REPLACED:** Yearly.
**HEIGHT OF LIGHTS ABOVE WATER:** 12 inches.
**LIGHTING CONTROLLER(S):** Three Intermatic timers.

## SYSTEM PARAMETERS & CHEMISTRY
**WATER TEMPERATURE:** 76 to 78°F.
**SPECIFIC GRAVITY:** 1.023-1.025.
**PH:** 8.0 to 8.3.
**ALKALINITY:** 9-11 dKH.
**CALCIUM:** 400 ppm.
**NITRATE:** Less than 10 ppm.
**PHOSPHATE:** 0.001-0.002.
**NATURAL SEAWATER:** Yes.
**REVERSE OSMOSIS:** Kent RO/DI system.
**WATER CHANGE SCHEDULE:** Every 3 months.
**ADDITIVES OR SUPPLEMENTS USED:** CombiSan ESV I/2.
**MONITORING EQUIPMENT:** Large display thermometer.
**MAINTENANCE SCHEDULE:** Clean glass weekly; harvest *Caulerpa* two times per month; ESV Calcium Part 1 and Part 2, 16 ounces per week each.

## LIVESTOCK
**FISHES:** 40.
**STONY CORALS:** 38.
**SOFT CORALS:** 21.
**OTHER LIVESTOCK:** Sea cucumbers, starfishes, serpent stars, brittlestars, *Tridacna* clams, *Astraea* snails.
**NOTEWORTHY SPECIMENS:** Beautiful assortment of stony and soft corals with many corals 6 to 8 years old.
**SPAWNING EVENTS:** Anthias, damsels, clams (once).

## FEEDING
**REGIMEN FOR FISHES:** Daily auto feeder 2 times per day. Mixed dry foods, lettuce and frozen foods 2 to 3 times per week.
**REGIMEN FOR CORALS/INVERTS:** Fish wastes + water changes.

## NOTES
**PROBLEMS OVERCOME WITH THIS SYSTEM:** Chiller relocated to outside of house with larger unit.
**THINGS THE OWNER WOULD LIKE TO CHANGE:** Larger tank with Starfire glass, mechanical systems in separate room.
**SUCCESSES:** Has been running continuously for 10 years and counting.
**WHAT IS SPECIAL ABOUT THIS SYSTEM:** Great sit-down area in front of tank to relax and enjoy the reef. Truly a focal point.
**FAVORITE COMMENT BY OTHERS ABOUT THIS AQUARIUM:** "Most beautiful aquarium I have ever seen."
**OVERALL POSITIVES:**
1. Quality of design.
2. Solid mechanical systems.
3. Thriving coral reef.

# Through the Looking Glass

*After a succession of smaller tanks, Gregory Schiemer built this 500-gallon system for his collection of corals and giant clams.*

## AQUARIUM PROFILE

**OWNER & DESIGNER:** Gregory Schiemer.
**LOCATION:** Hawthorne, NY.
**DATE ESTABLISHED:** 1989.
**DATE PHOTOGRAPHED:** 1999.

### TANK
**DISPLAY TANK VOLUME:** 500 gallons.
**DISPLAY TANK DIMENSIONS:** 10' X 30" X 32".
**DISPLAY TANK MATERIAL:** Glass.
**SUMP VOLUME:** 150 gallons.
**LOCATION:** Basement on solid concrete slab.

### CIRCULATION
**MAIN SYSTEM PUMP:** 3/4 hp Hayward; approx 5,000 gph.
**WATER RETURNS:** 4 returns using Locline pipe inside aquarium.
**HEATER:** Medusa controller-heaters in sump.

FOR A LOOK AT THE FUTURE OF REEF TANKS, one need search no further than Greg Schiemer's basement fish room where one of the best examples of a homegrown stony coral reef is on display. One of a handful of aquarists who helped unlock the secrets of keeping small-polyp stony corals and who is spreading the word through his writings and photography, Greg is also known for having a very extensive collection of the hard-to-keep fairy wrasses.

Success with smaller systems finally led Greg to combine several tanks into a single large 500-gallon tank that offers a 10-foot expanse of corals that never fail to astonish visitors with their robust growth and coloration. By going to a single large system instead of three smaller tanks, Greg says he was able to accomplish several things. First, all his attention could be focused on a single tank rather than several. This reduced the time spent on mundane maintenance tasks and increased the one thing some aquarists crave most: relaxing periods for simply viewing and enjoying the tank. Second, the large footprint of the tank allowed the fishes to settle into more natural behaviors. A group of six different surgeonfishes, for example, is getting along in this tank,

*BEFORE: Young Acropora formosa photographed by Greg to document its growth over time. See photograph at right.*

*AFTER: The same staghorn coral shown at left, six months later. Note areas (1) where the coral has grown onto the glass.*

*BEFORE: Young finger gorgonian was just a 1-inch cutting when given to Greg, who has kept track of its growth.*

*AFTER: The same gorgonian shown at left, as it has grown in stature and mass in Greg's 500-gallon reef.*

**SKIMMER:** ETS 1000 skimmer run with a dedicated Iwaki 70 RLT pump; plumbed in and out of sump.

**MECHANICAL FILTER:** Drip tray covered in 50-micron polyester pad; rinsed weekly.

**CARBON:** 16 ounces used continuously and changed every 6 weeks.

**AMOUNT AND TYPE OF LIVE ROCK:** 500+ lbs. mixed Hawaiian, Indonesian, Marshall Island, Fiji, and Haiti.

**SAND:** 300 lbs. Caribbean live sand.

## LIGHTING

**FLUORESCENT:** Two 6-foot and two 4-foot URI VHO actinic lamps.

**PHOTOPERIOD:** 14 hours.

**REPLACED:** every 9-12 months.

**METAL HALIDE:** Five 400-watt Iwasaki 6,500 K.

**PHOTOPERIOD:** 9 hours.

**REPLACED:** Annually.

## SYSTEM PARAMETERS & CHEMISTRY

**SPECIFIC GRAVITY:** 1.025.

**PH:** 8.25.

**ALKALINITY:** 8.4 dKH.

**CALCIUM:** 425 ppm.

**NITRATE, PHOSPHATE:** Unmeasurable.

**WATER SOURCE:** RO/DI.

**SALT:** Instant Ocean; Tropic Marin.

**WATER CHANGE SCHEDULE:** 20% semi-annually.

**ADDITIVES:** Lugol's solution: 10 drops weekly.

**DOSING EQUIPMENT:** Calcium reactor: Largest Knop Ca Reactor used continuously. Kalkwasser: 5 gallons daily through a peristaltic pump.

**MAINTENANCE SCHEDULE:** 2 hours weekly for cleaning skimmer and overflow.

## LIVESTOCK

**FISHES:** 40, including a Red Sea Regal Angel that is 5 years old.

**STONY CORALS:** 20 species.

**SOFT CORALS:** 12 species.

**INVERTEBRATES:** 4 tridacnid clams. The oldest is an 11-year-old *Tridacna crocea*.

## FEEDING

**REGIMEN FOR FISHES:** Multiple daily feedings of a mix containing krill, Pacifica plankton, *Mysis* shrimp, brine shrimp, and larval silversides. Sheet of dried macroalgae every other day.

## NOTES

**OVERALL POSITIVES:** The behavior of the fishes has been a surprise. For example, I have three pairs of pseudochromids, a school of 12 anthias (comprised of three different species), and six different species of tangs and surgeonfishes all cohabiting in the same aquarium.

---

while they would constantly battle in a smaller space. Also, a dozen flamboyant anthias, even though of different species, act like a school in nature—swimming in and out of the corals as they would on the reef. Finally, the availability of open water has allowed for explosive growth in many of his corals.

As a record of just how quickly this reef has developed, Greg has documented the growth of his corals over time in a series of photographs. Greg's images provide case histories showing that a properly set up and maintained closed system can support growth rates of SPS corals at least as fast and possibly faster than reported on reefs in nature.

This has caught the attention of many reef enthusiasts. As the keeping of corals has become more widespread, some critics have suggested that the aquarium trade is taking too many corals and that keeping them alive was nearly impossible. It has also been reported—erroneously—that stony corals are so slow growing that there is no way possible for them to be considered a renewable resource. The growth of corals in Greg's tank is a living refutation of these warnings. In a relatively short time, the small colonies of *Acropora* and *Montipora* that Greg transferred to this tank rapidly filled the tank. By giving the corals adequate space and care, Greg has been able to show by example how quickly corals can be grown in captivity.

By not overcrowding the tank and restricting his stocking to no more than approximately 20 species of coral, Greg has set the stage for an aquascape that mimics the look of a wild reef. This approach means giving smallish corals plenty of space in the early stages and having the patience not to overcrowd them. Greg provides the reef with strong water movement, and total tank volume is turned over approximately 10 times per hour. This level of water motion is a critical aspect for good coral growth, and one that is lacking in many systems.

The corals are also provided with more than four watts of high-intensity metal halide lighting per gallon plus actinic lighting. Water conditions are optimal as well. This tank has extremely low levels of dissolved nutrients, allowing the corals to predominate, rather than troublesome algae.

"I went to a larger aquarium to accommodate the corals and clams," says Greg, "but I've discovered that the best thing about a large aquarium is the fishes. Fishes behave more naturally in a large aquarium and many fishes that normally would not live together in a smaller system do wonderfully given the room." Greg has been able to keep a beautiful school of anthias alive and as vividly colored as any found on the reef. Greg also has had success with several difficult-to-keep fairy wrasses, as well as three pairs of pseudochromids. The latter fishes are often thought to be too aggressive to house except as a single species per tank, but the size of this aquarium and the many nooks and crannies provided by the live rock seem to make it possible in this case. Most impressive, though, is his five-year-old Red Sea Regal Angelfish and 11-year-old *Tridacna crocea* clam.

The combination of adequate space and meticulous husbandry, learned by years of trial and error, has allowed Greg to create a remarkably realistic captive ecosystem—with, most the reef having been grown in the tank itself.

*Feeding frenzy around a piece of dried seaweed attracts Greg's Red Sea Regal Angel (Pygoplites diacanthus).*

*Multiple tiers of this plating Montipora capricornis colony are a mark of exceptional success in stony coral husbandry.*

*Aquarist Schiemer says that an unexpected bonus of moving to a larger aquarium has been more natural behaviors of reef fishes, including the mixed school of anthias (1) that do not always fare well in smaller systems. Note very large Tridacna clams (2).*

# Homegrown Reef

*Stocked with coral fragments, rather than large imported colonies, this 100-gallon reef displays about 40 different coral colonies.*

## AQUARIUM PROFILE

**OWNER & DESIGNER:** John Susbilla
  http://www.reef.esmartweb.com.
**LOCATION:** Milpitas, CA.
**DATE ESTABLISHED:** December 1999.
**DATE PHOTOGRAPHED:** Various.

### TANK
**CONFIGURATION:** Rectangular.
**DISPLAY TANK VOLUME:** 100 gallons.
**DISPLAY TANK DIMENSIONS:** 48" X 24" X 20".
**DISPLAY TANK MATERIAL:** Acrylic.
**SUMP VOLUME:** 30 gallons.
**LOCATION:** Dining area.
**CABINETRY/ARCHITECTURAL DETAILS:** DIY
  oak cabinet and canopy.

### CIRCULATION
**MAIN SYSTEM PUMP(S):** SEN 900 External
  Pump 900 gph.
**WATER RETURNS:** Same as main.
**ADDITIONAL PUMPS:** One Maxi-Jet 1200
  powerhead for internal circulation
  (constantly on).
**WAVEMAKING DEVICES:** Wavestrip
  wavemaker driving three Maxi-Jet 1200
  powerheads.

### CONTROLLERS
**TEMPERATURE CONTROLS:** Medusa Digital
  Dual Stage controller.

A LIVING EXAMPLE OF A NEW GENERATION of reef aquariums, John Susbilla's spectacular 100-gallon system may be proof that the old rulebooks need updating. Using just 1 pound of live rock per gallon of water in the display tank, John found it was still too much when his stony corals quickly filled the available space. "If I could start over, I'd use less rock," says John. "I consider the old rule of 2 to 3 lbs. of rock per gallon an outdated legacy based on much more dense and heavy Florida live rock. Indo-Pacific live rock has a more open structure and is much more porous. Less of it is needed than most people think—especially if you are serious about growing corals."

Remarkably, the expansive growth of corals in John's tank came out of small colonies and fragments rather than imported show specimens. Even more significant is the fact that the coral species with which this is being done were thought to be impossible to keep as little as 10 years ago.

The design of this tank is unique in that it utilizes several different methodologies to maximize nutrient removal. (John is now a stickler for this, after a near disaster in which a dying *Cladiella* coral triggered the bleaching and/or death of his stony corals.) The 100 pounds of Marshall Island live rock and an in-sump protein skimmer remove considerable waste and are the Berlin method portion of his nutrient-removal system. A 3-inch deep sand bed occupies the bottom of the display tank and also helps in nitrate reduction. A refugium is incorporated into the sump with *Caulerpa* and 1 inch of sand in the refugium. The *Caulerpa* is harvested when it overgrows the refugium, and this helps export nitrate and phosphate. Carbon is also employed to polish the water and to adsorb any yellowing compounds released by the *Caulerpa*. Lastly, a 10% water change is done every month to further prevent unwanted nutrients from accumulating over time. Well-planned methods of nutrient export allow John to maintain this well-stocked tank with very low nutrient levels. Both nitrate and phosphate levels are undetectable despite the fishes being fed daily, the corals getting some of the leftovers from the homemade fish food, and the anemone being fed regularly.

The use of multiple methods for nutrient removal may also allow John to keep his tank slightly warmer than most, at an average range of from 81 to 84 degrees. Only by keeping the nutrient levels ultra-low does John have enough margin for error to escape a catastrophe if something goes wrong. High temperature, low nutrient levels, and very strong lighting produce growth rates in his corals that are comparable to those reported in the wild. More than 10 watts of light per gallon are used on this tank with both 6,500 K metal halide lamps and VHO actinic fluorescent lamps being employed. Strong water motion also encourages

*A large, bright green carpet anemone (Stichodactyla gigantea) with resident Ocellaris (False Percula) Clownfish is a favorite of visitors to John's reef.*

rapid growth, with an external pump and several powerheads producing water movement in the aquarium of more than ten times the tank's volume per hour.

John's list of livestock includes more than 40 colonies of corals, the majority being stony corals. The genera represented include *Acropora, Pocillopora, Montipora, Stylophora, Favia,* and *Turbinaria.* In addition, four *Tridacna* clams reside in the tank, as well as John's pride and joy: a 2-year-old green carpet anemone (*Stichodactyla gigantea*) that hosts an Ocellaris Clownfish.

The most impressive aspect of this system is the rapid growth and size that some of these stony corals have demonstrated in a relatively short time. Clearly, many are destined to outgrow the tank. John is planning on upsizing to a 180-gallon tank to give his prized corals room to expand. His strategy will be to avoid filling the initial void with live rock. Instead, he will allot a great deal of open water space for corals to grow and fill in over time. By doing this John hopes to have the tank fill in naturally with a true living reef that is not dependent on live rock for its topography. This appears to be the next important step in the evolution of reefkeeping—and something that coral biologists not so long ago predicted could never be accomplished.

**FANS:** 5 RadioShack 4-inch Axial Fans.
**HEATERS:** One 300-watt Visitherm heater controlled by Medusa.
**CHILLER:** 1/4 hp Aqua Logic drop-in chiller controlled by Medusa.

### FILTRATION
**SKIMMER:** AquaC Urchin (in-sump model).
**UV STERILIZER:** Aquanetics in-line 15 watt (occasional use only).
**CARBON:** 2 cups, used for a few days each month.
**BIOLOGICAL FILTER:** Live rock/ live sand.
**REFUGIUM:** The 30-gallon sump doubles as a refugium, using a 175 5,000 K metal halide. This configuration is used mostly for nutrient export (via three types of *Caulerpa*) and also for grow-out of certain fragments such as *Xenia*, other soft corals, and some SPS.
**LIVE ROCK IN DISPLAY TANK:** 100 lbs. of Marshall Island. 10 lbs. of Monano.
**LIVE ROCK IN SUMP:** 10 lbs. of Monano.
**SUBSTRATE IN DISPLAY:** 3 inches aragonite sand.
**SUBSTRATE IN SUMP:** 1 inch aragonite sand.

*Images of coral colonies of various sizes are reflected by the water surface. Lighting includes two 400-watt metal halide bulbs and two VHO actinic fluorescents.*

## LIGHTING

**FLUORESCENT BULBS:** Two 110-watt URI VHO actinics.
**PHOTOPERIOD:** 12 hours.
**HOW OFTEN REPLACED:** Once per year.
**METAL HALIDE BULBS:** Two 400-watt Iwasaki 6.5 K.
**PHOTOPERIOD:** 10 hours.
**HOW OFTEN REPLACED:** Once per year.
**HEIGHT OF LIGHTS ABOVE WATER:** 8 inches.
**OTHER BULBS:** Sump lighting using 175 5,000 K metal halide.
**PHOTOPERIOD:** 12 hours.
**LIGHTING CONTROLLER(S):** Appliance timers.

## SYSTEM PARAMETERS & CHEMISTRY

**WATER TEMPERATURE:** 81 to 84.5°F.
**SPECIFIC GRAVITY:** 1.025.
**PH:** 8.1.
**ALKALINITY:** 12 dKH.
**CALCIUM:** 400.
**NITRATE:** 0.
**PHOSPHATE:** 0.
**MUNICIPAL WATER SUPPLY:** Yes.
**REVERSE OSMOSIS:** Yes.
**DEIONIZATION:** Yes.
**SALT USED:** Reef Crystals.
**WATER CHANGE SCHEDULE:** 10% per month.
**MONITORING EQUIPMENT:** pH, ORP.
**MAINTENANCE SCHEDULE:** Wipe-down film algae (diatoms) once per week using a combination of scrapers and magnets; clean skimmer once per week to keep it at top efficiency. Calcium and alkalinity are checked once per month. The calcium reactor is also checked each week for proper operation.

## LIVESTOCK

**FISHES:** 8.
**STONY CORALS:** 36 colonies and fragments of SPS. The largest of the colonies, especially the branching ones, were grown from small fragments.
**SOFT CORALS:** 5.
**OTHER LIVESTOCK:** 4 *Tridacna* clams, a cleanup crew consisting of various snails, crabs, and a cucumber.
**NOTEWORTHY SPECIMENS:** Large, bright green carpet anemone (*Stichodactyla gigantea*). Large colony of "green slimer" (*Acropora yongei*).

## FEEDING

**REGIMEN FOR FISHES:** Once per day using homemade food made with fresh seafoods from the local Asian grocery. Various types of nori with a half bottle of Tahitian Blend are ground into small bits using a blender, then fortified with Selcon.
**REGIMEN FOR CORALS/INVERTS:** Incidental feeding with fish food. Fish food also contains microalgae for various filter feeders. Anemone is occasionally fed directly with the same fish food.

## NOTES

**PROBLEMS OVERCOME WITH THIS SYSTEM:**
The system experienced an RTN (rapid tissue necrosis) event around May 2001, which was initially caused by a change from 10,000 K Aqualine bulbs to Iwasaki 6,500 K bulbs. Even though the photoperiod was cut in half for the bulb change, a healthy and growing *Cladiella* soft coral colony immediately began disintegrating even though it was at the bottom on the shadiest side of the tank. This started a chain reaction of RTN that harmed a good number of the SPS. A large water change and heavy use of carbon helped stop the event but not until after a few valuable losses. Most of the remaining corals lost coloration and took a few months to regain it through new growth. It is possible that there was a release of toxins by the soft coral that caused such a swift reaction.

**THINGS THE OWNER WOULD LIKE TO CHANGE:**
Use less live rock in favor of more open space for corals to grow into.
**SUCCESSES:** A good number of SPS that started out as small frags have grown to very large colonies even after continuous fragments have been taken. For instance, the green Bali staghorn started out as a 3-inch fragment. After a year and a half it is larger than a volleyball. Within a year, a fragment of *Acropora microphthalma* became the size of volleyball with dense growth until half of it succumbed to the major RTN event. Similar success has been seen with *Acropora formosa,* although it is not as dense and fast-growing.
**SPECIAL ABOUT THIS SYSTEM:** It's another slice of the ocean that could not be had just a few years ago.
**FAVORITE COMMENTS BY OTHERS ABOUT THIS AQUARIUM:**
  1. "AMAZING!"
  2. "Your tank is magnificent!"
  3. "I have fallen in love with your tank."
**OVERALL POSITIVES:**
  1. Tremendous success with thriving and fast growing SPS.
  2. 2-year-old carpet anemone still doing very well.
  3. Keeps me busy.
**OVERALL NEGATIVES (OR THINGS TO DO DIFFERENTLY NEXT TIME):**
  1. Get an even deeper tank (30 inches) for more versatility in aquascaping.
  2. Use a tank with European-style perimeter bracing.
  3. Use an additional external water pump for in-tank (loop) circulation rather than obtrusive powerheads.
  4. Do not add *Xenia elongata* to the system. It seems to be a pest worse than *Aiptasia,* as it grows at tremendous rates where you don't want it. Same can be said of mushroom anemones.
  5. Use even less live rock. Even at 100 lbs. for a 100-gallon tank I thought it was a bit much. I consider the rule of 2 to 3 lbs. per gallon a legacy since that rule was based on much more dense and heavy Florida live rock. Indo-Pacific live rock is structured more openly and much more porous and less of it is needed.

*Glorious blue Acropora gemmifera demands excellent water circulation, light, and low nutrient levels.*

*Colorful branch tips on this tricolor Acropora are typical of thriving specimens in this generally fast-growing genus.*

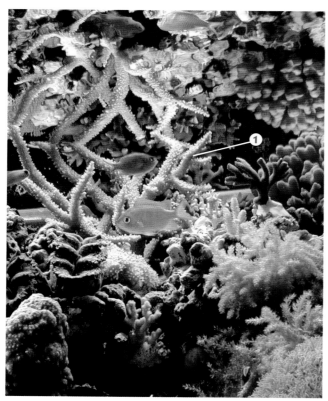

*Blue Green Chromis are excellent reef-safe fishes, adding movement to the tank. Note Acropora yongei staghorn (1).*

*A glowing pink Stylophora pistillata coral is an eye-catcher. Note pincers of coral crab nestled within the branches (1).*

# Trendsetting Reef

*This early 300-gallon reef by Richard Harker helped demonstrate the possibilities of keeping captive stony corals alive and well.*

## AQUARIUM PROFILE

**OWNER & DESIGNER:** Richard Harker.
**LOCATION:** Raleigh, NC.
**DATE ESTABLISHED:** August 1994.
**DATE PHOTOGRAPHED:** March 1995, 1996.

### TANK

**DISPLAY TANK VOLUME:** 300 gallons.
**DISPLAY TANK DIMENSIONS:** 8' X 2.5' X 2'.
**DISPLAY TANK MATERIAL:** Glass.
**SUMP VOLUME:** 33 gallons.
**CABINETRY:** Custom-built solid oak.

### CIRCULATION

**MAIN SYSTEM PUMP(S):** Iwaki 20 RLT.
**WATER RETURNS:** Pair of returns.
**ADDITIONAL PUMPS:** Six Tunze 2002 air-cooled pumps.
**WAVEMAKING DEVICES:** Two Tunze controllers.

### CONTROLLERS

**TEMPERATURE:** Room temperature-controlled.

I N A SPECIAL FISH ROOM in North Carolina between den and dining room sat one of the first reef tanks devoted almost exclusively to SPS corals in the United States. In this room was the 300-gallon reef tank of Richard Harker, who has spread the lessons learned here far and wide in marine aquarium circles.

In starting with the Berlin method of maintaining reef tanks that was introduced to the U.S. in the early 1990s, Richard Harker was a pioneer in using the system for small-polyp stony corals rather than the much easier to keep soft or large-polyped stony corals. At the time, many considered SPS corals either difficult or just plain impossible to keep alive. Richard says he did not employ a lot of technology or exotic equipment, but simply followed the guidelines for the Berlin method as laid out by Norwegian author Alf Jacob Nilsen in his books and articles on reefkeeping.

This tank was equipped with a very efficient protein skimmer, strong lighting provided by metal halide lamps, and good water motion provided by multiple pumps and powerheads. However, Richard took a different approach to turnover in the tank. Only a small sump was employed, and water from the display tank passed through the sump rather slowly—approximately once per

hour. This also resulted in a slow rate of feeding water to the skimmer, which repeatedly recirculated water from the sump and may have helped in keeping nutrients and dissolved organics low. A large fish load was not kept in the tank, and there was virtually no algae growth, with the exception of some calcareous algae that appeared on the intake to the skimmer box. These conditions—low nutrients and the absence of nuisance algae—have proved to be critical for success with SPS corals.

Since the opinion at that time was that *Acropora* species and other SPS corals either would do poorly or would not grow in captivity, Richard followed the common practice of filling every space on the live rock with small heads of coral. Even initially, there were very few bare spots on the live rock, and the tank was quite attractive. By the end of the first year, interesting things were happening in the tank. Despite predictions that the SPS corals would grow very slowly—if at all—in captivity, all of the corals were expanding rapidly. They grew so quickly, in fact, that they had filled virtually every space within the tank in the short span of a year. Pruning and keeping the corals from burning one another then became the main focus of Richard's maintenance, rather than simply trying to keep the water conditions stable.

**FILTRATION**
**SKIMMER:** MTC Powerpro venturi skimmer.
**OZONIZER:** Occasional use of Sanders 100.
**CARBON:** Changed one week each month.
**BIOLOGICAL FILTER:** Live rock only.
**REFUGIUM:** None, but there is significant growth of filter feeders in sump.
**LIVE ROCK IN DISPLAY TANK:** 300 lbs. of Fiji live rock.
**LIVE ROCK IN SUMP:** None.
**SAND/SUBSTRATE IN DISPLAY:** 2 inches of CaribSea aragonite seeded with sand from older tank.

**LIGHTING**
**FLUORESCENT BULBS:** Two 110-watt URI actinics.
**PHOTOPERIOD:** 12 hours.
**HOW OFTEN REPLACED:** Every two years.
**METAL HALIDE BULBS:** Three 400-watt Iwasaki 6,500 K.
**PHOTOPERIOD:** 10 hours.
**HOW OFTEN REPLACED:** Every two years.
**NATURAL LIGHT:** No.
**LIGHTING CONTROLLER(S):** Hardware store timers.

## SYSTEM PARAMETERS & CHEMISTRY

**WATER TEMPERATURE:** Winter 79°F; summer 83°F (average 81°F).
**SPECIFIC GRAVITY:** 1.024.
**PH:** 7.9-8.4.
**ALKALINITY:** 8 dKH.
**CALCIUM:** 350-400.
**NITRATE:** Unmeasurable.
**PHOSPHATE:** Unmeasurable.
**RESINS OR DEVICES USED TO REDUCE NITRATE OR PHOSPHATE:** None.
**MUNICIPAL WATER SUPPLY:** Yes.
**REVERSE OSMOSIS:** R.O./D.I.
**SALT USED:** Instant Ocean.
**WATER CHANGE SCHEDULE:** 10% about once per quarter.
**ADDITIVES OR SUPPLEMENTS USED:** Marinevit, Lugol's, calcium hydroxide, calcium chloride, ESV B-Ionic, strontium chloride. Weekly for trace elements; as needed for calcium.
**MONITORING EQUIPMENT:** Sandpoint controller, Aquadyne Octopus controller.
**DOSING EQUIPMENT USED:** MTC doser.

## LIVESTOCK

**FISHES:** 6.
**STONY CORALS:** 85.
**SOFT CORALS:** 20.
**OTHER LIVESTOCK:** Miscellaneous invertebrates: cleaner shrimp, brittlestars, blue leg hermits, *Astraea* snails.
**NOTEWORTHY SPECIMENS:** 11-year-old *Turbinaria peltata*, 7-year-old *Acropora*, *Porites*, *Favia*.
**SPAWNING EVENTS:** Planulae release of *Pocillopora* and growth to golf-ball size.

## FEEDING

**REGIMEN FOR FISHES:** Flake food and weekly romaine lettuce.
**REGIMEN FOR CORALS/INVERTS:** None.

## NOTES

**PROBLEMS OVERCOME WITH THIS SYSTEM:**
1. High biodiversity maintained by limiting predators.
2. High volume of filter feeders, including naturally occurring sponges, helps maintain quality of water.

**THINGS THE OWNER WOULD LIKE TO CHANGE:** More open design with less rock.
**THINGS OWNER LIKES BEST ABOUT THIS SYSTEM:** Biodiversity.
**FAVORITE COMMENTS BY OTHERS:** "The corals came to fill virtually every spot in the tank."
**OVERALL NEGATIVES:** Not enough open swimming space for fishes.
**SPECIAL NOTE:** Much of the collection in this tank was lost after an extended power outage in 1996. Some corals were salvaged and have been reestablished in a new tank.

*A Red Sea Purple Tang (*Zebrasoma xanthurum*) performs desirable grazing services in the reef. Note sweeper tentacles extending from large-polyped stony coral (1).*

This was also one of the first home tanks where SPS corals began to reproduce regularly. Small *Pocillopora damicornis* colonies began to appear throughout the tank after the first year. At the time it was not well understood how this coral reproduced, but it was viewed as quite an achievement to have small colonies—not simply fragments—spontaneously appearing in virtually any empty space on the live rock, as well as on the overflow box, return pipes, and heater. Richard's experiences have since led to a better understanding of how this coral can reproduce and how it comes to predominate in areas where it is located.

This tank also helped disprove the statements of coral biologists who said that stony corals would never be successfully kept alive for any length of time in captivity. From this tank, Richard now has an 11-year-old *Turbinaria peltata* and some 7-year-old colonies of *Acropora*, *Porites*, and *Favia*. The *Acropora* species and other SPS corals in this tank were predominantly brown, as those were the only stony corals available at that time. However, even with brown corals, this tank was quite dramatic to view and an astonishing sight at the time. Some of these corals were salvaged from the tank after much of the collection was lost during a hurricane and prolonged power loss several years ago. Fortunately pictures taken prior to the storm and shown here prove how successful it was and have motivated Richard to expand his expertise to a truly colossal 3,000-gallon home tank in a specially built addition to his home. If Richard matches the level of success he has had in the past, his new tank may set the reefkeeping bar even higher for other advanced home reefkeepers.

*To quell the chemical defenses used by the large soft and stony corals to establish their territories, Richard uses activated carbon, which is replaced monthly. Note large colonies of finger leather (Sinularia—1) and lobed brain coral (Lobophyllia—2).*

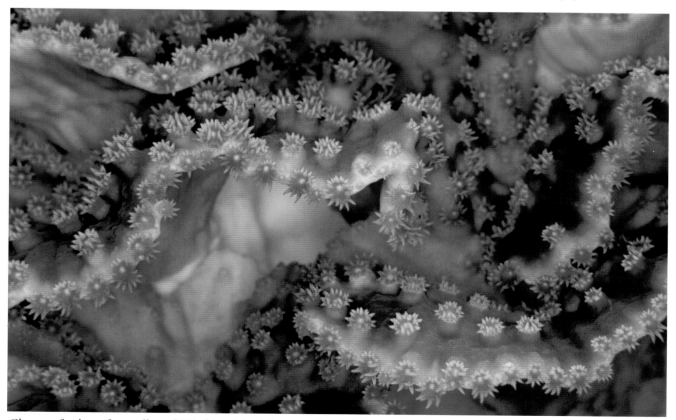

*Closeup of polyps of a scroll coral (Turbinaria) with a convoluted skeleton. During a power outage following a hurricane, Richard lost some of his coral collection, but has since reestablished the surviving colonies in a new 3,000-gallon system.*

# Walk-Around Reef

*Tapio Haaparanta's San Diego 300-gallon tank can be viewed from three sides and is designed to model an outer-reef habitat.*

PERHAPS IT'S OUR TELEVISION CULTURE AT WORK—leading most marine aquarists to position their tanks flat against a wall to be viewed only through the front window. Tapio Haaparanta planned his 300-gallon stony coral system differently, placing it in a spacious family room where it could be viewed from three sides. This required some creative thinking about the placement of equipment, as well as aquascaping. The unusual live rock structure touches only one of the short end walls of the tank. Extra large pieces of live rock were used to provide a very stable and self-supporting structure that Tapio says was actually easier to build than the usual aggregation of smaller rock pieces. Surprisingly, this design required only a few hundred pounds of live rock, less than normally required when the rock is stacked against the back wall. As a result, live corals—rather than a mass of rock—are now the dominant component of this aquascape. Walking around the aquarium, the viewer is treated to a different and unique view of the reef from many angles.

This tank and its custom stand were designed as a focal point in the family room and a dominant feature that can be seen from adjacent rooms as well. Tapio set up the tank to mimic a South Pacific outer-reef habitat where small-polyped stony corals dominate. These reefs receive intense sunlight and strong water motion—two technical challenges for the reefkeeper. To simulate the tropical sunlight, an elaborate array of lights consisting of four 400-watt metal

The holy grail of coral keepers, brightly colored Acroporas—such as this blue A. pulchra—proliferate in this tank.

A Regal Angelfish (Pygoplites diacanthus) finds the water conditions and profusion of hiding places to its liking.

A leafy, convoluted cactus coral (Pavona cactus) is developing into a sprawling, impressive specimen.

Large staghorns such as this Acropora pulchra require intense light, strong currents, and ever-available calcium to grow.

**ADDITIONAL PUMPS:** Six Gemini pumps, 960 gph each. Two Eheim 1060 pumps at the bottom of the tank near the overflow, directed toward the opposite short end. Emergency 12 V battery pump (500 gph) runs from a deep-cycle marine battery and is activated by a relay that will turn on the pump when power is out to main pump.

**WAVEMAKING DEVICES:** Neptune controller operates the 6 Gemini and 2 Eheim 1060 pumps.

## CONTROLLERS

**TEMPERATURE CONTROLS:** Neptune with internal thermostat on heaters and external chiller controller as backups (set slightly above and below, respectively, for safety).

**FANS:** Two Comair Rotron Falcon fans (300 cfm) in the light hood and one Comair-Rotron Caravel fan (550 cfm) that blows over the sump inside the aquarium cabinet. All fans have speed regulation and are controlled by the Neptune.

**HEATERS:** Three 200-watt Tronic heaters in sump.

**CHILLER:** Aqua Logic in-line 1/3 hp ("needs to be larger").

## FILTRATION

**SKIMMER:** ETSS 1200 Gemini run with Iwaki 70 RLT.

**OZONIZER:** Sanders 50 mg/h bubbled into standpipe in overflow.

**CARBON:** 100-200 ml. Used rarely.

**BIOLOGICAL FILTER:** Live rock with associated life.

**REFUGIUM:** Live rock with sponges, etc. in the sump.

**LIVE ROCK IN DISPLAY TANK:** Fiji rock added at different times. Tank evolved from a previous 200 gallon setup. Perhaps a few hundred pounds, but very loosely stacked. Rock is also very porous and was ordered as extra-large pieces.

**LIVE ROCK IN SUMP:** Same type of rock as in display. Smaller chunks (100-200 lbs. total).

**SAND/SUBSTRATE IN DISPLAY:** The tank was originally set up with ESV oolitic sand, subsequently removed. Only traces of sand and small rock pieces under the live rock are present now.

## LIGHTING

**FLUORESCENT BULBS:** Two URI VHO actinic (160 watt) and two (110 watt). Run on IceCap 660 ballast. Four CustomSea Life 96 watt 6,500 K power compacts. Run on IceCap 660 ballast.

**PHOTOPERIOD:** VHO on for 14 hours. Power compacts on for 9 hours.

**HOW OFTEN REPLACED:** Once a year.

**METAL HALIDE BULBS:** Four Osram Blue 400 watt (20,000 K). Run on Taiwan-made HQI ballast.

**PHOTOPERIOD:** 6 hours.

**HOW OFTEN REPLACED:** Every 10-12 months.

**OTHER:** Custom-made polished aluminum parabolic reflector distributes light quite evenly into the tank.

**LIGHTING CONTROLLER(S):** Neptune.

halides, four 96-watt power compact fluorescent, and four VHO fluorescent lights (two 160-watt; two 110-watt) were mounted into a suspended hood. The metal halide bulbs are powered by HQI ballasts that maximize the output and produce a blue-white light spectrum. This combination of lights not only provides good illumination for the corals, but is pleasing to the eye. In addition, the lights have a polished parabolic aluminum reflector (custom-built) behind them to maximize light output and focus the light into the tank. The light produced seems much brighter as the parabolic reflector minimizes light loss into the room. With more than 2,500 watts of light, the many stony corals maintained in this system display exceptionally vibrant colors.

Another major factor contributing to the health of the corals is strong water movement. An external 1,080-gallon-per-hour pump provides water circulation through the sump. In addition, six air-cooled, above-water pumps and two submersible pumps produce almost 8,000 additional gallons per hour of water movement.

Tapio's aggressive approach to providing water movement both at the surface and at the bottom of the tank minimizes dead spots, provides maximum oxygenation throughout the system, and prevents most detritus from settling down. Unfortunately, the water motion is so strong it caused a fine sand bed initially placed in the tank to be blown over the live rock and corals and the substrate had to be removed.

The tank has been stocked with corals that were either imported colonies or fragments from captive colonies obtained from other hobbyists, all carefully selected for their bright colors. These corals have maintained or improved their coloration over time, reversing the trend toward brown seen in early stony coral systems.

The exact taxonomy of many of the numerous *Acropora* colonies is difficult to ascertain because these corals tend to morph over time—especially in a captive environment. Some of the outstanding corals in the system include a bright yellow table colony of *Acropora*, a purple *Acropora valida*, pink *Acropora secale* and *Pocillopora damicornis*, a peach-colored colony of *Montipora spumosa*, a green *Porites cylindrica,* and a rare colony of *Pavona maldivensis*. Despite the strong water motion, a large colony of *Pavona cactus* has grown from a small fragment. This coral is generally found in calm waters, but its rapid growth in these conditions shows that it can grow well even in strong currents when good conditions are present.

Surgeonfishes seem to do especially well in this reef, and anthias have thrived. The king of the tank, however, is a Regal Angelfish (*Pygoplites diacanthus*), often described as a species that does poorly in captivity. Tapio believes that the secret for its success is providing a good habitat and pristine water conditions as well as a varied diet that includes sponges.

Because of its prominent spot in the family home, this tank needs to be kept in prime viewing condition. One the things Tapio would do differently if starting over would be to locate pumps, all filtration, and chiller in a separate room to isolate noise and to make for ease of maintenance behind the scene. Still, the system is designed to requires very little maintenance and it allows Tapio and his family time to sit back and enjoy the multitude of views.

*Hardly distinguishable from a section of wild reef, Tapio's natural-looking aquascape represents a large investment of time in experimentation and learning by trial and error to determine workable equipment combinations and physical parameters.*

## SYSTEM PARAMETERS & CHEMISTRY

**WATER TEMPERATURE:** Winter 78 to 80°F; summer 81 to 84.5°F.

**SPECIFIC GRAVITY:** 1.025-1.026.

**PH:** 8.0-8.3.

**ALKALINITY:** 4.0-4.5 dKH.

**CALCIUM:** 400-430 ppm.

**NITRATE:** Laboratory tested June 1999: 0.69 ppm nitrate + nitrite.

**PHOSPHATE:** Laboratory tested June 1999: 0.02 ppm.

**RESINS OR DEVICES USED TO REDUCE NITRATE OR PHOSPHATE:** None.

**OTHER READINGS:** Laboratory tested June 1999: Magnesium 1,200-1,300 ppm, Silica 0 ppm, Ammonia 0.03 ppm.

**MUNICIPAL WATER SUPPLY:** San Diego municipal water.

**REVERSE OSMOSIS:** SpectraPure RO/DI.

**SALT USED:** Tropic Marin and occasionally Instant Ocean.

**WATER CHANGE SCHEDULE:** 45 gallons monthly-bimonthly.

**ADDITIVES OR SUPPLEMENTS USED:** 1 ml 5% potassium iodide every week; 10-20 ml 20% strontium chloride biweekly. Often not added as regularly.

**MONITORING EQUIPMENT:** Neptune datalog and modem pager hook up.

**DOSING EQUIPMENT USED:** SpectraPure Liter meter for evaporated water hooked up through Ultralife float switch.

**MAINTENANCE SCHEDULE:** Routine maintenance involves cleaning the aquarium glass with magnet cleaner every 3 days. Perform water changes. Clean all pump impellers in acid twice a year. Clean skimmer once a month.

## LIVESTOCK

**FISHES:** 35.

**STONY CORALS:** 80.

**SOFT CORALS:** 10.

**OTHER LIVESTOCK:** Various starfish. Pair of cleaner shrimp and blood shrimp. Snails, hermit crabs, other crabs, urchins, etc.

**NOTEWORTHY SPECIMENS:** Regal Angel for 3 years. *Pavona maldivensis* coral colony.

**SPAWNING EVENTS:** Various spawns have occurred, but the animals responsible were not identified.

## FEEDING

**REGIMEN FOR FISHES:** Fed once per day an amount equal to approximately 4 frozen cubes. A mix of Instant Ocean Formula One, Formula Two, and Angel Formula. Other frozen foods are sometimes given in this mix. Nori is given occasionally in a clip.

**REGIMEN FOR CORALS/INVERTS:** Not fed directly.

## NOTES

**PROBLEMS OVERCOME WITH THIS SYSTEM:** The system seems to be accepted by most stony corals as good current is provided by the multiple pumps.

**THINGS OWNER LIKES BEST ABOUT THIS SYSTEM:** Three viewable sides. Good SPS coral coloration.

**SPECIAL ABOUT THIS SYSTEM:** Very good water movement and high wattage lighting.

**FAVORITE COMMENTS BY OTHERS ABOUT THIS AQUARIUM:**
1. "Good coloration of stony corals."
2. "Several corals have reached good sizes for captive specimens."

**OVERALL POSITIVES:**
1. Supports healthy fish population.
2. Good coral growth and coloration.
3. Three viewable sides and therefore easy access to all areas of the aquarium.

**OVERALL NEGATIVES:**
1. Somewhat noisy because all equipment is in the cabinet.
2. The suspended light hood is a bit cumbersome to move up when reaching into the tank.

# Barebones Reef

*Started by aquarium chemist Bob Stark to test his theories and products, this 120-gallon tank runs with minimal technology.*

## AQUARIUM PROFILE

**OWNER & DESIGNER:** Bob Stark
  www.esvco.com.
**LOCATION:** Yorktown Heights, NY.
**DATE ESTABLISHED:** April 1999. (This
  system is an upgrade from a 75-gallon
  system set up 6 years prior that used
  essentially the same methodology and
  housed some of the same specimens.)
**DATE PHOTOGRAPHED:** July 2001.

### TANK
**CONFIGURATION:** Rectangular.
**DISPLAY TANK:** 120 gallons, glass.
**DISPLAY TANK DIMENSIONS:** 48" X 24" X
  24".
**LOCATION (ROOM):** Den.
**CABINETRY/ARCHITECTURAL DETAILS:**
  Stained pine stand.

### CIRCULATION
**MAIN SYSTEM PUMP(S):** 6 Aquarium
  Systems Maxi-Jet 750 powerheads (198
  gph each); 1 Marineland H.O.T.
  Magnum, for circulation only (250 gph).
**WATER RETURNS:** 4 of the 6 powerheads
  are stacked and cable-tied onto a PVC
  pipe lowered into the back left corner
  behind the rock structure. Flow from
  these 4 powerheads runs parallel along
  the back glass and behind the rock

IN JAKARTA IN THE 1960S, Lee Chin Eng started using a system for keeping marine life alive that has been dubbed "The Natural Method." It called for live rock and live sand and relied on very little equipment—nothing more than an air pump, to be precise—to keep it running. Today, most reef enthusiasts rely much more on technology to support their fishes and invertebrates. In his experimental 120-gallon tank, chemist Bob Stark has demonstrated an ability to keep marine organisms alive and well with simple methods and a lack of technology that harkens back to the ideas of Lee Chin Eng.

Rather than using filters, skimmers or other means of filtration, this tank relies on the natural processes that occur on every reef to provide nitrification, denitrification, and nutrient removal. Rather than using an external means for nutrient export, this tank allows the corals, live rock, and microfauna keep the nutrient levels low. To make this work, Bob has learned to respect the biological limitations of the system and to understand the chemical processes necessary to keep it in balance.

Using his formal training in chemistry and his expertise in formulating additives for reef aquarists—he is the founder of ESV Co. Inc., Bob has spent a number of years of trial and error to achieve a working balance between the food introduced and waste produced by the fishes and the natural capacity of the tank to use these nutrients. Using only small pumps to create essential water circulation, Bob avoids skimmers and all other filtration and water conditioning devices that make life easier for most aquarists. He does no regular water changes. Some regard his methods as spartan and difficult for others to match, but the thriving condition of his animals attests to a method behind the minimalist strategy.

To achieve success, Bob has had to limit the bioload of fishes that are kept in this system to no more than four modestly sized specimens. Adding more would overwhelm the nutrient-cycling capacity of the tank and defeat the design of the system. Also, because there is no means for increasing the dissolved oxygen level at night, the photoperiod for the lights needs to be slightly longer than in most tanks, so that the dissolved oxygen levels do not get too low during the dark phase. Bob uses four power compact fluorescent bulbs to generate light above the tank. While not nearly as strong as the tropical sun, which Mr. Eng employed, they still provide more than 3 watts per gallon of light. Mr. Eng employed a simple airstone as a means for water movement, while this system has much better circulation with powerheads and a small pump that turn the tank's volume over at least 10 times per hour.

*Proving that expensive lighting and skimming are not absolutely essential for good coral growth, Bob's reef includes this hardy branching green Montipora digitata.*

The only chemical export done on this system is the harvesting and removal of the fast-growing soft corals and the use of activated carbon, which scavenges some dissolved wastes, on a regular basis. To cope with the lack of water changes, critical chemicals must be added as supplements. Calcium, buffer, iodine, strontium, and magnesium, all of which are constantly consumed by the corals, are added regularly. The fishes are fed daily, but not at the aggressive rates that occur in most reef tanks.

The success of this system can be seen not only in the overall health of the corals, but also in the longevity of the animals. Most of the corals are over 7 years old with some older than 9. New colonies of the soft corals develop regularly, and the stony corals such as the *Turbinaria* and the *Caulastrea* are budding into additional new colonies. This complete system shows that expensive technology need not be essential for a tank's success, provided that the owner offers attention to detail and an understanding of the biological and chemical processes at work in such a living system. Ever curious and eager try new ideas, Bob Stark may consider this a work in progress, but he has clearly mastered the basics of balancing a small captive reef system with methods that Lee Chin Eng would appreciate.

structure, which is arranged to create a space a few inches wide between the rock and back glass. The PVC pipe can easily be lifted from the tank for powerhead maintenance. The 5th powerhead is at the back top right corner with water flow aimed at a 45° angle toward the front glass. The 6th powerhead is attached to an Osci-Wave device located just to the left of the 5th powerhead. The H.O.T. Magnum is near the left side of the back glass with its output directed toward the SPS coral area. This canister filter contains no media and is used for circulation.

**CONTROLLERS:** None.
**FANS:** None (system is located next to a window AC unit).
**HEATERS:** 200 watt (used only in winter).
**CHILLER:** None.

## FILTRATION

**CARBON:** 12 fluid ounces (1 fl. oz. per 10 gals.); replaced monthly.
**BIOLOGICAL FILTER:** This system relies extensively on natural biological filtration

*A suspended shelf of eggcrate material, now covered with pink coralline algae, serves as a platform for establishing coral fragments and new colonies.*

within the system. These processes include nitrification, denitrification, and nutrient assimilation by photosynthetic organisms. Soft corals, predominantly *Xenia*, grow very rapidly and their periodic removal provides nutrient export from the system.

**REFUGIUM:** None intended, but the H.O.T. Magnum has gradually become a refuge for a dense population of sponges and other filter feeders that have taken up residence inside the dark canister.

**LIVE ROCK:** Live rock takes up approximately 25-30% of the area in the aquarium. The rock is predominantly homemade (Portland cement/Oolitic sand/oyster shell blend) seeded with Sea Critters aquacultured rock and rock from previously established aquariums.

**SAND/SUBSTRATE:** 2 inches of ESV Fine Grade Oolitic Aragonite sand originally added. No sand located behind rock structure where water current is very strong.

## LIGHTING

**FLUORESCENT BULBS:** CustomSealife hood with four 96-watt Power Compact bulbs.

**PHOTOPERIOD:** 2 actinics on for 17 hours; 1 Daylite plus 1 Smart bulb (1/2 actinic and daylight) both on for 14 hours.

**REPLACEMENT SCHEDULE:** Yearly unless bulb failure requires replacement.

**LIGHTING CONTROLLERS:** Standard lamp timer for each of the two ballasts.

## SYSTEM PARAMETERS & CHEMISTRY:

**WATER TEMPERATURE:** 78 to 81°F.
**SPECIFIC GRAVITY:** 1.024-1.025.
**PH:** 7.9 (a.m.) to 8.35 (p.m.).
**ALKALINITY:** 2.75-3.0 meq/L.
**CALCIUM:** 380-450 ppm.
**NITRATE:** Not detectable.
**PHOSPHATE:** Not detectable.
**RESINS OR DEVICES USED TO REDUCE NITRATE OR PHOSPHATE:** None.
**OTHER READINGS:** Magnesium 1,300 ppm.
**WATER SOURCE:** Municipal water supply.

**REVERSE OSMOSIS:** Yes.
**DEIONIZATION:** No.
**SALT USED:** Initial salt used was Aquarium Systems Instant Ocean.
**WATER CHANGE SCHEDULE:** None except for very small amounts of aquarium water removed each month and replaced with fresh RO water to offset the gradual increase in salinity due to the residual ions added by B-Ionic Calcium Buffer.

**ADDITIVES OR SUPPLEMENTS:**
1. ESV's B-Ionic Calcium Buffer (enough added daily to maintain alkalinity, usually 1 ml of each component per 2-4 gallons).
2. ESV's 1% Potassium Iodide, 20% Strontium Chloride, and Bromide Fluoride supplements, all added as per manufacturer's instructions.
3. ESV's B-Ionic Magnesium as aquarium testing warrants.

**MONITORING EQUIPMENT:** American Marine's Pinpoint pH meter and occasional use of the Pinpoint dissolved oxygen meter.

**DOSING EQUIPMENT:** None.

**MAINTENANCE SCHEDULE:** Approximately 2 hours maintenance per month consisting of daily feeding and supplement addition, weekly cleaning and supplement addition, and monthly testing and carbon change.

## LIVESTOCK:

**FISHES:** 4.
**STONY CORALS:** 16 SPS corals and 8 LPS corals.
**SOFT CORALS:** 11 species with too many colonies to count.
**OTHER LIVESTOCK:** Blue-leg hermits, *Astraea* snails, *Columbella* snails, plus countless tubeworms and other filter feeders.
**NOTEWORTHY SPECIMENS:** Most corals are over 7 years old, a few are 9 years old. *Turbinaria* cup coral is budding.
**SPAWNING EVENTS:** Occasional *Astraea* snail spawning. *Columbella* snails reproduce regularly with excellent survival rates as they have no planktonic stage.

## FEEDING

**REGIMEN FOR FISHES:** Pinch of OSI *Spirulina* Flakes daily. Frozen *Mysis* once per week.

**REGIMEN FOR CORALS/INVERTS:** 6 measuring spoons ESV Spray-Dried Marine Phytoplankton added twice per week.

## NOTES

**PROBLEMS OVERCOME WITH THIS SYSTEM:**
1. This system pushes the envelope of simplicity and low cost to the maximum while still delivering a healthy environment for coral aquaculture.
2. This system is practically silent except for the sound of the lighting hood cooling fan.
3. No external plumbing dramatically reduces the chance of system failure and flooding.

**THINGS THE OWNER WOULD LIKE TO CHANGE:** While such a simple reef system can result in a beautiful reef tank, it is limited as far as the number of fish that can be maintained due to the lack of an aggressive export mechanism (skimmer, algae filter, etc.) and an aggressive gas exchange device (aeration, skimmer, wet dry filter, or reverse/daylight algae filter). Reef aquarists who desire a large fish population should seriously consider adding one of these peripheral devices.

**THINGS OWNER LIKES BEST ABOUT THIS SYSTEM:** This system serves as an important prototype for the commercial culture of photosynthetic aquarium organisms with minimal overhead in energy and maintenance costs.The key to to this system's simplicity relies on the important balance between heterotrophic and autotrophic organisms. It provides an important educational tool in understanding ecosystems. For example, the effect of the varying photoperiod is much more dramatic on this system compared to a heavily aerated system. For this particular aquarium, the extended photoperiod is critical with regard to preventing dangerously low dissolved oxygen levels during the dark phase.

**FAVORITE COMMENTS BY OTHERS ABOUT THIS AQUARIUM:**
1. Other aquarists can't believe how good the animals look in such a barebones system. I've had fellow aquarists probe the system in search of a hidden skimmer, sump, etc.
2. "The lack of noise adds a certain degree of serenity and peacefulness to the system."

**OVERALL POSITIVES:**
1. Low cost.
2. Low noise.
3. Low maintenance.

**OVERALL NEGATIVES (OR THINGS TO DO DIFFERENTLY NEXT TIME):** Not much I would do differently except limit the number of soft corals as their rapid growth leads to problems as they encroach upon the stony corals.

# Desktop Coral Paradise

*A microcosmic reef scene in a 40-gallon tank created on a student budget by Tim Herman in his Illinois dorm room.*

T HE CONVENTIONAL WISDOM SAYS that you need a very large tank bristling with expensive technology to have a successful and visually appealing reef aquarium. Tim Herman's 40-gallon system is living proof of just how flawed this thinking is. As a college student with a small dormitory room, Tim had neither the space nor the huge finances to set up a large, state-of-the-art system. Undeterred, he set up a tank using the guidelines for the best systems he had seen and to fill it he acquired cuttings and fragments of the best-colored and rarest corals he had seen. He planned the system so that the beauty and colors of the corals would be the predominant feature, with an intentionally small fish load that provides some movement but not much waste.

When Tim was assembling his system, one of the hot topics in reef keeping was whether refugium-based systems had advantages over skimmer-based systems. Finding no definitive conclusion about which was better, Tim decided to utilize the positive attributes of both for his aquarium. However, while this system employs a hang-on-the-tank skimmer, unresolved pump problems limited its use and the tank is essentially skimmerless. Because of this, most of the filtration occurs in the five-gallon plastic waste can refugium that contains a 2-inch sand bed, live rock, various genera of marine algae and *Xenia*. Although a battle with keeping the alga *Dictyota* under control has been

## AQUARIUM PROFILE

**OWNER:** Tim Herman.
**LOCATION:** Champaign, IL.
**DATE ESTABLISHED:** June 2000.
**DATE PHOTOGRAPHED:** August 2001.

### TANK
**CONFIGURATION:** Rectangular.
**DISPLAY TANK VOLUME:** 40 gallons.
**DISPLAY TANK DIMENSIONS:** 36" X 18" X 16".
**DISPLAY TANK MATERIAL:** Glass.
**REFUGIUM VOLUME:** 5 gallons.
**PROPAGATION TANK VOLUME:** 20 gallons.
**LOCATION:** Dormitory room.
**CABINETRY:** On an oak desk.

### CIRCULATION
**WATER RETURNS:** Mini-Jet 606 pumping water up to a 20 gallon prop tank; gravity return through 1 inch vinyl tubing.
**ADDITIONAL PUMPS:** Hagen AquaClear 500 filter with media removed, replaced with live rock. Three Maxi-Jet 1200s on Wavemaster. Maxi-Jet 900 in prop tank also on Wavemaster.

**WAVEMAKING DEVICES:** Red Sea Wavemaster Pro.

## CONTROLLERS
**FANS:** IceCap 4-inch fan blowing on metal halide bulb; 10-inch Honeywell turbo fan blowing across tank surface.
**HEATERS:** Ebo-Jager 200 watt.
**CHILLER:** None.

## FILTRATION
**SKIMMER:** AquaC Remora Pro. Tried various alternative pumps to the Rio pump, none of which produced much skimmate at all, so system was essentially skimmerless most of the time.
**CARBON:** 1 cup, changed once per month.
**BIOLOGICAL FILTER:** None (other than live rock).
**REFUGIUM:** 5-gallon Rubbermaid wastebasket, holding about 8 lbs. Fiji live rock, assorted *Caulerpa* spp., *Sargassum* sp., *Dictyota* sp., *Xenia elongata*.
**LIVE ROCK IN DISPLAY TANK:** About 100 lbs. Fiji live rock.
**SAND/SUBSTRATE IN DISPLAY:** 3-inch sand bed, 50/50 mixture of oolitic and larger (2-3 mm diameter) aragonite sand.
**SAND/SUBSTRATE IN SUMP/REFUGIUM:** 2 inches of 2-3 mm diameter aragonite sand.

## LIGHTING
**FLUORESCENT BULBS:** Four 110-watt VHO URI Superactinic.
**PHOTOPERIOD:** 12 hours per day, replaced every 8 months.
**METAL HALIDE BULBS:** One 400-watt 6,500 K Iwasaki over display tank; one 250-watt 10,000 K Ushio HQI lamp over propagation tank.
**PHOTOPERIOD:** 9 hours per day, replaced every 12 months.
**REFUGIUM:** Lit by 65-watt Lights of America power compact fluorescent.
**REFUGIUM PHOTOPERIOD:** Reverse 10-hour.
**NATURAL LIGHT:** About 1.5 hours natural sunlight in the morning.
**LIGHTING CONTROLLER(S):** Intermatic appliance timers.

## SYSTEM PARAMETERS & CHEMISTRY
**WATER TEMPERATURE:** 81 to 84°F.
**SPECIFIC GRAVITY:** 1.026.
**PH:** ~8.0.
**ALKALINITY:** 10 dKH.
**CALCIUM:** 425 ppm.
**NITRATE:** 0.
**PHOSPHATE:** 0.
**RESINS OR DEVICES USED TO REDUCE NITRATE OR PHOSPHATE:** None.
**REVERSE OSMOSIS:** Kent 60 gpd Hi-S RO processed municipal water.
**DEIONIZATION:** No.
**SALT USED:** Instant Ocean.
**WATER CHANGE SCHEDULE:** 10 gallons every 6 to 8 weeks.
**DOSING EQUIPMENT USED:** DIY single-chamber calcium reactor. CaribSea Special Grade Reef Sand as media.

one of the problems with this setup, Tim feels that its rapid growth has helped with nutrient export. The only other filtration in this system is provided by the use of a small amount of carbon that is changed monthly and a 10-gallon water change performed every six to eight weeks. The limited filtration works because of the low fish load—coupled with a large population of microfauna to consume waste or detritus. This microfauna is reproducing at such a rapid rate that even in this relatively small tank a pair of Psychedelic or Spotted Mandarinfish (*Synchiropus splendidus*) are not only surviving but are also showing signs of spawning.

Considerable quantities of nutrients were also undoubtedly consumed by the rapidly growing corals and other invertebrates. Coral growth is encouraged by very strong light for a system of this size. A 400-watt 6,500 K bulb supplemented with four 110-watt Actinic bulbs provide approximately 20 watts of light per gallon. In addition, this tank was placed to receive approximately 1.5 hours per day of morning sunlight. The refugium was also provided with strong lighting from four 65-watt power compact fluorescent tubes. The bright light over the refugium allows for rapid growth of the algae present and has helped to keep the nutrient levels within the system very low. The only additions that are made to this tank are calcium and buffer via a calcium reactor. No other additives except food for the fish and corals are used.

Tim found that one of the advantages of using only inexpensive or free fragments from other captive systems is being able to accrue a collection of corals that consistently do well in captivity, but also that have brilliant colors when kept under optimum conditions. By trading with other hobbyists, Tim has put together a collection of more than 30 encrusting and plating *Montipora* and 70 different species and morphs of *Acropora*. These include many colonies of bi- and tricolored *Acropora* that are not widely available. (Tim uses a 20-gallon propagation tank linked to the system to acclimate and nurture cuttings outside the display aquarium.) In addition, this tank houses an additional 30 colonies of various soft corals. The combination of soft and hard corals in a tightly confined space is considered difficult to do successfully, owing to the growth inhibiting compounds produced by the soft corals, but this system has managed to do this with little apparent difficulty.

Through proper planning and consideration of the animals' needs, Tim has been able to establish a relatively small tank with a diversity of corals and other animals that is rarely seen in even much larger systems. Remarkably, the entire system requires little time and maintenance to run properly. Still, the constraints of the tank size will eventually prevent the corals from growing to full size, and Tim is modest in describing how meticulous he has had to be in order to keep the animals from overgrowing one another. Seeing the kind of growth, color, and success that Tim has had in such a small system illustrates that, even when space is limited, an imaginative and conscientious aquarist can produce an absolutely stunning display of coral beauty.

Editor's note: Tim Herman has completed his studies and this system has now been dismantled and the livestock moved to a larger system.

*A Caribbean Sailfin Blenny (Emblemaria pandionis) perches on the reef and shares the small system with a breeding pair of Psychedelic Mandarinfish.*

**AUTOMATIC TOP OFF:** Grainger float switches wired to Maxi-Jet 1200 pumping from RO reservoir.

## LIVESTOCK

**FISHES:** 5.
1 Firefish (*Nemateleotris magnifica*)
1 Caribbean Sailfin Blenny (*Emblemaria pandionis*)
2 Psychedelic Mandarinfish (*Synchiropus picturatus*)
1 Yellow-headed Jawfish (*Opistognathus aurifrons*)

**STONY CORALS:** Total approx. 120.
34 morphs/species of plating and encrusting *Montipora*
Approx. 70 morphs/species of *Acropora*
Assorted other SPS corals, including *Pavona, Porites, Psammocora, Seriatopora, Trachyphyllia, Euphyllia, Tubastraea, Caulastrea, Lobophyllia, Blastomussa*

**SOFT CORALS:** Total approx. 30.
*Tubipora, Heliopora, Clavularia, Pachyclavularia, Erythropodium, Xenia, Ricordea, Zoanthus, Palythoa, Sinularia, Sarcophyton, Rhodactis, Discosoma*

**OTHER LIVESTOCK:**
2 Fire Shrimp (*Lysmata debelius*)
1 brittle star
2 *Tridacna maxima*
1 *Tridacna derasa*

**NOTEWORTHY SPECIMENS:** Many unique soft and hard corals, pulsing *Sinularia*, several exceptional plating and encrusting *Montipora* spp.

**SPAWNING EVENTS:** *Synchiropus picturatus* regularly engaged in breeding behavior. No eggs actually seen.

## FEEDING

**REGIMEN FOR FISHES:** Formula One, flake, frozen *Artemia*, New Life Spectrum pellets, any of the preceding fed about twice per day.

**REGIMEN FOR CORALS/INVERTS:** 10 drops Tahitian Blend, 1/2 tsp. Golden Pearls fed 4 times weekly. New Life Spectrum pellets for *Tubastraea* and sand bed.

## NOTES

**THINGS THE OWNER WOULD LIKE TO CHANGE:** Fewer *Aiptasia*, not adding evil peppermint shrimp that ate all my *Stomatella*.

**THINGS OWNER LIKES BEST ABOUT THIS SYSTEM:**
1. Excellent growth rate and coloration of SPS.
2. Low fish load and extremely abundant microfauna population combined with calcium reactor and automatic top off made the system essentially maintenance free and self-sustaining. Could leave for over 1 week with no problems. Very natural system that basically took care of itself.
3. Abundant macroalgae provided food and cover for microfauna, allowing *S. picturatus* to thrive with no supplemental feeding for the 10 months I had them before the tank was taken down.

**SPECIAL ABOUT THIS SYSTEM:**
1. All but 2 of the over 100 SPS grown from captive grown fragments.
2. Successful keeping of *Synchiropus picturatus* in such a small tank (I don't recommend attempting this).
3. SPS flourishing in such a young system, due in part to beginning with some rock and sand from an established tank, large quantities of macroalgae maintaining low nutrient levels, and intense lighting keeping corals happy.
4. Feeding Golden Pearls, phytoplankton, and New Life Spectrum pellets (for *Tubastraea* and sand bed) also helped microfauna populations, which in turn fed corals.

**FAVORITE COMMENTS BY OTHERS:** "Holy *Montipora*!"

**OVERALL POSITIVES:**
1. Almost completely tank-raised corals.
2. Almost maintenance-free.
3. Great coloration and growth rates.

**OVERALL NEGATIVES (OR THINGS TO DO DIFFERENTLY NEXT TIME):**
1. *Aiptasia*.
2. *Dictyota* (love/hate relationship: it grew like mad and was annoying to keep in check, but it also provided lots of cover for microfauna and took up a lot of nutrients).
3. Must do a bigger system next time, real estate was at a premium.

# 20,000-Gallon Dream

*A home aquarist in his spare hours, Joe Yaiullo's job called for the creation of this 20,000-gallon reef at Atlantis Marine World.*

## AQUARIUM PROFILE

**OWNER:** Atlantis Marine World Aquarium
www.atlantismarineworld.com.
**DESIGNER:** Joseph Yaiullo.
**LOCATION:** Riverhead, NY.
**DATE ESTABLISHED:** July 2000.
**DATE PHOTOGRAPHED:** June 2001.
**PHOTOGRAPHER:** Charles Glatzer.

### TANK
**CONFIGURATION:** Rectangular.
**DISPLAY TANK VOLUME:** 20,420 gallons
(~77,000 L).
**DISPLAY TANK DIMENSIONS:** 30' X 14' X 6.5'.
**DISPLAY TANK MATERIAL:** Steel-reinforced
concrete with sprayed-on liner.
**SUMP VOLUME:** 750 gallons.
**LOCATION:** Public aquarium display.
**CABINETRY/ARCHITECTURAL DETAILS:** Lost
City of Atlantis "ruins."

### CIRCULATION
**MAIN SYSTEM PUMP(S):**
1. 3 hp Hayward II Super Pump (140
gpm/540 lpm) on high-rate sand
filter.
2. 5 hp PacFab Challenger pump (220
gpm/846 lpm).
3. 5 hp PacFab Challenger pump (220
gpm/846 lpm) on skimmer.

I MAGINE, IF YOU CAN, HAVING THE CHANCE TO SET UP a reef aquarium to fulfill your wildest fantasy. How large would it be? 1,000 gallons? 5,000 gallons? In the Living Reef exhibit at Atlantis Marine World, Joe Yaiullo had just such an opportunity to plan and create a dream reef system. At 20,420 gallons, the tank is beyond even the imaginary bounds of most home aquarists. It measures 30 feet across, 14 feet front to back, and is 6 1/2 feet deep. The sump adds another 750 gallons—bigger than the vast majority of reef display aquariums. The structure is not the traditional glass box, but rather it is made of concrete reinforced with steel with a special sprayed-on liner. Two 10-foot long and 6-foot-high acrylic panels are set into the concrete structure to provide viewing access.

More than 15 tons of quarried ancient limestone provide a base for the reef, covered by a living skin of 5 tons of live rock from Fiji and Tonga. This provides a reef structure to support approximately 600 coral colonies that represent the initial stocking in this tank. Interestingly, the corals are two-thirds stony corals (400) and one-third soft corals (200). The rock is arranged to provide large caves and open areas within the rocky structure, giving even small and shy fishes many places in which to hide and swim. This is a departure from most large public aquarium displays, which are typically designed to house sizable display species. However, because Joe is an avid home reefkeeper, he was determined to place some small species in this tank, such as firefishes, blennies, and gobies. With close observation, these relatively tiny specimens can be seen occupying safe shelter on or near the reef structure—just as they would in the wild.

Other aspects of this unique system are designed to mimic nature. This size tank requires a lot of water motion, and more than 3,500 gallons of water are moved per minute. Even so, the tank's total volume is only turned over slightly more then once per hour. Due to its great depth, lighting this tank requires the use of 1,000-watt metal halide lamps. More than 18,000 watts of light are provided, and while this may seem an awesome show of power (don't think about the utility bill), it is really less than one watt per gallon. Only metal halide lamps are used and there is approximately a 4:1 ratio of 6,500 K bulbs to higher temperature blue bulbs.

Filtration is achieved through the use of a custom-made 9-foot tall venturi-driven protein skimmer. The reaction chamber alone is 4 feet in diameter and 6 feet tall, and the riser tube for foam collection is 18 inches in diameter. Fifteen gallons of activated carbon are used constantly in a custom-made reverse flow chamber that filters 900 gallons per hour. Constant ozone is also used to keep the water crystal clear. Additionally, 10% of the water is changed per month. This filtration system produces water that is very low in nutrients despite the large fish load. Phosphate is undetectable and nitrate is less then 2 ppm.

A tank this size gives the 800 fishes room to behave in a natural manner. As a result, several fish species as well as clams and snails have spawned. Particularly interesting for many home aquarists is the school of over 200 anthias of several species that appear to exhibit the same social behaviors seen in the wild. The success that Joe has achieved with these anthias, typically a challenge in captive reefs, is due in large part to his aggressive feeding schedule. Joe feeds them New Life Spectrum pellet food, *Mysis* shrimp, frozen brine shrimp and frozen Cyclop-eeze (a small, aquacultured red copepod that is highly nutritious and a good substitute for the tiny plankton that wild anthias eat with relish). The special attribute of this food is that it remains suspended in the water column for extended periods so the anthias and other grazers can pick at it throughout the day. This closely mimics how they naturally feed in the water column and is one of the reasons why Joe feels they are doing so well in this system. Also, the more aggressive and belligerent feeders tend to leave this food alone because of its small size.

In addition, there are several schools of tangs, fairy wrasses, and damselfishes that interact as if they had never left their original reef. Banggai Cardinals have spawned and the young have grown to adulthood within the tank. This display also contains numerous herbivores and detritivores such as sea cucumbers, serpent stars, snails, and hermit crabs that work to keep any detritus or algae from gaining a foothold. Joe has also placed numerous anemones in the tank, including long-tentacle or corkscrew anemone (*Macrodactyla doreensis*), and the magnificent sea anemone (*Heteractis magnifica*). There is also a colony of elephant ear anemones that are over 18 inches across.

This tank is still relatively young at this writing, and as a result the corals have not had much time to fully grow in and cover the available space. Some observers think this tank may become more like an actual reef than any other known captive system in the country. Sheer size is part of the story, but the spirit and expertise of a home aquarist given the opportunity to build a dream reef is also a key to the success of this system.

**WATER RETURNS:** Five fixed 1 inch return lines and six 1 inch Sea Swirl oscillators.

**ADDITIONAL PUMPS:**
1. One 3/4 hp Kasco Aerator/Deicer: ~520 gpm/2000 lpm.
2. One 3/4 hp Scott Aquasweep (www.scottaerator.com): ~520 gpm/2,000 l pm.

## CONTROLLERS
**FANS:** Building air conditioned; vent fan to outside air.
**CHILLER:** Geothermal cooling with Polaris titanium heat exchanger (manually controlled water flow).

## FILTRATION
**SKIMMER:** Self-designed, fabricated polyethylene foam fractionator—4 inch diameter/6 inch reaction area/18 inch diameter riser tube/total height of 9' 4"/2 foot venturi uses 2 inch Mazzei venturi injector driven with 5 hp PacFab Challenger pump.
**MECHANICAL FILTER:** PacFab TR140 high-rate sand filter. Hayward DE filter used to vacuum tank.
**OZONIZER:** DEL CD ozone generator.
**CARBON:** 15 gallons in custom-made 18 inch diameter unit, ~900 gph, continuous use reverse flow.
**HOW OFTEN USED OR CHANGED:** Every 2-3 months.
**BIOLOGICAL FILTER:** 5 feet tall/6 inch diameter calcium reactors under construction.
**REFUGIUM:** To be added. Tank has various areas within the tank from very fine sand to large coral rubble zones, wide variety of small crustaceans throughout.
**LIVE ROCK IN DISPLAY TANK:** ~10,000 lbs. from Fiji and Tonga; ~30,000 lbs. quarried limestone from Eden Stone, Wisconsin. This rock is 300 million years old.
**SUBSTRATE IN DISPLAY:** Varies from 1/2-6 inches deep. Substrate varies from fine sand to large coral rubble zones.

## LIGHTING
**FLUORESCENT BULBS:** None.
**METAL HALIDE BULBS:** Twelve 1,000-watt Sunmaster 6,500 K on for 10-11 hours. Six 400-watt Iwasaki 6,500 K on for 10.5-11.5 hours. Four 1,000-watt Venture Blue Bulb/CDX series on for 12 hours.
**HOW OFTEN REPLACED:** 1000-watt 6,500 K every 10-12 months. 400-watt Iwasaki every 12 months. 1,000-watt Blue/CDX every 6-8 months.
**HEIGHT OF LIGHTS ABOVE WATER SURFACE:** 400-watt Iwasaki are wall mounted, 12 inches above water surface at 45° angle. 1,000-watt 6,500 K bulbs vary from 24-36 inches. 1,000-watt Blue/CDX at ~24 inches.
**NATURAL LIGHT:** 4 small skylights, insignificant amount of light, but does provide early a.m. light.
**LIGHTING CONTROLLER(S):** Digital timers.

*Joe takes particular pride in the natural behaviors of the large population of anthias, which are fed a ration that includes a new food called Cyclop-eeze—frozen plankton that satisfies these fishes' need to pluck protein-rich food from the water column.*

*The next generation of Yaiullos study their father's handiwork through one of the tank's two 10-foot-by-6-foot acrylic viewing panels.*

## SYSTEM PARAMETERS & CHEMISTRY

**WATER TEMPERATURE:** 75 to 78°F.
**SPECIFIC GRAVITY:** 1.021-1.022.
**PH:** 8.3-8.45.
**ALKALINITY:** 10-14 dKH.
**CALCIUM:** 400-430 ppm.
**NITRATE:** <2 ppm.
**PHOSPHATE:** 0.
**RESINS OR DEVICES USED TO REDUCE NITRATE OR PHOSPHATE:** None.
**OTHER READINGS:**
   Magnesium: ~1100-1300.
   Stontium: 8-12 ppm.
   Iodine: 0.04.
**NATURAL SEAWATER:** Mechanically filtered NY Atlantic Ocean water (KoldSteril treatment of seawater).
**WATER CHANGE SCHEDULE:** At most, 10% per month.
**ADDITIVES OR SUPPLEMENTS USED:** 160-240 grams/day of milky ESV CaO. ESV Magnesium, Iodine, Strontium and B-Ionic as needed.
**CALCIUM REACTOR:** Dual chamber in series flow, each chamber holds 56 lbs. of media. Flow is currently 400-600 ml/min.
**MONITORING EQUIPMENT:**
   PinPoint pH meter; PinPoint ORP controller; PinPoint pH controller on Ca reactors; Pocket thermometer.
**DOSING EQUIPMENT:** Rola Chem Model 503/80 gpd.

## LIVESTOCK

**FISHES:** 800.
**STONY CORALS:** 400.
**SOFT CORALS:** 200.
**OTHER LIVESTOCK:** Blue-leg hermit crabs, sea cucumbers, variety of algae-eating snails, serpent stars, banded coral shrimp, cleaner shrimps, magnificent sea anemones, long-tentacle anemones, sponges, feather dusters, strong population of amphipods, mysids, other crustaceans.
**NOTEWORTHY SPECIMENS:** Vlamingi Tangs.
**SPAWNING EVENTS:** *Tridacna* clams, Green Chromis, anthias, Banggai Cardinalfish and snails.

## FEEDING

**REGIMEN FOR FISHES:** Daily from 1 to 3x/day, some days heavier than others.
   Frozen: *Mysis, Euphasia pacifica*, brine shrimp, Cyclop-eeze, sand eels, silversides, clam.
   Flake foods: Aquatrol *Spirulina*, Aquatrol Brine, and SeaVeggies.
   Pellets: New Life Spectrum (all three sizes) (setting up auto feeder for NLS pellets which will feed tank small amounts 10x/day).
   Some fresh macroalgae on occasion.
**REGIMEN FOR CORALS/INVERTS:**
   Varies from 1 to 3x/week.
   Target-feed the anemones.
   ESV Spray Dried Algae, AlgaeFeast *Spirulina* powder (Earthrise).
   Frozen foods: Target feed some LPS with clam, shrimp, sand eels, silversides.
   Entire tank is fed Cyclop-eeze (frozen red copepods) 4 to 7x/week.

## NOTES

**PROBLEMS OVERCOME WITH THIS SYSTEM:**
   1. Bubbles back to tank from sump.
   2. Detritus buildup.
   3. Bacterial infections using 10 mg/gallon doxycycline.
**THINGS THE OWNER WOULD LIKE TO CHANGE:**
   1. Increase size of sump.
   2. Make the tank bigger.
**BEST ABOUT THIS SYSTEM:**
   1. Live rock/reef structures.
   2. Watching fish behave naturally.
   3. Setting up "stands" of corals.
**SPECIAL ABOUT THIS SYSTEM:**
   1. Largest closed system in USA and 4th largest in the world.
   2. Lighting designed to highlight the reef and not the walls of the tank.
**FAVORITE COMMENTS BY OTHERS ABOUT THIS AQUARIUM:**
   1. Silence. Then: "Wow."
   2. "You've inspired me to work harder."
**OVERALL POSITIVES:**
   1. Size.
   2. Species diversity/natural setting.
   3. I can SCUBA dive in it.

# Turf Scrubber Reef

*Greeting visitors to Louisville's most popular marine shop is this 180-gallon open reefscape designed by Bruce Davidson.*

## AQUARIUM PROFILE

**OWNER & DESIGNER:** Bruce Davidson.
**LOCATION:** Sandy's Pet Shop, Louisville, KY.
**DATE ESTABLISHED:** August 1999.
**DATE PHOTOGRAPHED:** May 2001.

### TANK
**DISPLAY TANK VOLUME:** All-Glass brand 180 gallons with corner overflow system.
**DISPLAY TANK DIMENSIONS:** 72" X 24" X 24".
**SUMP VOLUME:** Approximately 25 gallons.
**LOCATION (ROOM):** Behind sales counter with tank inside lavatory/utility room.

### CIRCULATION
**MAIN SYSTEM PUMP(S):** Iwaki WMD-40 RLXT ~1,000 gph.
**WATER RETURNS:** Two 0.75-inch knuckle tubing returns.
**WAVEMAKING DEVICES:** Algae turf scrubber uses a dump bucket that dumps ~4 gallons every 40-60 seconds.

### CONTROLLERS:
**TEMPERATURE CONTROLS:** Exhaust fans on metal halide lights.
**HEATERS:** 14 inch 300-watt submersible.

### FILTRATION
Algae Turf Scrubber.

A
S CAPTIVE REEFKEEPING HAS EVOLVED, two schools of husbandry have emerged. One group relies on sophisticated equipment and new technology to achieve a balanced and healthy system. The other group tries to employ natural processes to achieve the same goal. For those who don't ask, the impressive 180-gallon display reef behind the checkout counter at Sandy's Pet Shop in Louisville, Kentucky, could be just another example of a tank running the latest skimmers, UV-filters, ozonizers, and nutrient reactors.

In fact, owner Bruce Davidson uses an ingenious piece of equipment called an algae turf scrubber to achieve a balanced ecosystem in his store's showpiece reef. Hidden behind the wall in a lavatory/utility room, the scrubber is mounted on top of the display tank. Water from the tank is pumped up and into the acrylic unit, where it flows across a screen of dense, green turf algae that grows under compact fluorescent lights. The water, having been scoured of nutrients by its close contact with the fast-growing algae, then collects in a dump bucket, which tips a surge of approximately 4 gallons of water back into the tank every minute in natural, wavelike flushes.

Algae filters have been used, primarily in public aquariums, for years, but with mixed success in the eyes of many expert reef aquarists. Bruce Davidson's system has benefited by some operating modifications that appear to be an improvement on older algae filter systems. First, activated carbon is used continuously to keep the water from turning yellow from compounds released by the growing algae and to prevent any chemical inhibitors from the algae from affecting the corals. Second, even though a relatively deep sand bed is used, it is not the primary source of buffer or calcium. Instead a two-part additive is used daily to keep the calcium and alkalinity at their proper levels. This allows for the corals to grow quickly, utilizing available nutrients and creating a situation in which nuisance algae cannot compete in the aquarium. In addition, snails and other herbivores including fishes are used to keep the algae from getting out of control. This heavily stocked tank is fed approximately 20 times per day, and algae could easily spin out of control if steps were not taken to keep it at bay.

The aquascaping in this system is also quite unlike most reefs found in aquarium shops. Just 175 pounds of live rock were utilized, leaving an unusual amount of open water—and swimming space—in the tank. Bruce has a total of only 26 colonies of coral within the tank. Although still a relatively young reef, the corals have grown extensively and have nicely filled out the aquascape. A "screaming green" colony of *Acropora yongei* fills the center of the tank and now grows to its surface. An impressive green colony of *Montipora capricornis* fills the adjacent space next to it but lower in the aquarium. Befitting a store that caters to avid marine aquarists, the tank helps illustrate how healthy fishes can look with the proper care. The tangs, including a Clown and Kole, have maintained their color and still look quite robust, as do the Fiji and Orange-spotted Rabbitfishes. The show fish of this tank is the large Red Sea Map Angelfish (*Pomacanthus maculosus*) whose adult coloration is as intense as when it was added to the tank.

Lighting comes from three 250-watt metal halide lamps coupled with two VHO super actinic bulbs. The lack of aquarium technology extends even to the conspicuous absence of a chiller. Instead, Bruce has designed an exhaust system using inexpensive clothes dryer ductwork and fans to pull the heat away from the tank. Bruce does no regular water changes or water testing but depends on regular viewing of the tank and its inhabitants to determine if anything needs adjusting. While these practices may not work for the average aquarist, they have combined to provide a sight that greets Bruce's customers and sends them home wanting to duplicate the robust look in their own homes. This reef is a pleasure to observe and requires very little maintenance. This level of success—measured by the growth and health of the animals—with minimal maintenance is the goal of virtually every hobbyist.

*Hidden behind a wall, the tank has a utilitarian "black-box" algae-scrubber filter (at rear) and metal halide lamp fans that vent into flexible dryer ductwork.*

**CARBON:** 2 cups in continuous use (changed monthly).
**LIVE ROCK IN DISPLAY TANK:** Approximately 175 lbs. of Fiji rock.
**SAND/SUBSTRATE IN DISPLAY:** From 3-6 inches of mixed aggregate coral sand.

## LIGHTING
**FLUORESCENT BULBS:** Two 60-inch VHO Super actinic bulbs fired with IceCap 660 ballast.
**PHOTOPERIOD:** 12 hours.
**HOW OFTEN REPLACED:** Every 8 months.
**METAL HALIDE BULBS:** Three 250-watt 10,000 K bulbs.
**PHOTOPERIOD:** 10 hours.
**HOW OFTEN REPLACED:** Every 8 months.

## SYSTEM PARAMETERS & CHEMISTRY
**WATER TEMPERATURE:** 79 to 82°F.
**SPECIFIC GRAVITY:** 1.024.
**ALKALINITY:** 3 meq/L.
**CALCIUM:** 480 ppm.
**NITRATE:** Below detectable levels.
**PHOSPHATE:** Below detectable levels.
**WATER SUPPLY:** Municipal tapwater.
**REVERSE OSMOSIS:** Yes.
**SALT USED:** Instant Ocean.
**ADDITIVES OR SUPPLEMENTS USED:** ESV B-Ionic calcium buffer; 60 ml daily.
**MAINTENANCE SCHEDULE:** Every Friday the screen and dump bucket for the algae turf scrubber gets scraped and rinsed.

## LIVESTOCK
**FISHES:** 19.
**STONY CORALS:** 19.
**SOFT CORALS:** 7.
**OTHER LIVESTOCK:** Two handfuls each of blue-legged hermit crabs and turbo snails, 3 tiger-tail cucumbers, 6 serpent starfish, and 6 brittle stars.
**NOTEWORTHY SPECIMENS:** All animals were introduced within 2 weeks of the initial setup with the exception of the clown tang. Clown tang was introduced March 8, 2001. Red *Goniopora* has done well and has even grown.
**SPAWNING EVENTS:** Clownfish.

## FEEDING
**FEEDING REGIMEN:** The aquarium gets fed from 9 to 20 times daily. We feed mostly flake and pellet food and some frozen. All employees are encouraged to feed as often as they like.

## NOTES
**THINGS OWNER LIKES BEST ABOUT THIS SYSTEM:** Very low maintenance. Store visitors want one in their living room.
**FAVORITE COMMENTS BY OTHERS ABOUT THIS AQUARIUM:** "It looks so natural. That's great, I've got to have one."
**OVERALL NEGATIVES (OR THINGS TO DO DIFFERENTLY NEXT TIME):** Use a larger tank (550 gallons) when I move the tank to our new location. The rabbitfishes nip on the clams so I may have to remove them. The squirrelfishes eat shrimps so I may remove them, as I do like shrimps in a reef aquarium.

# Bedroom Reef

*A mesmerizing sight, this long-established Texas reef dominates the view in the master bedroom of Larry and Laura Jackson.*

## AQUARIUM PROFILE

**OWNERS/DESIGNERS:** Larry & Laura Jackson.
**LOCATION:** San Angelo, TX.
**DATE ESTABLISHED:** March 1990.
**DATE PHOTOGRAPHED:** June 2001.

### TANK
**CONFIGURATION:** Rectangular.
**DISPLAY TANK VOLUME:** 200 gallons, glass.
**DISPLAY TANK DIMENSIONS:** 84" X 24" X 24".
**SUMP VOLUME:** 20 gallons working volume.
**LOCATION:** Master bedroom.
**CABINETRY/ARCHITECTURAL DETAILS:** Plywood.

### CIRCULATION
**MAIN SYSTEM PUMP(S):** Iwaki 30 RLXT-115, maximum flow 1,140 gph.
**WATER RETURNS:** 5 inch surface spray bar.
**ADDITIONAL PUMPS:** 2 Gemini pumps, one in each front corner
**WAVEMAKING DEVICES:** Lifereef, Wavetech II.

### CONTROLLERS
**FANS:** Muffin fan in light skirt and clip fan blowing across water surface in the sump is controlled by Medusa two-stage controller, muffin fan in sump cabinet runs continuously.

WHILE MANY PEOPLE COUNT SHEEP to fall asleep, Larry Jackson can count reef fishes or corals. With a 200-gallon reef tank located in the master bedroom of his spacious Texas home, this well-known aquarist can relax to the sounds of rushing water, as more than 2,000 gallons flow through the system each hour, providing a peaceful, mesmerizing prelude to sleep. Through his many years of online tutoring of new reefkeepers and his public presentations on the subject of demystifying reef aquarium technology and husbandry, Larry Jackson has helped countless hobbyists solve dilemmas and start successful reefs.

Passing along the tricks that he knows best, Larry teaches hobbyists the textbook way to maintain a tank using the Berlin method. By the book may sound mundane, but as demonstrated in Larry's own tank, now entering its second decade of operation, the results can be quite stunning when this approach is properly followed.

A large, efficient skimmer is used to keep the water sparkling, while 500-plus pounds of live rock act as a biological filter. Kalkwasser is used to replace the water that has evaporated and support the large size and rapid growth of the corals and clams. Strong water movement is employed throughout the tank to keep detritus from settling and to keep the water well oxygenated. Approximately 5 watts of light per gallon are employed to illuminate the tank, and small lights are employed during artificial "dawn" and "dusk" periods to keep the corals and other animals from suffering light shock. All of this creates conditions that Larry hopes will approximate those found on wild reefs. In

fact, the temperature, pH, specific gravity, alkalinity, and calcium are all just about at optimum levels. Even the nutrients that are of great concern, such as nitrate and phosphate, are at reef-like levels—undetectable with standard test kits. Amazingly, this level of success is achieved with Larry spending only a little more than an hour per week maintaining the 200-gallon tank and several small breeder setups. This is a clear illustration that choosing a reliable methodology, sticking to it, and performing maintenance on a regular basis can produce a reef tank that is not as time consuming as is generally thought.

Larry's dedication to having his tank mimic actual reef conditions as closely as possible has resulted in

*Fighting for turf, Larry's diverse assemblage of corals has crowded the tank, forcing him to remove live rock and rigorously prune back a number of large specimens.*

many thriving colonies of coral as well as healthy, vividly colored fishes. The corals are diverse, impressive in size, and several have been with him throughout the life of this system. Large 11-year old colonies of hammer coral (*Euphyllia ancora*), bubble coral (*Plerogyra sinuosa*), and flowerpot coral (*Goniopora* sp.) dominate the tank. Larry also has cardinalfish and a couple of tangs that have been in the aquarium as long as the corals. Spawning events involving both fishes and invertebrates have also been recorded in the tank. The reproductive displays put on by clams, corals, snails, limpets, and sand worms are a convincing indication of the success that Larry has achieved with this system. The spawning activities may also be a result of the attention that he pays to nutrition. Both the fishes and corals are fed an extremely varied diet that changes from day to day.

Small-polyped stony corals dominate much of the upper third of the tank, where they can take advantage of the most intense light. Because of Larry's diligence, there are few signs of die-back or burning among the corals as he regularly prunes them to reduce the size of any offending colonies. This constant need to cope with the aggressive growth of the SPS corals is actually one of the drawbacks that he sees with this tank, but his cutting sessions have allowed him to distribute many hundreds of fragments to other aquarists to stock in their own tanks.

This tank has grown in so much that mushroom anemones now fill all of the voids between the live rock, giving the tank the look of a full-blown reef. All of this has caused Larry to have one concern: the corals have grown so much that much of the swimming space for the fishes has now been filled. This is the kind of problem that all of his beginning pupils would like to have, but Larry has since started to reconfigure his aquascape, using half the live rock, removing most of the small-polyped coral colonies and focusing on slower-growing large-polyp species. Given his attention to the smallest detail and a keen sense of what his animals need, there is little doubt that his new bedroom reef will soon be just as impressive as the incarnation shown here.

**HEATERS:** Two 300-watt submersible heaters controlled by Medusa two-stage controller.
**CHILLER:** None.

### FILTRATION
**SKIMMER:** Euro-Reef F8-1.
**CARBON:** 2 cups, changed monthly, dripped through slowly.
**BIOLOGICAL FILTER:** Live rock and sand.
**LIVE ROCK IN DISPLAY TANK:** 500-600 lbs. of mostly Florida Keys live rock.
**LIVE ROCK IN SUMP:** None.
**SAND/SUBSTRATE IN DISPLAY:** 3 inches of sugar-fine calcium carbonate sand.

### LIGHTING
**FLUORESCENT BULBS:** Two 6-inch VHO, 110 watts each, Actinic 03 front, AquaSun in the rear.
**PHOTOPERIOD:** 12 hours, 10 a.m. to 10 p.m.
**HOW OFTEN REPLACED:** "When burned out."
**METAL HALIDE BULBS:** Three 250-watt Iwasaki 6,500 K.
**PHOTOPERIOD:** 10 hours, 11 a.m. to 9 p.m.
**HOW OFTEN REPLACED:** "When burned out."
**OTHER BULBS:** Three 15-watt incandescent bulbs that begin and end the light period.
**PHOTOPERIOD:** 8 a.m. to 10:05 a.m., 9:55 p.m. to 10:30 p.m.
**LIGHTING CONTROLLER(S):** Digital timers, IceCap for metal halides, Intermatic DT1C timers for remaining lights.

### SYSTEM PARAMETERS & CHEMISTRY
**WATER TEMPERATURE:** 78 to 80°F.
**SPECIFIC GRAVITY:** 1.026.
**PH:** 8.0.
**ALKALINITY:** 3.0.
**CALCIUM:** 400 ppm.
**NITRATE:** Undetectable.

*This aquascape achieves the look of a wild reef, with corals everywhere vying for space and colorful mushroom anemones (1) filling most gaps. Note under-tank sump (2), spreading brain coral (3) and two massive Tridacna clams (4).*

**PHOSPHATE:** Undetectable.
**RESINS OR DEVICES USED TO REDUCE NITRATE OR PHOSPHATE:** None.
**MUNICIPAL WATER SUPPLY:** Yes.
**REVERSE OSMOSIS:** SpectraPure.
**DEIONIZATION:** None.
**SALT USED:** Instant Ocean.
**WATER CHANGE SCHEDULE:** 15% per month.
**ADDITIVES OR SUPPLEMENTS USED:** 10 drops of Lugol's solution per month, 7 ml of 20% strontium chloride per month.
**MONITORING EQUIPMENT:** PinPoint pH monitor, Hanna ORP meter.
**DOSING EQUIPMENT USED:** Litermeter replaces all evaporation with limewater.
**MAINTENANCE SCHEDULE:** Clean glass once per week, 30 minutes; water change once per month, 2 hours; misc. maintenance, 5 hours per month.

## LIVESTOCK
**FISHES:** 28.
**STONY CORALS:** 45 species.
**SOFT CORALS:** 5 species.
**OTHER LIVESTOCK:** Sea cucumbers, sea stars, snails, hermit crabs, *Tridacna* clams.
**NOTEWORTHY SPECIMENS:** 11 years, *Euphyllia glabrescens*, *Plerogyra sinuosa*, *Goniopora* sp., *Sphaeramia*
*nematoptera* male and female, *Zebrasoma flavescens*, *Paracanthurus hepatus*.
**SPAWNING EVENTS:** *Sphaeramia nematoptera*, *Amphiprion ocellaris*, *Synchiropus splendidus*, *Centropyge argi*, *Tridacna derasa*, *Pocillopora damicornis* (possibly polyp bailout), snails, limpets, sand worms.

## FEEDING
**REGIMEN FOR FISHES:**
Mon., Wed., Fri. = 2 tbsp. rinsed, frozen brine shrimp, nori, and chunks of raw table shrimp for triggerfish.
Tues., Thurs. = 2 tbsp. rinsed mysid shrimp plus flake algae and finely ground fish flake food, and chunks of shrimp for triggerfish.
Sat. = fast day.
Sun. = finely grated raw shrimp for corals that show feeding response and food fish, chunk shrimp, and diced silversides for larger fishes and sea stars.
**REGIMEN FOR CORALS/INVERTS:**
Sun. = finely grated raw shrimp for corals that show a feeding response (*Fungia*, *Euphyllia*, *Plerogyra*, *Lobophyllia*, *Symphyllia*, *Cynarina*).

## NOTES
**THINGS THE OWNER WOULD LIKE TO CHANGE:** Too much coral, frequent need to trim small polyped stonies, too little swimming room for the fishes, too little sand showing. These changes were made over a 2-week period of time after the photographs were taken. More than half the live rock was removed and most of the small-polyped corals were sent away.
**THINGS OWNER LIKES BEST ABOUT THIS SYSTEM:** Healthy creatures.
**SPECIAL ABOUT THIS SYSTEM:**
1. Low noise.
2. Low maintenance, long-lived creatures, colorful.
**FAVORITE COMMENTS BY OTHERS ABOUT THIS AQUARIUM:** "Always impressive."
**OVERALL POSITIVES:** Large enough to have significant diversity, shares wall with TV to form part of every evening's entertainment, colorful.
**OVERALL NEGATIVES (OR THINGS TO DO DIFFERENTLY NEXT TIME):** Tank isn't quite level; drill tank for overflow box instead of siphon box; place further from wall for easier access to plumbing and electrical.

# Saltwater Paradise

*Bathed in blue-spectrum light, Joe Kozak's 125-gallon reef near Buffalo, New York, appears to fluoresce with life.*

PART OF THE CHAUVINISM OF THOSE WHO KEEP SPS corals is the belief that soft corals and LPS (large-polyped stony) corals do not possess the bright colors of small-polyped species. However, when chosen properly and lighted in a manner that brings out their colors, these corals can be every bit as dazzling—as demonstrated by Joe Kozak of Saltwater Paradise. Joe has filled his tank with bright green leather corals (*Sinularia* spp.) as well as orange, red, and green *Cynarina, Blastomussa*, and *Scolymia* corals that he's selectively plucked from the many corals that pass through his store.

Joe has also found that by lighting his tank with actinic-blue lights and metal halide lamps in the blue range of the spectrum, he has been able to maximize the coloration and health of the corals. As a result, his aquascapes literally glow and biofluoresce. The bright contrasting colors of the corals, coupled with the swaying movement of the *Sinularia*, is quite striking and is easily as appealing as any tank containing only SPS corals.

The 125-gallon tank is set up in traditional Berlin style with a few modifications. A custom-built counter-current protein skimmer provides most of the filtration with 2 pounds of carbon removing any chemical impurities that remain. Four VHO actinic fluorescent tubes and two 400-watt 20,000 K metal halide lamps supply lighting. In addition, the tank receives three hours per day of morning sunlight. One variation from the Berlin method is a 75-gallon refugium, which acts not only as a sump, but also houses some *Caulerpa* as well as a couple of angelfish. This helps to keep the dissolved nutrient levels low, and it also supplies some microfauna to the tank. Kalkwasser is not used

## AQUARIUM PROFILE

**OWNER:** Joseph M. Kozak
www.geocities.com/saltwaterparadise/.
**LOCATION:** North Tonawanda, NY.
**DATE ESTABLISHED:** October 1998.
**DATE PHOTOGRAPHED:** October 2001.

### TANK
**DISPLAY TANK VOLUME:** 125 gallons.
**DISPLAY TANK DIMENSIONS:** 72" X 18" X 22".
**DISPLAY TANK MATERIAL:** Glass.
**SUMP VOLUME:** 75 gallons.
**LOCATION:** Display tank in retail shop.
**CABINETRY/ARCHITECTURAL DETAILS:** Sitting on rack.

### CIRCULATION
**MAIN SYSTEM PUMP(S):** Rio 2500.
**WATER RETURNS:** Magnum diffuser hose.
**ADDITIONAL PUMPS:** Three powerheads, 250 gph each.

### CONTROLLERS
**TEMPERATURE CONTROLS:** CustomSea Life.
**FANS:** 2.
**HEATERS:** One 250 watt.

### FILTRATION
**SKIMMER:** Custom-built counter-current skimmer.

**MECHANICAL FILTER:** Pre-filter sponge.
**CARBON:** 2 lbs., changed every 4 months.
**BIOLOGICAL FILTER:** 250 lbs. of Fiji live rock.
**REFUGIUM:** 75-gallon tank containing 1 or 2 angelfish and some plants.
**LIVE ROCK IN DISPLAY TANK:** 250 lbs. Fiji live rock.
**LIVE ROCK IN SUMP:** 25 lbs. Tonga branch rock.
**SAND/SUBSTRATE IN SUMP/REFUGIUM:** 1 inch of sand in sump.

## LIGHTING
**FLUORESCENT BULBS:** Four 36-inch VHO actinics by URI, 95 watts
**PHOTOPERIOD:** 10 hours.
**HOW OFTEN REPLACED:** Twice per year.
**METAL HALIDE BULBS:** Two Radium 400-watt 20,000 K.
**PHOTOPERIOD:** 6 hours per day.
**HOW OFTEN REPLACED:** Every 18 months.
**HEIGHT OF LIGHTS ABOVE WATER SURFACE:** 12 inches.
**NATURAL LIGHT:** 3 hours of morning light per day.
**LIGHTING CONTROLLER(S):** Timer.

## SYSTEM PARAMETERS & CHEMISTRY
**WATER TEMPERATURE:** 76 to 79°F.
**PH:** 8.2.
**ALKALINITY:** 2.5.
**CALCIUM:** 420.
**NITRATE:** 5 ppm.
**PHOSPHATE:** 0.02.
**REVERSE OSMOSIS:** RO unit.
**SALT USED:** Coralife.
**WATER CHANGE SCHEDULE:** 10% every two weeks.
**ADDITIVES OR SUPPLEMENTS USED:** ESV B-Ionic 30 ml every other day.
**MAINTENANCE SCHEDULE:** 2 hours per week.

## LIVESTOCK
**FISHES:** 4.
**STONY CORALS:** 18.
**SOFT CORALS:** 18.
**OTHER LIVESTOCK:** Noteworthy specimens: Zebra Eel, Green *Sinularia* that has filled the tank. *Blastomussa* corals with exceptional colors.

## FEEDING
**REGIMEN FOR FISHES:** Brine shrimp, bloodworms, and Marine Supreme once per day.
**REGIMEN FOR CORALS/INVERTS:** Powdered plankton once every two weeks.

## NOTES
**PROBLEMS OVERCOME WITH THIS SYSTEM:** Bubble algae remedied with a Foxface Rabbitfish. *Aiptasia* anemones remedied with peppermint shrimp.
**OVERALL POSITIVES:**
1. Health of the system.
2. Growth of the corals.
3. Simplicity of the set-up.
**OVERALL NEGATIVES:**
1. Red slime algae (occasional).
2. Brick stand.

to supplement calcium; instead a two-part daily additive is used to maintain calcium levels and alkalinity. Powdered plankton is fed to the corals once every two weeks. The simplicity of this system is one of the things that Joe likes best, and his only real maintenance is cleaning the glass and doing a 10% water change every two weeks.

This simplicity carries over to the aquascaping—or lack of aquascaping. Thirty-six of the brightest soft and stony corals to come through his shop were selected and placed in this tank and allowed to grow over the past three years. The most impressive of these is the bright green *Sinularia* that was initially only four small cuttings. The colonies now occupy one-third of the tank. This *Sinularia* grows above and behind numerous colonies of brightly colored *Blastomussa* corals, which thrive in subdued light and offer an interesting contrast. Intermingled among these corals are several colonies of multi-colored *Cynarina* corals. In addition, several colonies of bright green leather corals and open brain corals show up brilliantly under the actinic lights.

In addition to allowing lush coral growth to fill the tank, Joe has selected some interesting fishes to add movement and to provide biocontrols for several potential nuisances. Rabbitfish, along with a couple of tangs, have been used to reduce bubble algae. Two pygmy angelfish help to pick microalgae from the rocks before it starts to grow. These are fascinating and beautiful fishes, but the crown jewel of this tank is the Zebra Moray Eel that lives in a cave formed by live rock. Joe keeps this eel well fed, a tactic that has kept it from bothering the other fishes. The large pieces of live rock in the aquascape keep the eel from knocking over the structure. This healthy and remarkable eel provides an unexpected exclamation point to an exceptionally attractive reef tank.

*Spreading green Sinularia (1) started as small cuttings. Note colorful Cynarinas (2), Trachyphyllia or open brain coral (3), and Blastomussa wellsi (4).*

# Algae-Filtered System

*This unusual 115-gallon system uses algal turf scrubbing as a primary form of nutrient export. Note healthy red Goniopora (1).*

THE INCREDIBLE ABILITY OF PLANTS to scavenge nutrients out of the water has long preoccupied aquarists seeking more natural methods of keeping their closed systems healthy and in balance.

Unfortunately, it has often proved difficult to harness the filtering capabilities of marine algae and plants and to use them as a primary mode of nutrient export. One innovative approach that appears to offer promise is the use of algal filters, sometimes called "turf scrubbers," mostly custom-built and found in institutional settings and public aquariums.

Fred and Carrie Draper have a small, home-scale version of an algal turf scrubber, manufactured and installed for them by Morgan Lidster of Inland Aquatics in Terre Haute, Indiana. Although hardly a conventional piece of equipment, an algal scrubber, in conjunction with other management techniques, can provide results that rival other filtration methods. In some ways, according to its proponents, it may be superior.

The 115-gallon tank sits in the Drapers' living room, and because very little technology is employed, the system is quiet enough not to intrude on family activities. It is primarily filtered with a small acrylic box sitting atop the tank, through which the entire volume of water flows approximately four times per hour. Water from the display tank flows over a set of screens positioned in a dump tray under a pair of power compact fluorescent lights. A dense, carpetlike turf of algae covers the screen and extracts nutrients from the water as it washes through the scrubber. The tray is designed to tip every 20 to 30 seconds, releasing a wave of purified water back into the tank.

## AQUARIUM PROFILE

**OWNER:** Fred & Carrie Draper.
**DESIGNER:** Morgan Lidster of Inland Aquatics (www.inlandaquatics.com).
**LOCATION:** Terre Haute, IN.
**DATE ESTABLISHED:** August 1999.
**DATE PHOTOGRAPHED:** August 2001.

### TANK
**CONFIGURATION:** Rectangular.
**DISPLAY TANK VOLUME:** 115 gallons.
**DISPLAY TANK DIMENSIONS:** 48" X 24" X 24".
**DISPLAY TANK MATERIAL:** Acrylic.
**SUMP/REFUGIUM VOLUME:** 5 gallons.
**LOCATION:** Living room.

### CIRCULATION
**MAIN SYSTEM PUMP(S):** Supreme Mag-Drive Model 5 (500 gph).
**WATER RETURNS:** Overflow with teeth in center of tank.
**ADDITIONAL PUMPS:** Mini-Jet 404 Mini-Pump (refugium pump).
**WAVEMAKING DEVICES:** ATScrubber.
**CONTROLLERS:** Neptune.

### TEMPERATURE CONTROLS:
**FANS:** Two 3-inch muffin fans in canopy.
**HEATERS:** Visi-Therm 300 watt.

## FILTRATION

**MECHANICAL FILTER:** Inland Aquatics ATScrubber Model 100.

**BIOLOGICAL FILTER:** Live rock and refugium.

**REFUGIUM:** *Caulerpa sertularoides*, *Ochodes* sp., *Anthelia*, pair of *Lysmata debelius* shrimp, rich population of microfauna.

**LIVE ROCK IN DISPLAY TANK:** 100 lbs. Fiji and base rock, 250 lbs. substrate.

**SAND/SUBSTRATE IN DISPLAY:** 65% sugar fine oolitic sand, 30% CaribSea ReefSand, 5% crushed shell. Average depth 5 inches.

**SAND/SUBSTRATE IN SUMP/REFUGIUM:** Up to 2.5 inches average (same kinds as in tank).

## LIGHTING

**FLUORESCENT BULBS:** Four 55-watt CustomSea Life power compacts (two 7,100 K and two 6,500 K).

**PHOTOPERIOD:** 12 hours.

**HOW OFTEN REPLACED:** Every 12 months.

**HEIGHT OF LIGHTS ABOVE WATER SURFACE:** 9 inches.

**OTHER BULBS:** ATS: 55-watt power compacts (6,500 K) above refugium.

**PHOTOPERIOD:** 16 hours.

**LIGHTING CONTROLLER(S):** Neptune.

## SYSTEM PARAMETERS & CHEMISTRY

**WATER TEMPERATURE:** 74 to 80°F.

**SPECIFIC GRAVITY:** 1.023.

**PH:** 8.2-8.4.

**WATER SOURCE:** Original saltwater from Inland Aquatics.

**MUNICIPAL WATER SUPPLY:** Yes (poor quality).

**REVERSE OSMOSIS:** SpectraPlus 60 gpd with auto top-off.

**WATER CHANGE SCHEDULE:** Typically 10% every 24 months.

**ADDITIVES OR SUPPLEMENTS USED:** ESV B-Ionic once weekly or as needed, Bio-Trace once weekly.

**MONITORING EQUIPMENT:** Neptune.

**DOSING EQUIPMENT USED:** Manual.

**MAINTENANCE SCHEDULE:** 35 minutes weekly of glass and general maintenance.

## LIVESTOCK

**FISHES:** 23—nearly all captive-bred and reared. Pair *Pseudochromis fridmani*, pair *Cryptocentrus cinctus*, pair Onyx Perculas, pair Banggai Cardinalfish (reproducing with young), 6 Blue Green Chromis, pair Neon Gobies, pair Bicolor Blennies, pair Cherub Angels, Yellow Tang, Palette (Blue) Surgeonfish.

**STONY CORALS:** 8—red *Goniopora*, several *Caulastrea furcata*, red *Trachyphyllia*, several *Pocillopora damicornis*, one *Acropora*.

**SOFT CORALS:** 20.

**OTHER LIVESTOCK:** 12 inch *Macrodactyla doreensis*, 2 gorgonians, cleaner shrimp, sea cucumbers, emerald crabs, *Nassarius* snails, *Alpheus* shrimp, tunicates, sponges.

*Looking down into the turf scrubber, with its plates of dense algal growth that extract nutrient wastes. A dump tray mechanism creates waves in the aquarium.*

A 5-gallon refugium also actually sits within the tank itself, partitioned off at the rear so that it is separated from the display area but with a small viewing window that adds an unusual dimension to the system. Water from the tank is pumped slowly through the refugium, which is stocked with *Caulerpa racemosa* and has a deep bed of sand. As with the turf scrubber, the algae and other fauna within the chamber extract nutrients as the water passes through. They can live and reproduce in the refugium without danger of predation by fishes in the display tank.

The algae scrubber is illuminated for 16 hours each day, while the tank itself is lit for a typical 12 hours. The scrubber is on a partial "reverse light cycle" from the tank to reduce pH fluctuations (the filter lights are mostly on while the aquarium is dark) with a two-hour overlap after the lights in the tank come on and before they go off. Both the tank and the scrubber are illuminated with 55-watt power compact fluorescents. The tank illumination works out to just 2 watts of light per gallon, yet all of the corals appear to be doing well.

Two and a half inches of sand are also present in the refugium and act as a locus for much microfauna, including live *Mysis* shrimp, amphipods, copepods, and many other organisms, which are another benefit of this system. The filtration is so effective that no water changes have been made to date. The only augmentations are weekly additions of a calcium and buffer in the form of a two-part additive and a trace element supplement.

The health of the corals, despite the relatively modest level of light, may be explained by the nutrition they receive in the form of live microfauna that are flushed into the tank from the refugium. (The rhythmic wave motions created by the dumping of water from the scrubber is another benefit.) The fish in the tank are fed three times per day with flake and pellet food and once per week with *Mysis* shrimp. These foods may also provide some nutrients for the corals, but the corals are not fed directly.

*An in-tank refugium (1) serves as a breeding chamber for Caulerpa racemosa and numerous small invertebrates, such as Mysis shrimp, that provide a constant source of live food for the display aquarium inhabitants. Note worm population (2) in sand.*

The centerpiece of this tank is a red *Goniopora* that has grown from a 50-cent-coin-sized piece to the equivalent of a pair of softballs. When expanded, the polyp mass is roughly the size of a basketball, and this one coral now threatens to outgrow the tank. This coral is typically thought of as being one of the least likely to survive in a closed system, yet in this aquarium it is not showing the gradual decline and tissue recession that is often the case with these animals. Morgan is not sure why this coral is doing so well, but possibilities include the availability of live food, lack of skimming, avoidance of activated carbon, or a combination of factors. Other stony corals, such as *Caulastrea, Montipora, Pocillopora,* and *Acropora,* are also doing extremely well.

The collection of fishes is noteworthy in that they are nearly all captive bred. Several spawn on a regular basis with the pair of Banggai cardinalfish constantly reproducing. Other animals that seem to find these conditions to their liking include sponges, tunicates, pistol shrimp, gorgonians, sea cucumbers, and various types of microfauna.

This system requires very little work, with a short weekly session to clean the glass and scrape algae from the screens in the scrubber. There is very little to add, no water changes, no filters or skimmer to clean—and more time can be spent enjoying the tank. That being one of the main goals of any tank, Morgan has succeeded in designing just such an aquarium for the Drapers.

**NOTEWORTHY SPECIMENS:** Red *Goniopora*: introduced on August 1, 2001 has tripled in size and attached to rock.
**SPAWNING EVENTS:** All fish pairs, except watchman gobies.

### FEEDING
**REGIMEN FOR FISHES:** Autofeeder with Formula Flake and New Life Spectrum pellet 3X daily, Beta meal weekly, and *Mysis* shrimp weekly.

### NOTES
**PROBLEMS OVERCOME WITH THIS SYSTEM:** *Aiptasia* and cf. *Anemonia majano* anemones, also *Xenia* and *Anthelia.*
**THINGS THE OWNER WOULD LIKE TO CHANGE:** More and bigger fishes.
**THINGS OWNER LIKES BEST ABOUT THIS SYSTEM:** Lack of difficult problems.
**SPECIAL ABOUT THIS SYSTEM:**
  1. Using all *Nassarius* and Inland Aquatics "detritivores kit" with no hermit crabs.
  2. Using power compact lighting over SPS corals.
**OVERALL NEGATIVES:** *Goniopora* is growing out of control and will have to be removed soon.

# Impossible Reef

*Lit entirely by fluorescent lighting is Ron Hunsiker's 715-gallon "big tank," populated with some 250 fishes and 190 corals.*

## AQUARIUM PROFILE

**OWNER:** Ron Hunsiker
www.bomani.com/saltwaterheaven.html.
**LOCATION:** Williamsport, PA.
**DATE ESTABLISHED:** August 1998.
**DATE PHOTOGRAPHED:** August 2001.
**PHOTOGRAPHER:** Keto Gyekis.

### TANK
**CONFIGURATION:** Rectangular.
**DISPLAY TANK VOLUME:** 715 gallons.
**DISPLAY TANK DIMENSIONS:** 8' X 4' X 3'.
**DISPLAY TANK MATERIAL:** Glass.
**SUMP VOLUME:** 250 gallons.
**LOCATION:** Retail storefront.
**CABINETRY:** Inexpensive pine and plywood.

### CIRCULATION
**MAIN SYSTEM PUMP(S):** Two Iwaki 70 RLT
and 1 RK2 5,900 gph pump.
**WATER RETURNS:** Spray bar and six PVC
returns.
**WAVEMAKING DEVICES:** Two 3/4-inch Sea
Swirl wavemakers.

### CONTROLLERS
**FANS:** Four 4-inch.
**HEATERS:** Two 200 watt.
**CHILLER:** CSL 1 hp.

GOING IN TWO DIRECTIONS AT ONCE, the marine aquarium hobby is seeing many people experimenting with smaller tanks, while others are moving to larger and larger systems. Many in the latter group are coping with one of the problems that reefkeeping success has bred—their corals are simply growing too big.

Rather than continually trimming, pruning, and fragmenting the corals in his basement tanks, Ron Hunsiker chose to move them into a much bigger 715-gallon display tank in his retail store, Saltwater Heaven. If the 8-foot length, 4-foot width, and 3-foot height of the tank itself are not awesome enough, the corals within make a mind-boggling display, filling the space within as if it were a crowded segment of a healthy, wild reef.

This tank breaks one of the entrenched rules of reefkeeping by avoiding the use of metal halide lighting, usually said to be essential for large systems. Even with a depth of 3 feet, the aquarium is illuminated entirely with fluorescent lights. Approximately 3,300 watts of fluorescent lighting are used, with virtually every inch of the canopy above the tank filled with tubes, including 20 VHO lamps, that hang a mere 5-inches above the water's surface. Ron has also skewed the color spectrum toward blue with the use of actinic lighting in an approximately 2:1 ratio with daylight fluorescent bulbs. The effect is dramatic. The colors in the soft corals and mushroom anemones are intensified, and corals with green pigments biofluoresce and cast an almost magical glow throughout the tank.

*Despite a 3-foot depth, Ron's aquarium thrives under an array of 24 fluorescent lighting tubes of different types. Nutrient removal is accomplished with a bank of five homemade countercurrent skimmers, an ozonizer, and activated carbon.*

Stocking is mixed, with more than 90 colonies of stony corals and 100 colonies of soft corals. This is a potential recipe for disaster, as both types of corals produce potent defensive or aggressive chemicals. Significant filtration is employed to keep the toxic by-products of the corals from harming each other.

A bank of five 6-foot-tall counter-current protein skimmers built by Ron are employed to perform much of the filtration. In addition, a 500 mg Ozonizer is employed constantly, along with 7 pounds of carbon in the outflow from the Ozonizer to prevent any ozone from reaching the tank. Mechanical filtration is accomplished by the use of quilted acrylic batting in the overflows, and these are changed weekly. Additional chemical filtration is performed with the use of seven bags of Chemi-Pure that are changed bimonthly. A 160-watt UV sterilizer is used to reduce the risk of a disease outbreak in the large fish population. Water motion is provided to the tank via three pumps producing over 9,000-gallons of water movement per hour. This is necessary not only to keep the detritus in suspension, but also to keep coral chemical by-products from accumulating. Lastly, 120 gallons of water are changed weekly by draining the sump and refilling it with new synthetic seawater. Ron believes that all of this is necessary to cope with the huge bioload in this system, which seems to defy many of the notions of what is possible in home-scale reef tanks.

In addition to rigorous maintenance of the filtration and lighting systems, several other frequent tasks are performed as well. The tank is fed three times

## FILTRATION

**SKIMMER:** Five homemade 4-inch diameter, 6-foot-tall counter-current skimmers.

**MECHANICAL FILTER:** Quilted batting in overflows.

**UV STERILIZER:** 160-watt Rainbow Lifeguard.

**OZONIZER:** 500 mg Ozotech.

**CARBON:** Seven Chemi-pure in carbon reactor for ozone, changed every 60 days.

**BIOLOGICAL FILTER:** Live rock.

**LIVE ROCK IN DISPLAY TANK:** 1,640 lbs. live rock from Fiji.

**LIVE ROCK IN SUMP:** 200 lbs. Fiji.

**SAND/SUBSTRATE IN DISPLAY:** 1 inch Fiji live sand.

## LIGHTING

**FLUORESCENT BULBS:** Fourteen 160-watt VHO actinic, six 160-watt VHO daylight, two 40-watt actinic, and two 40-watt Ultralume.

**PHOTOPERIOD:** Approximately 12 hours.

**HOW OFTEN REPLACED:** 6 months.

**HEIGHT OF LIGHTS ABOVE WATER:** 5 inches.

**LIGHTING CONTROLLER(S):** Appliance timers.

## SYSTEM PARAMETERS & CHEMISTRY

**WATER TEMPERATURE:** 77.6 to 78.2°F.

**SPECIFIC GRAVITY:** 1.025.

**PH:** 8.1-8.3.

**ALKALINITY:** 12-15 dKH.

**CALCIUM:** 320.

**NITRATE:** 4 ppm.

**RESINS OR DEVICES USED TO REDUCE NITRATE OR PHOSPHATE:** Chemi-pure.

**MUNICIPAL WATER SUPPLY:** Yes.

**REVERSE OSMOSIS:** Yes.

**DEIONIZATION:** Yes.

**SALT USED:** Reef Crystals.

**WATER CHANGE SCHEDULE:** 120 gallons per week.

**ADDITIVES OR SUPPLEMENTS USED:** CaCl, 1 cup per day; Thiel Vital Gold, 4 tbsp. every day; KSM Iodine, 1 tbsp. every day.

**MAINTENANCE SCHEDULE:** Water change by pumping sump empty weekly, change overflow sponges and rinse Chemi-pure in Magnums.

## LIVESTOCK

**FISHES:** 250.

**STONY CORALS:** 90.

**SOFT CORALS:** 101.

**OTHER LIVESTOCK:** Shrimp, cucumbers, starfish, and clams.

**NOTEWORTHY SPECIMENS:** Sea anemone 12 years old, large leather coral 10 years old.

**SPAWNING EVENTS:** Percula Clowns every 14 days, Banggai Cardinals.

## FEEDING

**REGIMEN FOR FISHES:** Three times per day. Morning: brine shrimp, peas, carrots, and broccoli. Afternoon and evening: mixed seafood and three kinds of Omega foods mixed with Vitachem.

**CORALS/INVERTS:** Phytoplankton, brine shrimp and seafood mix offered once per week before water change.

## NOTES

**PROBLEMS OVERCOME WITH THIS SYSTEM:** Lack of current under center brace, but Sea Swirl did the trick.

**THINGS THE OWNER WOULD LIKE TO CHANGE:** Nothing except center brace.

**THINGS OWNER LIKES BEST ABOUT THIS SYSTEM:** How real it looks: wall-to-wall corals and fishes.

**SPECIAL ABOUT THIS SYSTEM:** So much of it is impossible according to all the "experts."

**FAVORITE COMMENTS BY OTHERS:** "According to everything I've read, this tank cannot be real."

**OVERALL POSITIVES:** Health of fishes, fullness and size of animals.

**OVERALL NEGATIVES (OR THINGS TO DO DIFFERENTLY NEXT TIME):**
1. Center brace.
2. Tank is 4 inches too deep to reach the bottom.
3. The holes in spray bar should be drilled in a straight line.

*Schools of anthias—which number more than 100—and Blue Green Chromis mix with an assortment of surgeonfishes, which serve as active algae grazers.*

per day with brine shrimp, various marine foods, and vegetables, including broccoli, carrots, and peas. The corals and other inverts are fed once per week with a phytoplankton-zooplankton mix just before the water change. In addition, calcium, trace elements and iodine are added to the tank daily.

The livestock in the tank offer proof that Ron's design and methods are working. A large leather coral is now over 10 years old, and it weighed more than 120 pounds before Ron divided it. A beautiful purple-tipped long-tentacled anemone is more than 12 years old and has been in three of Ron's tanks over the years. The health and size of the other corals is further testament to how well this system works. Unlike many reef systems, this tank is rich in fishes, with more than 250 specimens living in the reef. Perhaps most spectacular is a school of more than 100 assorted anthias that act as though they were on a natural reef face. Too see this school of fishes come out to feed is as awe-inspiring for veteran Indo-Pacific divers as it is for landlocked schoolchildren who never find themselves any closer to a real coral reef.

*Some corals have been in Ron's care for more than a decade, and the large purple-tipped, long tentacle anemone at bottom center has been growing for more than 12 years. Percula Clownfish and Banggai Cardinals spawn regularly in the tank.*

# Low-Tech Reef

*Simplicity works in Randy Donowitz's 75-gallon New York reef with its long-lived collection of clams, corals, and fishes.*

## AQUARIUM PROFILE

**OWNER:** Randy Donowitz.
**LOCATION:** Brooklyn, NY.
**DATE ESTABLISHED:** January 1999.
**DATE PHOTOGRAPHED:** June 2001.

### TANK
**DISPLAY TANK VOLUME:** 75 gallons.
**DISPLAY TANK DIMENSIONS:** 48" X 18" X 22".
**DISPLAY TANK MATERIAL:** Glass.
**SUMP VOLUME:** None.
**LOCATION:** Living room.
**CABINETRY:** Iron Stand.

### CIRCULATION
**MAIN SYSTEM PUMP(S):** 1 Rio 1700 (600 gph).
**WATER RETURNS:** None.
**ADDITIONAL PUMPS:** 2 Maxi-Jet 1200 power heads, plus return from skimmer and H.O.T. Magnum canister filter.
**WAVEMAKING DEVICES:** Lifereef wavemaker.

### CONTROLLERS
**FANS:** 2 IceCap variable speed fans.
**HEATERS:** 1 Ebo-Jager 250 watt submersible.
**CHILLER:** None.

ONE OF THE COMMON MISCONCEPTIONS about saltwater tanks, and reef systems in particular, is that you need to have all kinds of technical equipment and a Ph.D. in marine biology to succeed. In reality, the demands are rather simple: an elementary understanding of the biological processes occurring, an appreciation for the basic needs of the animals, and a desire and willingness to look after the details on a regular schedule. For Randy Donowitz, keen attention to detail seems to allow him to maintain an outstanding 75-gallon tank using minimal equipment in a simple setup.

Unlike most reef systems that employ elaborate plumbing schemes, numerous pumps, and multiple controllers, Randy's tank depends on a hang-on-the back skimmer that receives the water for skimming via a powerhead. Water motion within the tank is provided by two modest 500 gph powerheads and the water return from a canister filter. The flow from the powerheads is varied by the use of an electronic wavemaker—just about the only piece of advanced technology used on this system.

Two 250-watt 6,500 K metal halide lamps and two VHO actinic fluorescent lamps provide intense lighting amounting to almost 10 watts per gallon. This tank is just 18-inches deep and the lights are a mere 2 to 3 inches above the water's surface, allowing strong light to penetrate into virtually every space in the tank. To maximize light penetration even more, carbon is run constantly, preventing any yellowing compounds from accumulating and keeping the water exceptionally clear. Despite the concentration of light present and the concomitant heat that is produced, no chiller is required for this tank. Instead, Randy utilizes two variable-speed fans to draw the heat away from the tank. This tank does run a little warmer than most—at 78 to 84 degrees F, but this does not seem to have a measurably negative effect on the corals.

Water changes are done infrequently and the only additive used is a daily dose of a liquid two-part calcium-buffer supplement to maintain the calcium and alkalinity levels. The only testing or monitoring that is done is for pH, temperature, and salinity. As a result, maintenance on this tank only requires approximately one hour of time each week, with the better part of one day each month when Randy cleans out any accumulated detritus and makes sure that everything is working properly. This once-a-month thorough maintenance is crucial for keeping the tank's parameters at optimal levels.

If the hardware used on this tank is nothing out of the ordinary, the biological success of the system is obvious to all who visit. The nine fishes, including a small school of iridescent Green Chromis, provide an interesting contrast to the immobile stony corals. These corals have come to dominate the aquascape, and some have been with Randy for quite some time. The two *Favia* corals are now close to 10 years old, and the colony of *Montipora spumosa* has grown from a small fragment into a large colony. The *Tridacna* clams in this tank are also quite impressive and have grown significantly. Over time, Randy expects the stony corals to encase some of these clams so that they will appear as they often do on the reef.

One curiosity in this tank is the widespread encrustation of coralline algae. In most tanks with this much light and where stony corals dominate, coralline algae tends to be less than obvious. In this tank, the back and sidewalls as well

## FILTRATION
**SKIMMER:** Aqua C Remora Pro hang-on-tank skimmer powered by a Rio 1700 pump.
**CARBON:** 3-5 ounces run continuously in a H.O.T. Magnum canister filter; changed every 2 months.
**LIVE ROCK IN DISPLAY TANK:** 100 lbs. of Indo-Pacific Rock, primarily Purple Fiji, but also Branch and Slab from Tonga.
**SAND/SUBSTRATE IN DISPLAY:** 2 inch layer of CaribSea Seaflor aragonite sand, seeded with live sand from a variety of sources.

## LIGHTING
**FLUORESCENT BULBS:** Two 110-watt VHO actinics from URI.
**PHOTOPERIOD:** 12 hours.
**HOW OFTEN REPLACED:** Once per year.
**METAL HALIDE BULBS:** Two Iwasaki 250-watt 6,500 K.
**PHOTOPERIOD:** 10 hours.
**HOW OFTEN REPLACED:** Once per year.
**HEIGHT OF LIGHTS ABOVE WATER SURFACE:** 2-3 inches.
**OTHER BULBS:** None.
**NATURAL LIGHT:** Minimal.
**LIGHTING CONTROLLER(S):** Lamp timers.

## SYSTEM PARAMETERS & CHEMISTRY
**WATER TEMPERATURE:** 78 to 84°F.
**SPECIFIC GRAVITY:** 1.024-1.025.
**PH:** 8.1-8.5.
**ALKALINITY:** Approximately 2.5-3.5 meq/L.
**CALCIUM:** Approximately 400 ppm.
**MUNICIPAL WATER SUPPLY:** Yes.

*As his reef develops, Randy anticipates that some of his Tridacna clams may become encased in growing coral, as they are often found in the wild. Calcium and alkalinity parameters are kept up with a two-part liquid additive used daily.*

**REVERSE OSMOSIS:** Yes.

**DEIONIZATION:** Yes.

**SALT USED:** Instant Ocean.

**WATER CHANGE SCHEDULE:** Infrequent.

**ADDITIVES OR SUPPLEMENTS USED:** ESV B-Ionic Alkalinity/Calcium supplement 40 ml daily.

**MONITORING EQUIPMENT:** American Marine pH monitor, Radio Shack indoor/outdoor thermometer.

**DOSING EQUIPMENT USED:** None.

**MAINTENANCE SCHEDULE:** 5 to 10 minutes daily, 1 hour weekly, better part of a day monthly. Clean glass, skimmer, change carbon, test water, etc.

## LIVESTOCK

**FISHES:** 9.

**STONY CORALS:** 25 colonies.

**SOFT CORALS:** 1 gorgonian.

**OTHER LIVESTOCK:** 5 tridacnid clams: 2 *maxima*, 2 *crocea*, 1 *squamosa*, 1 coral banded shrimp, numerous hermit crabs and snails, 1 small serpent star.

**NOTEWORTHY SPECIMENS:** A colony of *Montipora spumosa* is particularly attractive and fast growing. There are also colonies of *Echinopora lamellosa* and *E. horrida* of which I am very fond. The 2 *Favia* species inherited from Terry Siegel are nearly 10 years old.

## FEEDING

**REGIMEN FOR FISHES:** A combination of flake food, *Spirulina*, frozen brine shrimp, and *Mysis* shrimp; 1 to 2 heavy feedings daily.

**REGIMEN FOR CORALS/INVERTS:** I am experimenting with a variety of foods including cryo-preserved phytoplankton, decapsulated brine shrimp eggs, and Golden Pearls artificial rotifers.

## NOTES

**PROBLEMS OVERCOME WITH THIS SYSTEM:**
1. A seemingly *Acropora*-specific disease outbreak that killed or damaged many colonies.
2. Reaching equilibrium with an outbreak of *Anemonia majano* anemones. This is an ongoing battle.

**THINGS THE OWNER WOULD LIKE TO CHANGE:**
1. Upgrade lighting to 400-watt metal halides.
2. Add a deeper and finer sand substrate.
3. Avoid introducing the *A. majano* anemones.

**THINGS THE OWNER LIKES BEST ABOUT THIS SYSTEM:**
1. Variety and color of SPS corals and clams.
2. Good growth rates of corals. Able to fragment mother colonies often.
3. Perhaps the best aquascaping of my three systems.

**SPECIAL ABOUT THIS SYSTEM:**
1. Pretty low-tech except for the lighting system.
2. In excess of 80% of the livestock is captive bred/propagated.

**FAVORITE COMMENTS BY OTHERS ABOUT THIS AQUARIUM:** "Beautiful colors."

*The tank's modest population of fishes are fed once or twice daily with a variety of high-quality flake, frozen, and dried foods, including Mysis shrimp and Spirulina.*

as much of the live rock, the shells of the *Tridacna* clams, and even the powerheads are covered in lovely pink coralline algae. Randy does not have an explanation as to why he is so successful in keeping this often-difficult algae thriving, but some other regular users of two-part calcium and buffer additives report similar results.

This 75-gallon reef tank is a perfect example of how beautiful and healthy a tank can be when proper husbandry techniques are employed with the right equipment.

# Aquatic Reflections

*Given time and space to grow, Robert Dalton's stony corals now present one of the most natural aquascapes imaginable.*

CLEAN WATER, INTENSE LIGHTING, strong water movement. Anyone familiar with modern reefkeeping fundamentals knows that these are essentials for success. However, Robert Dalton's exceptionally natural-looking 337-gallon tank illustrates two more—often under-appreciated—factors: time and space. Unlike most reef tank owners, who place a wide variety of small animals as closely together as possible, Robert has taken a different tack and stocked his system with only a few choice specimens. Small coral colonies or fragments were sited carefully in the aquascape and allowed to grow without crowding or disturbance.

This approach, coupled with excellent water conditions, has resulted in extraordinary coral specimens with natural growth forms. Robert says that the tank, located at his small Aquatic Reflections online retail workshop, looked somewhat sparse when first set up, but the rapid growth of the corals quickly filled every space with color. It appears that the stony coral colonies have been able to channel their energy into growth rather than into aggressive strategies to battle for territory with other nearby corals. *Acropora* and *Montipora* specimens developed into show-size colonies in a relatively short period of time, and within 18 months most of the empty spaces in this tank were nicely filled with new growth. There is very little burning going on between the colonies, which tend to grow up and away from each other rather than battling their neighbors.

## AQUARIUM PROFILE

**OWNER:** Robert Dalton
www.aquatic-reflections.com.
**LOCATION:** Dublin, CA.
**DATE ESTABLISHED:** September 1999.
**DATE PHOTOGRAPHED:** March 2001.

### TANK
**CONFIGURATION:** Rectangular.
**DISPLAY TANK VOLUME:** 404 gallons.
**DISPLAY TANK DIMENSIONS:** 72" X 36" X 36".
**DISPLAY TANK MATERIAL:** Starfire glass.
**SUMP VOLUME:** 120 gallons.
**LOCATION:** Garage.
**CABINETRY:** Custom white-lacquered stand and canopy.

### CIRCULATION
**MAIN SYSTEM PUMP(S):** Dolphin (3,000 gph).
**WATER RETURNS:** Two water returns built into overflow box. Center overflow in the back panel directly in the middle.
**ADDITIONAL PUMPS:** Four Maxi-Jet 1200s.
**WAVEMAKING DEVICES:** Four Osci-Wave oscillating devices.

## CONTROLLERS:

**TEMPERATURE CONTROLS:** Neptune AquaController.
**FANS:** None.
**HEATERS:** Two 250-watt Ebo-Jager heaters.
**CHILLER:** Inline Universal Marine Industries chiller.

## FILTRATION

**SKIMMER:** Euro-Reef CS-12-2 recirculating venturi skimmer.
**UV STERILIZER:** 40-watt unit.
**CARBON:** Never used.
**BIOLOGICAL FILTER:** Live rock and live sand.
**LIVE ROCK IN DISPLAY TANK:** 250 lbs. Fiji live rock.
**SAND/SUBSTRATE IN DISPLAY:** 350 lbs. Bio-Active, producing a 3-4 inch sand bed.

## LIGHTING

**FLUORESCENT BULBS:** None.
**PHOTOPERIOD:** 7 a.m. to 10 p.m.
**HOW OFTEN REPLACED:** Every 6 months.
**METAL HALIDE BULBS:** Six 400 watt 10,000 K HQI bulbs.
**PHOTOPERIOD:** 12 hours.
**HOW OFTEN REPLACED:** Every six months.
**HEIGHT OF LIGHTS ABOVE WATER SURFACE:** 24 inches.
**OTHER BULBS:** Four 96-watt power compacts, seven 100-watt actinics.
**PHOTOPERIOD:** 12 hours.
**LIGHTING CONTROLLER(S):** Neptune.

## SYSTEM PARAMETERS & CHEMISTRY

**WATER TEMPERATURE:** 75 to 76°F.
**SPECIFIC GRAVITY:** 1.024.
**PH:** 8.0-8.2.
**ALKALINITY:** 4.0-5.0.
**CALCIUM:** 400 to 450 ppm, with calcium reactor
**RESINS OR DEVICES USED TO REDUCE NITRATE OR PHOSPHATE:** None.
**REVERSE OSMOSIS:** SpectraPure Ultimate DI.
**SALT USED:** Kent.
**WATER CHANGE SCHEDULE:** 20% per month.
**ADDITIVES OR SUPPLEMENTS USED:** ESV iodine and strontium, 30 ml per week.
**MONITORING EQUIPMENT:** Neptune.
**DOSING EQUIPMENT:** Dosing pump for evaporated water.
**MAINTENANCE SCHEDULE:** Daily observation and adjustments.

## LIVESTOCK

**FISHES:** 60.
**STONY CORALS:** 30 different species of *Acropora* and *Montipora.*
**SOFT CORALS:** 10.
**OTHER LIVESTOCK:** Hermits and snails.
**NOTEWORTHY SPECIMENS:** Blue *Montipora capricornis* and deep blue *Acropora tortuosa.*
**SPAWNING EVENTS:** *Maxima* clams and *Fungia* corals.

## FEEDING

**REGIMEN FOR FISHES:** 20 cubes of various formula foods, *Spirulina, Mysis* fed twice daily (10 morning, 10 evening).

*Large plating Montipora capricornis colonies in pink and blue morphs complement each other and are interspersed with Acroporas in many shapes and colors.*

It should be pointed out that the hand of the aquarist has also assisted, as Robert has taken the cuttings from colonies that were growing too large and used the fragments to fill in the empty spaces within his reefscape. This has produced a unique and very pleasing scene. Rather than having a large number of species with different colors, the tank contains either large colonies of a single species or multiple colonies of the same species with the same color. This creates the dramatic effect seen from in front of the tank as well as when looking down on the reef. Large colonies of rare blue, orange, or green plating *Montipora* species are the centerpieces of the tank, but interspersed among them are deep blue colonies of *Acropora tortuosa*, green *Acropora formosa,* and pink *Montipora digitata.*

The coloration of these corals is especially intense, and Robert credits the use of high temperature metal halide lamps powered by HQI ballasts—a combination that produces a large percentage of the light in the blue spectrum. To some, this choice of lighting may make the tank appear somewhat dim, but it is close to how a reef looks at 30 feet underwater. The water is virtually free of nitrate and phosphate, despite the large number of planktivorous anthias and damselfishes. These fishes provide a bright contrast to the deep coloration of the corals. However, they also produce a great deal of waste. Robert copes with this by following a 20% water change schedule per month, and using a very efficient recirculating venturi skimmer that is rated for a tank twice as large.

Among coral aficionados, this is a tank that commands remarkable respect. The lessons to be learned from it are obvious: give corals adequate space so that they can grow naturally and allow them the time needed to develop their beautiful potential. Jamming a hodgepodge of different corals together for the sake of immediate effect should be avoided if the health of the animals and the expression of natural growth patterns is considered important. By thinking about the spatial distribution of coral colonies, one can aquascape a tank to be visually appealing not only from the front, but from virtually any perspective—including looking down into the system. Robert Dalton has done all of this and the result, even after a relatively short period of time, is one of the most stunning tanks most of us have ever seen.

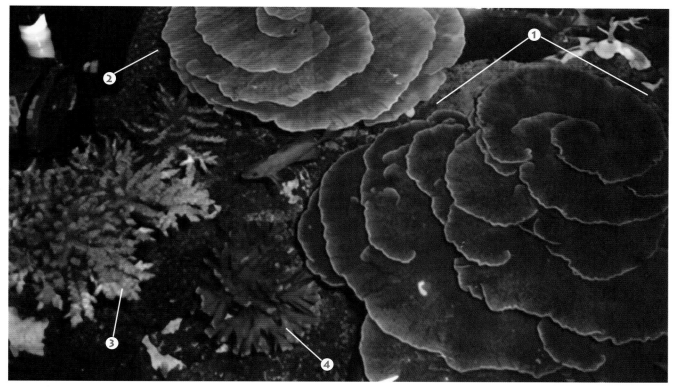

*A top-down view provides a glimpse of exceptional coral husbandry success: gorgeous tiered colonies of Montipora capricornis (1) and (2), a purple cluster Acropora (3), and a small orange colony of finger Montipora (4).*

*A perfect reef-safe species for stony coral tanks, Blue Green Chromis (1) are at home among the corals. Note the massive plating blue Montipora capricornis (2). Robert credits low-nutrient water and high alkalinity provided by a calcium reactor.*

## NOTES

**PROBLEMS OVERCOME WITH THIS SYSTEM:**
None. SPS corals have dominated tank from the onset, due to low-nutrient water and high alkalinity—thanks to calcium reactor.

**THINGS THE OWNER WOULD LIKE TO CHANGE:**
None.

**THINGS OWNER LIKES BEST ABOUT THIS SYSTEM:**
1. Growth rates.
2. No fatalities.

**SPECIAL ABOUT THIS SYSTEM:** It is a perfectly balanced system containing many different organisms.

**FAVORITE COMMENTS BY OTHERS:** How fast the corals are growing and how well they have kept their coloration.

**OVERALL POSITIVES:**
1. Water quality.
2. Design and good equipment such as the calcium reactor and the HQI lighting.

**OVERALL NEGATIVES (OR THINGS TO DO DIFFERENTLY NEXT TIME):** Would like to increase and improve random water currents, either with a better developed wavemaker or a dump bucket design.

# Enhanced Plenum System

*Using a Jaubert plenum beneath the sand, Greg Smith has created a system with an open look and a relatively light bioload.*

## AQUARIUM PROFILE

**OWNER:** Aquatic Technology.
**DESIGNER:** Greg Smith,
  www.aquatictech.com.
**LOCATION:** Columbia Station, OH.
**DATE ESTABLISHED:** November 1999.
**DATE PHOTOGRAPHED:** June 2001.

### TANK
**TANK MATERIAL:** All-Glass with built in
  overflows.
**DISPLAY TANK VOLUME:** 120 gallons.
**DISPLAY TANK DIMENSIONS:** 48" x 24" x
  24".
**DISPLAY TANK MATERIAL:** Glass.
**SUMP VOLUME:** Approximately 40 gallons.
**LOCATION (ROOM):** Aquarium shop.
**CABINETRY/ARCHITECTURAL DETAILS:**
  All-Glass Classic Oak.

### CIRCULATION
**MAIN SYSTEM PUMP(S):** Little Giant 3-MDQX-
  SC.
**WATER RETURNS:** Split between one
  directional jet nozzle and one return
  hooked up to a Sea Swirl oscillator.

### CONTROLLERS
**HEATERS:** Ebo-Jager 100-watt.

HYBRID SYSTEMS SEEM TO TEMPT ADVENTUROUS aquarists, and at the back of his store, in the middle of Ohio, Greg Smith of Aquatic Technology has equipped a 120-gallon tank with two of the most popular nutrient-control methods of reef tank husbandry of the 1990s: protein skimming and a plenum. Protein skimming, of course, is now the approach of choice for most hobbyists, while the plenum system devised by Jean Jaubert of the Monaco Aquarium (Musée Océanographique) is more controversial, with both advocates and detractors. When done according to the description of Dr. Jaubert, this system can work extraordinarily well at reducing nitrate and maintaining calcium and alkalinity levels. However, it does not remove dissolved organics. Furthermore, when not set up according to Jaubert's strict guidelines, the plenum system frequently fails to live up to its expectations. Thinking he could reduce one obvious downside to the Jaubert system, Greg hybridized it by adding some of the components of the Berlin method, most notably the foam fractionator or skimmer.

Unlike most Berlin tanks that employ no substrate or a substrate that is largely covered with live rock, Greg follows Jaubert's tenets and has considerable areas of open live sand, with just 20-25% of the substrate covered by live rock. Just 80 pounds of live rock is used, and this is placed parallel to the back and one side of the tank, with open space between the rock and glass, giving fishes swimming room and ample space where they can retreat. The open expanse of white coral sand causes light to be reflected, so the tank appears brighter than most, even though it is lit without metal halide bulbs.

*Greg reports good growth in the system, provided that calcium and buffer supplements are added regularly. Note green Sinularia (1) and rare pink Clavularia (2).*

The corals have responded with exceptional growth and noteworthy polyp extension. Unfortunately, the plenum system, with its deep (4-inch) bed of substrate slowly dissolving, does not release enough calcium into the system to meet the needs of the corals. Therefore, calcium and buffer are added on a regular basis.

Greg has several corals in this tank that seem to do remarkably well against the bright white bottom. These include several colonies of red *Goniopora*, bright green *Sinularia*, pink-tipped frogspawn *Euphyllia*, and a huge colony of *Xenia*. The *Goniopora*, in particular, stands out against the white sand on which it rests. One of the toughest stony corals to keep alive, this genus seems to be doing well in this system, resting on the bottom of the tank as far away from the lights as possible. The light being reflected from the white sand and the strong water movement may account for part of this success.

Greg has avoided overstocking the tank with fishes, placing just 14 specimens in this 120-gallon tank. The species chosen also tend to be rather small and docile and spend much of their time hiding behind the live rock. Only the *Anthias* require frequent feeding to stay healthy, and this is achieved with daily feedings of brine or *Mysis* shrimp.

This hybrid system has not been without its problems. Despite claims to the contrary, buffer and calcium still need to be added or else their levels are rapidly depleted. Greg has also found that the sand needs to be stirred weekly and the detritus removed—or else noxious conditions develop and fishes die. This concern over toxic compounds accumulating has resulted in Greg doing at least a 10% water change weekly. Nuisance algae has not proved to be a problem, and this is may be the largest benefit of using this system. Despite having to do slightly more work in the form of substrate stirring and water changes, Greg has shown that a hybrid system can produce results at least as impressive as many of the other methods now being employed.

## FILTRATION
**SKIMMER:** HSA 250 protein skimmer.
**CHEMICAL FILTER:** Rainbow Lifeguard module with Kent phosphate remover.
**BIOLOGICAL FILTER:** Live rock.
**LIVE ROCK IN DISPLAY TANK:** Samoan, about 60 lbs.; Tonga, one big piece about 20 lbs.
**SAND/SUBSTRATE IN DISPLAY:** 4 inches cultured live sand over plenum.
**JAUBERT PLENUM:** Yes.

## LIGHTING
**FLUORESCENT BULBS:** Six 48-inch URI VHO bulbs; three URI actinic white 110-watt; three URI Superactinic 03 110-watt.
**PHOTOPERIOD:** 12 hours.
**HOW OFTEN REPLACED:** Yearly.

## SYSTEM PARAMETERS & CHEMISTRY
**WATER TEMPERATURE:** 72 to 82°F.
**SPECIFIC GRAVITY:** 1.0235.
**PH:** 8.2.
**ALKALINITY:** 2.0.
**CALCIUM:** 350-400 ppm.
**NITRATE:** 0.
**PHOSPHATE:** 0.
**RESINS OR DEVICES USED TO REDUCE NITRATE OR PHOSPHATE:** Kent phosphate sponge.
**MUNICIPAL WATER SUPPLY:** Yes.
**RO/DI:** Yes.
**SALT USED:** Red Sea and Kent Marine.
**WATER CHANGE SCHEDULE:** 15 gallons per week.
**ADDITIVES OR SUPPLEMENTS USED:** Reagent-grade calcium chloride, reagent-grade buffer, weekly to bring to 450 ppm calcium and 2.5 meq/liter alkalinity.
**MAINTENANCE SCHEDULE:** Check water parameters and water changes weekly; sand vacuuming.

## LIVESTOCK
**FISHES:** 14.
**STONY CORALS:** 4.
**SOFT CORALS:** 3 species zoanthids, clove polyps, Young's soft coral, *Xenia*, 2 species of leather coral, green *Sinularia*.
**OTHER LIVESTOCK:** Rose anemone, long-tentacle anemone.

## FEEDING
**REGIMEN FOR FISHES:** Flake food, brine shrimp, or *Mysis* shrimp daily.
**REGIMEN FOR CORALS/INVERTS:** 1 or 2 times per week anemones and frogspawn get shrimp or silversides

## NOTES
**PROBLEMS OVERCOME WITH THIS SYSTEM:** Fish died unless weekly sand cleaning was performed.
**THINGS THE OWNER WOULD LIKE TO CHANGE:** Add a chiller.
**THINGS TO DO DIFFERENTLY NEXT TIME:** Varnish the stand and canopy before setting it up.

# Angel & Butterfly Reef

*A home aquarium wonder: Wayne Shang's Fremont, California, 300-gallon fish-only reef houses 17 marine angelfishes.*

## AQUARIUM PROFILE

**OWNER:** Wayne Shang
www.underseadiscovery.net.
**DESIGNER:** Wayne Shang.
**LOCATION:** Fremont, CA.
**DATE ESTABLISHED:** February 1997.
**DATE PHOTOGRAPHED:** August 2001.

### TANK
**CONFIGURATION:** Rectangular.
**DISPLAY TANK VOLUME:** 300 gallons (1,150 L).
**DISPLAY TANK DIMENSIONS:** 96" X 24" X 30".
**DISPLAY TANK MATERIAL:** Plexiglas.
**SUMP VOLUME:** 85 gallons.
**LOCATION:** Living room.
**CABINETRY:** Custom wood stand.

### CIRCULATION
**MAIN SYSTEM PUMP(S):** ATK MP 6560 6,500 L/h (1,700 gph).
**WATER RETURNS:** Direct from the top of the aquarium.

FOR CENTURIES ONE OF THE GREAT theological questions has been how many angels can fit on the head of a pin. In a less cosmic vein, the number of angelfish that could be fit in an aquarium has been the subject of lively debate among saltwater enthusiasts for decades. Wayne Shang has come close to providing one unforgettable answer in a 300-gallon system that many experts would classify as an impossibility—or a miracle.

This eye-catching tank is outfitted with live rock and much of the reefkeeping equipment used to sustain corals, but may be the ultimate home collection of coveted angelfishes. A meticulous aquarist, Wayne has been able to keep 14 large and three small angelfishes—along with a pair of beautiful Red Sea Golden Butterflyfish—together for as long as eight years. Conventional wisdom holds that only one member of the angelfish clan can be kept safely in a single tank. Among the most desirable of marine aquarium species, the angelfishes are favored for their intelligence, bright colors, large sizes, and dominating personalities. A number of species are rare and handsome enough to command very high prices when they occasionally become available.

Wayne has some of the most prized of these, and keeping a large group of relatively territorial and aggressive fishes together for such a long time is a true testament to his skills as a fishkeeper.

*Larger angelfishes are normally kept singly to avoid territorial aggression, but Wayne appears to have assembled enough different fishes to disperse the hostility and avoid fatalities. Shown here: Bluegirdled Angel (1), Flagfin Angel (2), Rock Beauty (3).*

*Virtually never seen in the same tank: Scribbled Angel (1), Red Sea Map Angel (2), Bluegirdled Angel (3), and the rarely seen Chaetodontoplus conspicillatus (4).*

**ADDITIONAL PUMPS:** Two Tunze 2002 (2,400 L/h).
**WAVEMAKING DEVICES:** Tunze 7082 Interval power timer.

## CONTROLLERS
**TEMPERATURE CONTROLS:** Aquadyne Octopus controller.
**HEATERS:** Two 250-watt Ebo-Jager.
**CHILLER:** 1/3 hp Aqua Logic Cyclone.

## FILTRATION
**SKIMMER:** ATK Maxi II.
**BIOLOGICAL FILTER:** Live rock.
**LIVE ROCK IN DISPLAY TANK:** Approximately 250 lbs.
**LIVE ROCK IN SUMP:** Approximately 175 lbs.
**SAND/SUBSTRATE IN DISPLAY:** 3 inches CaribSea aragonite.
**SAND/SUBSTRATE IN SUMP/REFUGIUM:** 2 inches CaribSea aragonite.

## LIGHTING
**FLUORESCENT BULBS:** Four 36-inch fluorescent (30 watts each).
**PHOTOPERIOD:** Two 10,000 K bulbs on 10 hours; two 50/50 on 12 hours per day. Powered by IceCap 430 ballasts.
**LIGHTING CONTROLLER(S):** Timer/dimmer.

## SYSTEM PARAMETERS & CHEMISTRY
**WATER TEMPERATURE:** Winter 78 to 79°F; summer 80 to 81°F.
**SPECIFIC GRAVITY:** 1.022-1.023.
**PH:** 8.2-8.3.
**NITRATE:** <10 ppm (LaMotte Test Kit).
**REVERSE OSMOSIS:** 6-stage RO/DI system.
**SALT USED:** Tropic Marin.

*A prize among a collection of fishes that leaves experienced marine fishkeepers breathless is this pair of Scribbled Angels (C. duboulayi). Wayne attributes his success to using reef methods to maintain pristine water conditions for his fishes.*

**WATER CHANGE SCHEDULE:** Approximately 25% every 3 weeks.
**MONITORING EQUIPMENT:** Aquadyne Octopus controller.
**DOSING EQUIPMENT USED:** AquaTune doser for topping off evaporated water.

### LIVESTOCK
**FISHES:** 20.

### FEEDING
**REGIMEN FOR FISHES:** Fish are fed twice a day. Morning: Hikari Marine A soaked in multi-vitamin supplement. Evening: Hikari Frozen Mysis & Ocean Plankton, Mega Marine and Mega Marine Algae.

### NOTES
**PROBLEMS OVERCOME WITH THIS SYSTEM:** Managing to keep 14 big angelfishes—most of them known for their aggressiveness to other angels—together in one tank.
**THINGS THE OWNER WOULD LIKE TO CHANGE:** These fish can definitely use a bigger home.
**THINGS OWNER LIKES BEST ABOUT THIS SYSTEM:** It includes almost every fish on my wish list.

The secrets of this system are simple enough. The water is kept low in nutrients through the use of a large protein skimmer and frequent water changes. Biological filtration occurs not only in and on the live rock (250 pounds in the main display and 175 pounds in the sump), but also in the aragonite sand beds in both the aquarium and sump. Water changes are performed at the rate of 25% every three weeks, using a multi-stage reverse osmosis deionization unit to purify all makeup and replacement water. Despite the daunting fish load, there is little algae within the tank, and the parameters of the water are near optimum.

The fishes are fed a well-balanced diet daily. These feedings consist of high-quality vegetable-based foods as well as high-protein foods including frozen *Mysis* shrimp and plankton. The dry foods are enriched with vitamins, Selcon, or Zoe vitamin complex. A varied diet coupled with the use of these supplements has not only kept the fishes growing, but it has also prevented any lateral line disease from occurring in these normally susceptible species. Because one of the biggest problems faced in setting up a tank of this type is the threat of a disease outbreak, each of the fishes have gone through a rigorous quarantine procedure before being added to the main population.

The live rock in this system is also a critical component, because it not only serves as a locus for biological filtration but also helps to break the tank up into different sections that allow the fishes to establish their own territories. Among this collection of angels, each has a small portion of the tank that it

*Wayne is particularly satisfied with the fact that this system uses "only natural filtration"—live rock, live sand, and foam fractionation or protein skimming. He feeds a varied diet enriched with vitamins and essential fatty acids.*

defends as its own. Wayne believes that the large number of fishes of similar dispositions actually works to diffuse the aggressiveness that would normally be focused on the weakest individual.

To the uninitiated, this is a wonderful tank, but experienced marine aquarists say that what Wayne has been able to achieve is nothing short of spectacular. Many of his specimens, including an almost impossible-to-keep cleaner wrasse, have lived for over five years and in the case of some of the angels, for more than eight. Just as remarkable is the rarity of many of these angels. The Goldflake (*Apolemichthys xanthopunctatus*), Blue Line (*Chaetodontoplus septentrionalis*), and Xanthotis Angels (*A. xanthotis*) are prized species. But these are commonplace in comparison to the *A. griffisi* and *C. conspicillatus* that swim amongst them. For some observers, the most interesting of all is a mated pair of Scribbled Angels (*C. duboulayi*).

Clearly, this is not a system meant to be imitated by average marine aquarists everywhere. The collection of fishes is remarkable and unique from many points of view—not the least being the extraordinary husbandry practiced by its owner. For some of us, the most impressive aspect of this aquarium is the willpower that Wayne continues to demonstrate. Unlike so many aquarists, he has the inner strength to refrain from continually adding "just one more fish"—and jeopardizing a delicate balance among angels impossibly clustered in a relative pinhead of underwater space.

**SPECIAL ABOUT THIS SYSTEM:**
This system shows that with all-natural filtration (live rock and sand) and proper care (water quality and diet), marine fishes—including those thought difficult to keep alive in captivity—can live and grow in a home aquarium for years.

**FAVORITE COMMENTS BY OTHERS:**
1. "Beautiful fish!"
2. "How did you do it?"

**OVERALL POSITIVES:**
1. All natural filtration.
2. Low maintenance required.

# Penthouse Reef

*The ultimate executive view: Greg Sachs's 505-gallon reef aquarium, located in the penthouse suite of a Chicago office building.*

## AQUARIUM PROFILE

**OWNER:** Greg Sachs.
**LOCATION:** Chicago, IL.
**DATE ESTABLISHED:** March 1999.
**DATE PHOTOGRAPHED:** June 2001.

### TANK
**DISPLAY TANK VOLUME:** 505 gallons.
**DISPLAY TANK DIMENSIONS:** 108" X 36" X 30".
**DISPLAY TANK MATERIAL:** Glass.
**SUMP VOLUME:** 180 gallons.
**LOCATION:** Office.
**CABINETRY/ARCHITECTURAL DETAILS:**
   Custom installation in office wall.

### CIRCULATION
**MAIN SYSTEM PUMP(S):** Dolphin HHS 5,100
   gph.
**WATER RETURNS:** 4 Sea Swirls.

### CONTROLLERS
**TEMPERATURE CONTROLS:** Aquadyne Octopus.
**FANS:** Exhaust fan in ceiling.
**CHILLER:** Universal Marine Industries.

### FILTRATION
**UV STERILIZER:** Rainbow Lifeguard 40 watt.
**CARBON:** 2 cups, 5 days per month.
**BIOLOGICAL FILTER:** Live rock and mud-
   bottom refugium.

OST OFFICE BUILDINGS OFFER PRECIOUS few spots where one can relax. Over time the inability to escape constant stress—even for a few minutes at a time—can wear you down. To remedy this situation, Greg Sachs decided to bring one of his personal passions to his penthouse office suite in Chicago. Despite being on the twelfth floor, Greg wanted a large reef tank in his office where he and his many visitors could enjoy it.

The demands of his location and situation required more than the usual planning of an appropriate system. Greg travels quite frequently, and he needed a system that would require minimal maintenance. Because the 505-gallon tank had to be custom-built to fit the space behind his executive desk, it was not something that could be bought off the shelves of a local store. In the end, the aquarium was designed and built in Canada and trucked to Chicago. Once there, it presented another problem when its nine-foot length would not fit into the building's elevator. The solution was to place the tank, along with several movers, on top of the elevator for the ride to the twelfth floor. Once there, it was carried into the office and placed on a stand made of steel I-beams. All of the plumbing, filling with water, and placement of live rock was carried out before the wall that would isolate it from the adjoining office was erected. This whole process took about seven weeks and effectively resulted in a room being erected around the tank and all of the equipment that supports it.

Being innovative is a hallmark of Greg's business and he wanted to use

cutting edge technology in setting up this tank. After considering the options, he elected to use an Ecosystem mud filter as the primary method of filtration. At the time, this was the largest aquarium ever set up using this method outside of those at Ecosystem itself.

With no protein skimmer in use, the mud filter had to be large enough to accommodate a tank of this size. A 180-gallon sump was retrofitted with the baffles and partitions to make it into a useable mud-based refugium. Ninety pounds of Ecosystem's proprietary Miracle Mud was introduced, creating a bed approximately 1 to 2 inches deep. The refugium was inoculated with two pounds of mud and related microfauna from an existing tank. The tank and live rock were allowed to acclimate for six weeks before the first livestock was brought in. After one week of curing, a 10% water change was made to remove a considerable amount of detritus shed by the live rock, and some *Caulerpa prolifera* was introduced into the lighted refugium to help with nutrient export.

After six weeks, a 25% water change was made and the ammonia, nitrite, nitrate, and phosphate levels were all near zero. Phosphate removing resins were put to use after a loss of fish due to an ich outbreak. To lessen the chances of further occurrences, a UV sterilizer was installed. In addition to the phosphate remover, a monthly introduction of activated carbon is made to keep the water clear. No protein skimming or other means of filtration have ever been used on this system. The *Caulerpa* has remained at a steady level and has neither been harvested nor removed for any reason.

VHO fluorescent lighting was chosen for this tank due to space and heat considerations and in recognition that the system would house only soft and LPS corals. This lighting has been more than adequate even with the depth of this tank for these types of corals. That it is more than adequate is seen not only by the health of the corals but also by the growth that has occurred. In this regard the colt coral has grown to over four times its initial size and several of the leather corals and *Sinularia* have more than doubled in two years.

The stability and nutrients provided by the large refugium appear to have a positive effect on the fishes, as well. The Flame Hawkfish has kept its brilliant red coloration and the anthias have not faded, as is often the case. Two difficult-to-keep species, a Clown Surgeonfish (*Acanthurus lineatus*) and a Copperbanded Butterflyfish (*Chelmon rostratus*) have not only survived but have grown appreciably in this tank. Numerous tangs and angelfishes have done well and show no signs of lateral line erosion, an all-too-common affliction.

Despite the logistics that had to be overcome to locate a large reef high above street level Chicago, Greg's system has lived up to expectations, with minimal maintenance after the initial stages. For owner and guests alike, it is an oasis of serene tropical life and light in the midst of all the frenetic activities and stresses of a large corporation.

**REFUGIUM:** 180-gallon mud filter filled with 90 lbs. of Miracle Mud.
**LIVE ROCK IN DISPLAY TANK:** 750 lbs. Fiji.
**SAND/SUBSTRATE IN DISPLAY:** 1 inch Fiji live sand.

## LIGHTING
**FLUORESCENT BULBS:** Twelve 48 inch 110-watt VHO fluorescent lamps, six actinic and six actinic white.
**PHOTOPERIOD:** 12 hours.
**HOW OFTEN REPLACED:** Every 6 months.
**HEIGHT OF LIGHTS ABOVE WATER:** 6 inches.
**OTHER BULBS:** Four 48-inch fluorescent lamps over sump.
**PHOTOPERIOD:** 24 hours per day.

## SYSTEM PARAMETERS & CHEMISTRY
**WATER TEMPERATURE:** 77 to 79°F.
**SPECIFIC GRAVITY:** 1.024.
**PH:** 8.1-8.3.
**ALKALINITY:** 8 dKH.
**CALCIUM:** 420.
**NITRATE:** 0.
**PHOSPHATE:** 0.01.
**RESINS OR DEVICES USED TO REDUCE NITRATE OR PHOSPHATE:** Phosphate removing resin (Rowaphos) needed from time to time.
**MUNICIPAL WATER SUPPLY:** Yes.
**REVERSE OSMOSIS:** Yes.
**DEIONIZATION:** SpectraPure 6-stage unit.
**SALT USED:** Instant Ocean.
**WATER CHANGE SCHEDULE:** 10% per month.
**ADDITIVES OR SUPPLEMENTS USED:** Tropic Marin Bio Calcium, ESV strontium .
**MAINTENANCE SCHEDULE:** Glass cleaned weekly and detritus removed during water changes.

## LIVESTOCK
**FISHES:** 28.
**STONY CORALS:** 5.
**SOFT CORALS:** 40.
**OTHER LIVESTOCK:** Snails and hermit crabs.

## FEEDING
**REGIMEN FOR FISHES:** Twice per day, 4 blocks of varied frozen foods.

## NOTES
**PROBLEMS OVERCOME WITH THIS SYSTEM:** *Valonia* controlled by *Mithrax* crabs; overheating of room behind tank fixed with better exhaust fans.
**THINGS THE OWNER WOULD LIKE TO CHANGE:** More space behind tank; greater depth (front to back) to balance height; upgrade cooling system.
**SPECIAL ABOUT THIS SYSTEM:** Low maintenance, how healthy everything looks and how full it has gotten in such a short time.
**FAVORITE COMMENTS BY OTHERS:**
1. "How did you ever get that up here?"
2. "How can I get one of these?"

# A System from Scratch

*A do-it-yourselfer's project, this 120-gallon reef created by Jamie Cross in British Columbia uses many home-built components.*

## AQUARIUM PROFILE

**OWNER & DESIGNER:** Jamie Cross
http://members.shaw.ca/jcross1/index.htm.
**LOCATION:** Abbotsford, British Columbia, Canada.
**DATE ESTABLISHED:** June 2000.
**DATE PHOTOGRAPHED:** November 2001.
**PHOTOGRAPHER:** Darren Hoglund.

### TANK
**CONFIGURATION:** Rectangular.
**DISPLAY TANK VOLUME:** 120 gallons.
**DISPLAY TANK DIMENSIONS:** 4' X 2' X 2'.
**DISPLAY TANK MATERIAL:** Glass.
**SUMP VOLUME:** 70 gallons.
**LOCATION (ROOM):** Living room.
**CABINETRY/ARCHITECTURAL DETAILS:** Main tank stand is extruded aluminum with a decorative pine skirt that can be pulled out for full sump access.

### CIRCULATION
**MAIN SYSTEM PUMP(S):** Supreme Mag-Drive 24 (2,400 gph).
**WATER RETURNS:** Two 1-inch Sea Swirls.
**ADDITIONAL PUMPS:** 2 Otto powerheads (500 gph each).

THE DO IT YOURSELFER SPIRIT IS ALIVE AND WELL in the world of marine aquarists, but Jamie Cross of British Columbia is inspiring proof that you can both build and grow a reef from scratch. Not only did he design, build, and aquascape his 120-gallon tank, he also planned and constructed the sump, protein skimmer, and stand for this system as well. Remarkably, his talents extend to the arts of marine husbandry, and the tank is home to some of the healthiest and most brightly colored corals imaginable. In fact, the vivid SPS corals more than give the nearby television set a run for its money, and a visiting aquarist would be hard pressed not to find at least one specimen that sets a new standard for intensity of color.

The success of the system may be traced to Jamie's hybridizing two of the methodologies that dominate the hobby. Most of the filtration is done by a homemade downdraft skimmer, which employs a Beckett injector to maximize foam output. This and the 160 pounds of live rock perform most of the filtration. The classic Berlin approach is enhanced by the presence of a refugium/sump that harbors a deep sand bed with numerous types of algae and various sand sifters. Like a seagrass bed adjacent to a coral reef, this biological refuge undoubtedly helps to keep the nutrient levels low, and Jamie no longer needs to test for them. This refugium also produces a steady supply of copepods and other microfauna that he believes help nourish his tank. He feeds only the fishes and relies on the production of the refugium to feed the corals.

*Brilliant colors characterize Jamie's corals, especially this blue branching Acropora that has not been positively identified.*

*A look-down view shows the diversity of life crowding the reef, illuminated by two 250-watt metal halides and four fluorescent bulbs.*

## CONTROLLERS
**TEMPERATURE CONTROLS:** None.
**FANS:** Main canopy fan has a 7-inch muffin fan; 4-inch fan ventilates the sump.
**HEATERS:** One 250 Ebo-Jager.

## FILTRATION
**SKIMMER:** DIY dual Beckett skimmer run by a Mag 24.
**CARBON:** Approximately 1 cup, 1-2 days per month.
**BIOLOGICAL FILTER:** Rock and deep sand bed.
**REFUGIUM:** Serves as a sump, a refugium, and a coral-fragment-growing tank. Has a deep sand bed with *Halimeda* and *Caulerpa serrulata*. Also has snails, some hermits, a *Halodeima* cucumber, and many pods and worms.
**LIVE ROCK IN DISPLAY TANK:** Approximately 160 lbs. Fiji.
**LIVE ROCK IN SUMP:** None.
**SAND/SUBSTRATE IN DISPLAY:** CaribSea Seaflor and Oolitic from 3-4 inches mixed.
**SAND/SUBSTRATE IN SUMP/REFUGIUM:** CaribSea Seaflor and Oolitic from 3-4 inches mixed.

## LIGHTING
**FLUORESCENT BULBS:** Four 4-foot 110-watt VHO, 2 actinic, and 2 actinic white by URI.
**PHOTOPERIOD:** 13 hours.
**HOW OFTEN REPLACED:** Every year.
**METAL HALIDE BULBS:** Two 250 watt double-ended HQIs 10,000 K by PFO Lighting.
**PHOTOPERIOD:** 11 hours.
**HOW OFTEN REPLACED:** Every year.
**HEIGHT OF LIGHTS ABOVE WATER SURFACE:** 5 inches.
**OTHER BULBS:** Four 3-foot VHOs 10,000 K on propagation tank.
**PHOTOPERIOD:** Reverse as main for 12 hours.
**LIGHTING CONTROLLER(S):** Appliance timers.

## SYSTEM PARAMETERS & CHEMISTRY
**WATER TEMPERATURE:** 80 to 83°F.
**SPECIFIC GRAVITY:** 1.025.
**PH:** 8.00-8.10.
**ALKALINITY:** 4.46 mg/L or 12.5 dKH.
**RESINS OR DEVICES USED TO REDUCE NITRATE OR PHOSPHATE:** None.
**REVERSE OSMOSIS:** Yes.
**DEIONIZATION:** Yes.
**SALT USED:** Instant Ocean.
**WATER CHANGE SCHEDULE:** 20-35 gallons monthly depending on the health of the system.
**ADDITIVES OR SUPPLEMENTS USED:** None.
**MONITORING EQUIPMENT:** pH probe and a digital thermometer.
**DOSING EQUIPMENT USED:** Calcium reactor K2R with DIY second chamber.
**MAINTENANCE SCHEDULE:** At least one hour a week with work also going into the refugium/sump.

## LIVESTOCK

**FISHES:** 6 midwater swimmers and 2 coral gobies.

**STONY CORALS:** About 65-70 SPS corals.

**SOFT CORALS:** About 6 not including unwanted mushrooms.

**OTHER LIVESTOCK:** 4 peppermint shrimp, 3 skunk cleaner shrimp, 2 sea cucumbers, 1 glass shrimp, *Tridacna* clams, many snails, hermits, and coral crabs.

**NOTEWORTHY SPECIMENS:** Christmas Wrasse (*Halichoeres ornatissimus*) is 4 years old.

## FEEDING

**REGIMEN FOR FISHES:** 4 times daily, 1 cube (per day) of frozen San Francisco Bay frozen foods; on weekends, 2 cubes; nori at least 2 times per week.

**REGIMEN FOR CORALS/INVERTS:** None. Hoping pod life can produce enough coral feed.

## NOTES

**PROBLEMS OVERCOME WITH THIS SYSTEM:** Bleaching due to overfeeding, flood due to owner error.

**THINGS THE OWNER WOULD LIKE TO CHANGE:** Would prefer an external return/skimmer pump to lessen heat transfer.

**THINGS OWNER LIKES BEST ABOUT THIS SYSTEM:**
1. Color and health of corals is excellent.
2. Refugium/sump aids in feeding main tank.
3. Money made from selling coral fragments helps pay for the hobby.

**WHAT IS SPECIAL ABOUT THIS SYSTEM:** The system is full of life that all visitors, reef hobbyist's or not, enjoy. After many trials and errors, the system is near complete. Many pieces of the system are hand crafted, including the skimmer, canopy, and stand.

**FAVORITE COMMENTS BY OTHERS:**
1. "Wow! The color and growth rates are incredible."
2. "Interesting specimens and well-stocked system."

**OVERALL POSITIVES:**
1. Calcium reactor.
2. Skimmer.
3. Sump/refuge/prop tank and lighting.

**OVERALL NEGATIVES (OR THINGS TO DO DIFFERENTLY NEXT TIME):**
1. Would use an external pump rather than the internals.
2. System is a little loud.
3. Don't like the center glass support.

The bright coloration of the corals is at least partially due to the intense lighting above the tank. More than 7-watts per gallon are provided from both 10,000 K HQI bulbs and VHO actinic and actinic white bulbs. This lighting is especially intense as these lights are only about 5 inches above the water surface. To ensure maximal light penetration, activated carbon is used monthly to remove any yellowing compounds that could significantly diminish the amount of light reaching the corals. Virtually every coral in Jamie's tank is vividly colored, with a dazzling array of pastels rather than the typical greens or browns seen in most tanks.

This aquarium houses approximately 70 stony coral colonies as well as 6 soft coral colonies. There are just 8 fishes in this tank, but they still put on a realistic show, assisted by numerous small invertebrates such as shrimps and hermit crabs. The robust health of the animals more than compensates for the light stocking load of fishes, with a beautiful Christmas Wrasse that has been in the tank for over 4 years, and blue and yellow tangs that provide flashing color in their constant swimming patterns.

The brilliant pinks and purples of the *Acroporas* provide an authentic backdrop for the fishes, and virtually every coral colony within the tank shows some bright coloration, whether it is only at the deep purple tips of an otherwise white colony of *Acropora cerealis* or the completely purple body of an unknown staghorn type of *Acropora*. The deep blues of the *Tridacna maxima* clams that reside on the substrate contrast with the hues of the corals to add to the beauty of this display. These clams have grown appreciably despite being at the bottom of the tank and having no food given to them directly.

Although this system is relatively new, Jamie says he has learned what is necessary for success through many years of trial and error with other tanks. Not only did he learn to build much of his own equipment, he also discovered how to aquascape a tank to allow its inhabitants to get the maximum benefits of light and water motion. The result is a reef that awes the senses not with sheer size, but with the brilliant colors and obvious good health of its corals and fishes.

*Modeled after the Ecosystem filter, Jamie's refugium is filled with a mass of Halimeda and Caulerpa (closeup inset) and a deep bed of fine coral sand.*

*Rampant stony coral growth, especially of the many staghorn Acroporas, gives this system a complexity that coral biologists until very recently predicted could never be achieved in a captive system.*

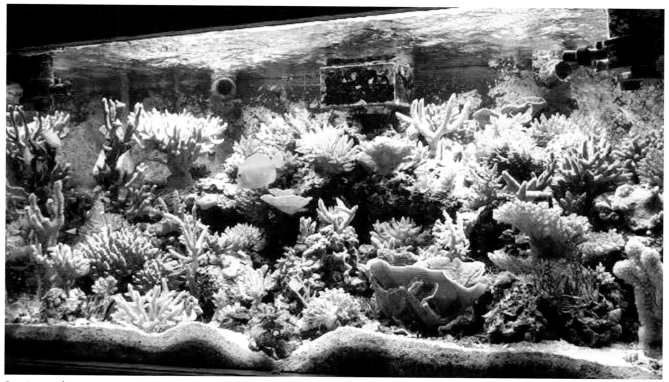

*Jamie uses his system as a working reef, harvesting coral fragments for sale to fellow hobbyists to defray his own costs. This shot was taken prior to the image shown on page 90 and shows some of the colonies in earlier stages of their development.*

# Acropora Treasure Chest

*Residing in a marine shop in Canoga Park, California, this specialized display houses many exceptional Acropora stony corals.*

## AQUARIUM PROFILE

**OWNER:** Aquarium City
www.theaquariumcity.com.
**DESIGNER:** Dustin Dorton, Aquarium City.
**LOCATION:** Canoga Park, CA.
**DATE ESTABLISHED:** March 1997.

### TANK
**DISPLAY TANK VOLUME:** 225 gallons.
**DISPLAY TANK DIMENSIONS:** 72" X 30" X 24".
**DISPLAY TANK MATERIAL:** Glass.
**SUMP VOLUME:** 100-gallon custom tank with 40 gallons of water.

### CIRCULATION
**MAIN SYSTEM PUMP(S):** Iwaki 100 RLT.
**WATER RETURNS:** 4 Sea Swirls.
**WAVEMAKING DEVICES:** Sea Swirl.

### CONTROLLERS
Octopus 3000, monitoring only.
**FANS:** 5 fans in canopy.
**CHILLER:** 1/3 hp Delta Star, located outside, 40-50 feet away, run with two Gen-X pumps run in series.

### FILTRATION
**SKIMMER:** ETS 1400, with an Iwaki 70 RLT.
**UV STERILIZER:** Aqua Ultraviolet 40-watt.

NIRVANA, FOR A CORAL KEEPER, would be the chance to cherry-pick from among the most brightly colored stony corals coming into the United States, hand selecting rare and exceptional specimens right out of their shipping boxes. This dream, unattainable but for a handful of individuals, is one of the secrets that contributes to the stunning display to be found at Aquarium City, a Los Angeles-area retail shop. Originally set up by Dustin Dorton in 1997, this outstanding system is now maintained by Mike Lascurain, Peter DeCaussin, and David Folgar. While they work in the store, they are also marine hobbyists with the enviable opportunity to stock and maintain a tank that is admired by every aquarist who finds his or her way to Aquarium City.

Every nook and cranny within this 225-gallon tank seems to be occupied by some of the most brightly colored stony corals imaginable. Assembled over a period of several years, this world-class collection is particularly rich in *Acropora* spp. staghorns. A huge colony of pink/purple *Acropora formosa* is on the left side of the tank, with a blue colony of *Acropora nobilis* on the right. Normally these large corals are seen in various shades of brown, but in this system they show some of the flamboyant hues found in nature.

Careful examination of the tank reveals other prized and much-sought-after corals. Both *Acropora valida* and *A. humilis* are common enough, but in this tank the tips are all bright purple, sometimes several inches long. Among the most dazzling corals are a bright pink colony of *Acropora millepora*, a tiny colony of *Acropora nana* that is deep purple throughout with vivid green

*Closeup of a young unidentified purple and green Acropora.*

*Acropora selago (lower) and blue Acropora secale (upper).*

*Closeup of bright pink Acropora millepora.*

*Polyp extension on pink-tipped green Acropora millepora.*

*Purple Acropora millepora.*

*Intense purple Acropora formosa.*

*With a volume of 225 gallons, this reef has a light fish load but corals that are "too many to count." Coral fragments are harvested for sales to visiting aquarists.*

polyps, and a pink colony of *Acropora robusta*. These are just a supporting cast for the star of this tank: a colony of *Acropora selago* that is a deep midnight blue.

In this *Acropora* tank, soft corals and reef fishes are lightly stocked—in part to keep the nutrient levels low. The fishes are not fed more than two to three times per week, and there is a large downdraft skimmer to extract dissolved wastes. Nutrients such as phosphate and nitrate are undetectable in this tank, an important factor in keeping the colors of the corals high. The low nutrient level may also be a function of the deep sand bed upon which the reef structure rests. In addition, more than 1,500 watts of light, both metal halide and actinic fluorescent, supply the energy these corals demand. This large amount of light, more than 6 watts per gallon, is shifted toward the blue spectrum with metal halides rated at 10,000 degrees Kelvin coupled with VHO actinic fluorescent lights.

One indication of the rapid growth rates in this aquarium are the previously noted long, brightly colored growth tips—a sure sign of thriving *Acroporas*. This has created a problem in trying to maintain calcium levels. A constantly running calcium reactor and a 5-gallon nightly supplement of Kalkwasser are not enough to keep the calcium level of the tank above 300. However, alkalinity is on the high side at 12 dKH, and this may offset the surprisingly low calcium level.

While the fish population is rather sparse, it is still quite striking, reminiscent of the manner in which many of the early European reef tanks were stocked. Small colorful fishes such as a Flame Hawkfish, a *Chrysiptera starkii* damselfish, a pair of Blackcap Basslets and a pair of Banggai Cardinalfish are examples. Several commensal gobies can be spotted living within the coral heads in which they were transported. Finding these small fishes within the reef requires some patience, but this merely adds to the pleasure for most visitors. A sharp-eyed aquarist will pick out the lovely pair of Randall's Gobies with their commensal pistol shrimp, as well as a rare hybrid Lemonpeel Angelfish.

If this aquarium is a treasure chest of corals, it is highly unusual in being open to picking by the public. Aquarium City is willing to make fragments of the many brilliant corals that they have. As a result, many of the jewels on display in this tank are also now available to hobbyists who can try their hands at matching the growth rates and vibrant colors of the parent colonies that set such a high standard for aquarium-kept stony corals.

**CARBON:** Almost never, very small amounts.
**BIOLOGICAL FILTER:** Live rock.
**REFUGIUM:** Just rock in sump with two PC bulbs. A few mangroves and some assorted macroalgae.
**LIVE ROCK IN DISPLAY TANK:** Fiji and Tonga branch. Approximately 300-500 lbs.
**LIVE ROCK IN SUMP:** Fiji and Tonga branch. Approximately 40-50 lbs.
**SAND/SUBSTRATE IN DISPLAY TANK:** 4-6 inches of Fiji live sand.

## LIGHTING
**FLUORESCENT BULBS:** Four 72-inch VHO actinics, run on two IceCap ballasts.
**PHOTOPERIOD:** 12 hours.
**HOW OFTEN REPLACED:** Exactly every 6 months.
**METAL HALIDE BULBS:** Three 400-watt 10,000 K bulbs. Alternate Aqualine Buschke and Hamiltons, all powered with HQI ballasts.
**PHOTOPERIOD:** 10 hours.
**HOW OFTEN REPLACED:** Exactly every 12 months.
**HEIGHT OF LIGHTS ABOVE WATER SURFACE:** About 12 inches.
**LIGHTING CONTROLLER(S):** Appliance timers.

## SYSTEM PARAMETERS & CHEMISTRY:
**WATER TEMPERATURE:** 77 to 78°F.
**SPECIFIC GRAVITY:** 1.023-1.024.
**PH:** 8.0-8.1.
**ALKALINITY:** 12 dKH.
**CALCIUM:** 300.
**SALT USED, IF APPLICABLE:** Tropic Marin.
**WATER CHANGE SCHEDULE:** Only when needed. Usually to clear settled detritus from sump every few months.
**ADDITIVES OR SUPPLEMENTS USED:** None.
**MONITORING EQUIPMENT:** Octopus 3000.
**DOSING EQUIPMENT USED:** ReefFiller pump adding 5 gallons of Kalkwasser every night. Also MTC Pro-Cal reactor.

## LIVESTOCK
**FISHES:** Approximately 12.
**STONY CORALS:** "Too many to count."
**SOFT CORALS:** Very few.
**NOTEWORTHY SPECIMENS:** Chevron Tang and hybrid Lemonpeel Angelfish.

## FEEDING
**REGIMEN FOR FISHES:** Mixed food two or three times per week.
**REGIMEN FOR CORALS/INVERTS:** Phytoplankton occasionally.

## NOTES:
**THINGS THE OWNER WOULD LIKE TO CHANGE:**
1. More flow and more light!
2. Growing corals block out light and current from other animals.
3. Might prefer to have less rock.
**THINGS OWNER LIKES BEST ABOUT THIS SYSTEM:** Growth!
**SPECIAL ABOUT THIS SYSTEM:** Not very much work.

# Sunshine Super Reef

*Touched by sunlight streaming across a northern California kitchen, Gregg Cook's 75-gallon reef grew into a mass of coral.*

L IKE FISHERMEN, AQUARISTS ARE KNOWN to exaggerate occasionally, and most of us have heard tales of reefs so successful that "the corals were literally growing out of the tank." In the case of the 75-gallon reef tank of Gregg Cook, this was indeed the case. Bolstered by good husbandry and a daily dose of northern California sunshine, a stand of *Acropora grandis* grew so robustly that it literally covered the surface of the tank and dominated so effectively that it was killing off the other corals by overgrowing or shading them out of existence. When the day came to move his coral collection to a much larger system, Gregg was forced to saw his acrylic tank in half in order to extricate the offending *Acropora*.

In looking for an explanation of the phenomenal coral growth, Gregg says that the system was set up and run by the traditional Berlin method, but with one major advantage: this tank received 4 hours of morning sunlight that flooded the kitchen of his family home every day. It wasn't really a planned situation—the tank was located against an interior wall and several strides away from the windows.

Despite our best efforts to mimic the light that is available on a reef, it is clear from tanks such as this that photosynthetic animals such as stony corals can show explosive growth if supplied with an extra kick of natural sunlight. In most tanks, artificial light is the limiting factor in setting rates of growth that

## AQUARIUM PROFILE

**OWNER & DESIGNER:** Gregg Cook.
**LOCATION:** Mountain View, CA; Palo Alto, CA.
**DATE ESTABLISHED:** 1989.
**DATE PHOTOGRAPHED:** 1992, 1993.

### TANK
**DISPLAY TANK VOLUME:** 75 gallons, acrylic.
**DISPLAY TANK DIMENSIONS:** 48" X 20" X 18".
**SUMP VOLUME:** 25 gallons.
**LOCATION (ROOM):** Kitchen.
**CABINETRY/ARCHITECTURAL DETAILS:** Bleached oak, standard aquarium cabinet.

### CIRCULATION
**MAIN SYSTEM PUMP(S):** Iwaki 540 gph.
**WATER RETURNS:** Flexible hose into top back of aquarium.
**ADDITIONAL PUMPS:** Two Gemini powerheads in front corners, two Maxi-Jet 1000s in back corners.
**WAVEMAKING DEVICES:** Homemade (switches two powerheads).

## CONTROLLERS

**TEMPERATURE CONTROLS:** Heater in sump, chiller.

**FANS:** Two small muffin fans in light hood and one inside cabinet.

**HEATERS:** Aquarium Systems 150 watt.

**CHILLER:** UMI 1/5 hp (plumbed outside of house).

## FILTRATION

**SKIMMER:** Homemade 48" tall X 4" diameter ABS.

**MECHANICAL FILTER:** Sometimes use polyester batting on standpipe in overflow of aquarium.

**CARBON:** 1 cup every month or so, changed every month or so.

**BIOLOGICAL FILTER:** Live rock.

**LIVE ROCK IN DISPLAY TANK:** Fiji 40 lbs. and Hawaiian 30 lbs.

**SAND/SUBSTRATE IN DISPLAY:** CaribSea aragonite for aesthetic purposes in front of rock structure.

## LIGHTING

**FLUORESCENT BULBS:** Two 48-inch VHO Phillips actinics.

**PHOTOPERIOD:** 13 hours.

**HOW OFTEN REPLACED:** 9-12 months.

**METAL HALIDE BULBS:** Two 6,500 K 150-watt Iwasaki.

**PHOTOPERIOD:** On 9 hours per day.

**HOW OFTEN REPLACED:** Every 9-12 months.

**HEIGHT OF LIGHTS ABOVE WATER SURFACE:** 8 inches (no glass between lamps and water surface).

**NATURAL LIGHT:** 3-4 hours of natural light per day from window into front of aquarium.

**LIGHTING CONTROLLER(S):** Standard mechanical timers.

## SYSTEM PARAMETERS & CHEMISTRY

**WATER TEMPERATURE:** 78 to 81°F.

**PH:** 7.8 to 8.4.

**ALKALINITY:** 2.5-3.5 meq/L.

**CALCIUM:** 300-400 ppm.

**NITRATE:** 0.0 (Aquarium Systems).

**PHOSPHATE:** 0.0 (Hach).

**OTHER READINGS:** Sr 8 ppm.

## WATER SOURCE

**MUNICIPAL WATER SUPPLY:** Hetch Hetchy Reservoir (Lake Tahoe).

**REVERSE OSMOSIS:** SpectraPure (TFC).

**DEIONIZATION:** SpectraPure single mixed bed, 10-inch cartridge.

**SALT USED:** Instant Ocean, Reef Crystals, sometimes Coralife.

**WATER CHANGE SCHEDULE:** 15% per month.

**ADDITIVES OR SUPPLEMENTS USED:** $SrCl_2$ (15 ml/week), KI (5 drops/week), sometimes use B-Ionic supplements to increase calcium/alkalinity during periods when I neglect water changes. Kalkwasser dosed using homemade reactor using magnetic spinner. ~1/3 cup of $Ca(OH)_2$ powder added weekly and dosed with RO/DI via dosing pump. I add $SrCl_2$ to Kalkwasser solution.

**MONITORING EQUIPMENT:** pH monitor.

*A huge colony of hammer coral (Euphyllia ancora) has grown to fill almost a third of the tank. Note Percula Clownfish using this coral as an anemone surrogate.*

may be lower than in the wild. When the lighting provided includes natural sunlight or is close to that of natural sunlight, growth rates can approach or exceed those seen in nature. In time Gregg found that the growth rates were so rapid that the limiting factor was no longer light, but rather calcium and carbon in the form of buffer. As the corals gained in size, his tank came to require close monitoring because if either the calcium or buffer levels fell, the corals would suffer and begin to bleach. Similarly, Gregg also found it crucial to closely monitor strontium and iodine levels as well, lest the corals suffer a shortage of these elements.

Despite the massive growth of the *Acropora grandis* and the amount of mucous it released into the water, Gregg was able to keep other corals, both soft and hard. He employed strong protein skimming along with activated carbon and vigorous water movement that turned the tank's water volume over more than 10 times per hour. Because of the *Acropora grandis* growth, Greg

*Wall-to-wall stony coral colonies, many grown from pass-along fragments provided by other marine aquarists, eventually forced Gregg to move on to a larger reef.*

had to keep moving the smaller coral colonies to prevent them from being overshadowed or killed by sloughed-off mucous. (This staghorn species is known to exude more mucous than virtually any other coral, soft or hard.)

The other corals in his tank also thrived, including not only colonies of *Acropora microphthalma* and *Acropora elseyi* grown from fragments provided by Bruce Carlson at the Waikiki Aquarium, but also leather corals and a huge colony of *Euphyllia ancora* that eventually filled almost a third of the tank. All grew so rapidly that much of Gregg's work was cutting and fragmenting the colonies before they got too large. Gregg was willing to share his good fortune by providing many friends and acquaintances with fragments from these corals—their progeny are now spread among reef tanks throughout the San Francisco area. Gregg notes that the one major advantage of having corals grow out of the tank is that it becomes much easier to convince your spouse that a much bigger tank is needed. Many of the same corals that started out fighting for space in the ill-fated 75-gallon tank are now thriving in a much larger and equally successful custom aquarium that dominates a whole wall of the Cook's Palo Alto kitchen.

**DOSING EQUIPMENT USED:** Dosing pump for Kalkwasser.
**MAINTENANCE SCHEDULE:** 2 hours per week.

## LIVESTOCK
**FISHES:** 12.
**STONY CORALS:** 30.
**SOFT CORALS:** 6.
**OTHER LIVESTOCK:** Snails, small hermit crabs.
**NOTEWORTHY SPECIMENS:** *Acropora grandis.*
**SPAWNING EVENTS:** *Tridacna derasa* clam.

## FEEDING
**REGIMEN FOR FISHES:** Once per week, 1 or 2 Prime Reef fish food cubes, occasional live brine shrimp. All food supplemented with vitamin C. All food consumed in 2-3 minutes.
**REGIMEN FOR CORALS/INVERTS:** None.

## NOTES
**PROBLEMS OVERCOME WITH THIS SYSTEM:** Large stony coral load caused significant calcium/alkalinity depletion.
**THINGS THE OWNER WOULD LIKE TO CHANGE:** I would have liked to make the live rock structure more interesting. Increasing the front to back dimension of the aquarium to add more depth would have helped in this respect. Keeping the powerheads more discrete would have also been more aesthetically pleasing.
**THINGS OWNER LIKES BEST ABOUT THIS SYSTEM:** Small, easy to maintain. Live rock and associated fauna minimizes need to feed often. Problem algae kept to a minimum.
**WHAT IS SPECIAL ABOUT THIS SYSTEM:** Density and diversity of stony corals. Lots of cuttings from Bruce Carlson from the Waikiki Aquarium (*Acropora microphthalma, A. elseyi, M. digitata*). The growth rate was quite high (approaching natural rates), which enabled me to share many fragments with other hobbyists.
**OVERALL POSITIVES:**
1. Healthy, growing corals.
2. Gives me the opportunity to meet and communicate with other people who have shared interests within and outside the hobby.
3. Intellectually stimulating and challenging.
**THINGS TO DO DIFFERENTLY NEXT TIME:**
1. More automation in terms of lighting, temperature, powerheads, pH, dosing, etc.
2. Build tank into a wall unit so that all pumps and filtration equipment are concealed and can be easily serviced.
3. Use a false back to give the illusion of depth. (In general, I am obsessed with enhancing the natural look and feel of the aquarium display and concealing those items that take away from it such as returns, powerheads, etc.)

# Mud & Acropora

*Determined to use natural filtration, Texas aquarist Sue Truett has found success with a number of difficult stony corals.*

## AQUARIUM PROFILE

**OWNER:** Sue Truett
   http://suetruett.homestead.com/home.
   html.
**DESIGNER:** Keith Gay, Aquatic Designs,
   Houston, TX.
**LOCATION:** Houston, TX.
**DATE ESTABLISHED:** December 2000.
**DATE PHOTOGRAPHED:** September 2001.

### TANK
**CONFIGURATION:** Rectangular.
**DISPLAY TANK VOLUME:** 180 gallons.
**DISPLAY TANK DIMENSIONS:** 72" X 24" X
   24".
**DISPLAY TANK MATERIAL:** Glass.
**SUMP VOLUME:** 65 gallons.
**LOCATION:** Den.
**CABINETRY:** 36 inch tall oak stand, 12 inch
   tall canopy.

### CIRCULATION
**MAIN SYSTEM PUMP:** Velocity T4 1,200 gph.
**WATER RETURNS:** Plumbed to return behind
   rock structure.

For years they were the holy grail of coral husbandry—beautiful, diverse, and difficult to keep. As the most important genus of reef-building stony corals, *Acropora* species are still coveted—although some grow like weeds in good conditions—and still near the top of the list of corals that can test an aquarist's skills. Particularly challenging are the bulkier species, such as *Acropora humilis*, *Acropora gemmifera*, and *Acropora sarmentosa*. For Sue Truett, these species of *Acropora* as well as numerous other corals and invertebrates are thriving. Of special interest is the fact that her tank is being filtered with a mud-bottomed refugium, completely without protein skimming or other conventional water-treatment technology.

Sue says that she wanted to use natural methods for nutrient export and before purchasing her system she researched many of the filtration methods available for reef systems. Having something of a pioneering spirit, she settled on a refugium-based system with a mud substrate and nutrient-extracting *Caulerpa*, even though at the time this method was still regarded by many as somewhat experimental.

For her 180-gallon reef, she chose a 65-gallon refugium using 2-inches of Ecosystem-brand mud as the substrate. Surface water from the display tank is siphoned off and flows across this mud and a mass of *Caulerpa taxifolia* that

*A lush growth of Caulerpa taxifolia in Sue's Ecosystem refugium assists in extracting dissolved organic nutrients.*

*Madly pulsing white Xenia (pulse coral) is reflected by the water's surface in this image.*

*Notoriously hard to keep, this colorful sea rod (Diodogorgia nodulifera) is shown with its snow-white polyps extended.*

*Plump, perfect polyps are indicative of a healthy anchor coral and are typical of the thriving specimens in this system.*

**ADDITIONAL PUMPS:** Three Rio 2100, two Maxi-Jet 1200.

**WAVEMAKING DEVICES:** Natural Wavemaker strip set to switch on/off every 45 seconds.

## CONTROLLER

**TEMPERATURE CONTROLLERS:** None.
**FANS:** None.
**HEATERS:** None.
**CHILLER:** CSL 1/3 hp.

## FILTRATION

**SKIMMER:** None.
**MECHANICAL FILTER:** None.
**CARBON:** One cup Kent reef carbon in bag, as needed.
**BIOLOGICAL FILTER:** Ecosystem with Miracle Mud substrate with *Caulerpa taxifolia*.
**REFUGIUM:** 65 gallons.
**LIVE ROCK IN DISPLAY TANK:** 250 lbs. live rock: 175 lbs. Samoan, 75 lbs. Fiji.
**SAND/SUBSTRATE IN DISPLAY:** Live sand less than 1/2 inch deep.
**SAND/SUBSTRATE IN SUMP/REFUGIUM:** 2 inches mud.

## LIGHTING

**FLUORESCENT BULBS:** Two URI 03 actinic 160-watt.
**PHOTOPERIOD:** 14 hours per day (7 a.m. to 9 p.m.), replaced every 12 months.
**METAL HALIDES:** Three Iwasaki 6,500 K 250-watt.
**PHOTOPERIOD:** 11 hours per day (8:30 a.m. to 7:30 p.m.), replaced every 10 months.
**HEIGHT OF LIGHTS ABOVE WATER SURFACE:** 8 inches.
**LIGHTING CONTROLLERS:** Digital timers.

## SYSTEM PARAMETERS & CHEMISTRY

**WATER TEMPERATURE:** 78°F.
**SPECIFIC GRAVITY:** 1.025.
**PH:** 8.1-8.4.
**ALKALINITY:** 11 to 12 dKH.
**CAL:** 450 ppm.
**NITRATE:** 0.
**MUNICIPAL WATER:** with RO/DI.
**SALT:** Kent Marine.
**WATER CHANGE:** 10 gallons per week.
**ADDITIVES:** Kent Superbuffer for alkalinity, Kent Kalkwasser 24/7.
**DOSING EQUIPMENT:** Kent Aquadoser for Kalkwasser.
**MAINTENANCE SCHEDULE:** With the Ecosystem, my time scraping glass and other cleaning is cut to a minimum.

## LIVESTOCK

**FISHES:** 6 Blue Green Chromis, 1 Sailfin Tang, 1 Kole Tang, 1 Maroon Clown with bubbletip anemone, 1 Copperbanded Butterfly, 1 Potter's Angel, 1 male Flame Wrasse.
**STONY CORALS:** 60, almost all SPS.
**SOFT CORALS:** A couple of polyp rocks and some blue *Anthelia*.
**OTHER LIVESTOCK:** 2 *Tridacna crocea* clams, 1 *T. maxima* clam, 1 *T. squamosa* clam, numerous blue-leg hermits, various snails.

*A beautiful Common Lionfish (Pterois volitans) is an atypical reef tank resident—harmless to corals but a realistic threat to smaller fishes and crustaceans.*

rests on top of it. Water passes through the refugium at a rate of 1,200 gallons per hour, and over time Sue has observed several things happening in the sump. The algae has grown and filled the tank to the surface, so that large handfuls of the green *Caulerpa* must be removed from time to time. Also the microfauna population within the sump has exploded, growing and reproducing so rapidly that some of their offspring are constantly being pumped into the display tank. These small amphipods and copepods seem to flourish in the detritus from the display tank that sinks to the bottom of the refugium. Thus a dynamic recycling system is at work, wherein the waste from fishes and corals acts as nutrients for the microfauna, which then reproduce and help to provide high-quality living foods for the fishes and corals. To remove any yellowing or other deleterious substances that may be produced by the *Caulerpa*, Sue uses a small amount of carbon periodically.

Equally important is the strong water motion provided both to move the waste products away from the corals and to distribute tiny food to the corals throughout the tank. To produce adequate water motion, five powerheads are employed, controlled by a wavemaker electric strip to keep the 2,700 gallons per hour of flow as random as possible.

Lighting is provided by a combination of 6,500 K metal halide lamps and

**NOTEWORTHY SPECIMENS:** Copperbanded Butterflyfish raised from a juvenile the size of a quarter. Solid blue staghorn coral, *Acropora exquisita*, from Lone Star Corals/John Moffet; *Acropora spicifera* from Ron Coleman.

## FEEDING

**REGIMEN FOR FISHES:** Frozen *Mysis* shrimp, frozen brine shrimp, *Spirulina* flakes.

**REGIMEN FOR CORALS:** Golden pearls and Tahitian Blend mixture once per week.

## NOTES

**PROBLEMS OVERCOME WITH THIS SYSTEM:** Ability to keep more difficult SPS corals for the long term.

**THINGS I WOULD LIKE TO CHANGE:** A larger system to start with!

**THINGS THE OWNER LIKES BEST ABOUT THIS SYSTEM:** My Ecosystem reef tank has been the easiest in terms of maintenance of any system I have ever had. The ability of the system to house the number of corals and the ease with which I have been able to do it says to me that the Ecosystem is a viable alternative to other filtration methods. I could not be happier with the appearance of this reef tank with my beloved SPS corals. (The pictures were taken when the system had been up 9 months.)

**FAVORITE COMMENTS BY OTHERS:**
1. "WOW."
2. "Oh my gosh."
3. "This is unbelievable."

**OVERALL POSITIVES:**
1. Ease of maintenance.
2. Growth of corals and no calcium reactor.
3. Beauty and health of corals and fishes.

actinic fluorescent tubes. These lights provide almost seven watts of light per gallon. This, coupled with low phosphate and nitrate levels as well as high calcium and alkalinity levels, supports significant growth rates for Sue's corals, many of which were started as small colonies or fragments. With space becoming scarce, she is now only adding fragments of rare corals, such as brightly colored additions of *Acropora spicifera* and *Acropora exquisita*.

As planned, stony corals predominate in this tank and the only soft corals to be seen are patches of a rare purple *Anthelia* that Sue received from her reef buddy Holly Lostracco. This coral now fills the few empty spots between the SPS corals in the tank. Ten gallons of water are changed each week, and the only additive used in addition to the Kalkwasser reactor is some buffer. No other additives have ever been used. The nutrient levels in this tank have remained low in part because of the filtration method, but also due to the low fish load. The fish are fed daily and the corals are fed directly once a week with a plankton substitute. Sue credits her success and the ease of maintenance to the Ecosystem filtration method, which she feels works to help the corals retain their bright coloration and encourage the exceptional polyp extension that is readily apparent.

# Living Art

*Howard Swimmer's 120-gallon aquarium was designed to bring a vivid, biologically rich scene into a Pittsburgh home.*

## AQUARIUM PROFILE

**OWNER:** Howard Swimmer.
**LOCATION:** Pittsburgh, PA.
**DATE ESTABLISHED:** October 1999.
**DATE PHOTOGRAPHED:** Fall 2001.

### TANK

**CONFIGURATION:** Rectangular.
**DISPLAY TANK VOLUME:** 120 gallons.
**DISPLAY TANK DIMENSIONS:** 48" X 24" X 24".
**DISPLAY TANK MATERIAL:** Glass.
**SUMP VOLUME:** 30 gallons.
**LOCATION:** Family room.
**CABINETRY/ARCHITECTURAL DETAILS:** Gray granite speckled finish.

### CIRCULATION

**MAIN SYSTEM PUMP(S):** Dolphin SM1212, 830 gph.
**WATER RETURNS:** Two overflow boxes, rear right and left corners, hard-plumbed to sump using PVC.
**WAVEMAKING DEVICES:** Two Sea Swirls used for water return.
**CONTROLLERS:** Aquadyne Octopus 3000.

### TEMPERATURE CONTROLS

**FANS:** Four IceCap variable speed fans.
**HEATERS:** Visi-Therm 150 watt.

A MARINE AQUARIUM CAN BE A SCENE STEALER, even in the most smartly decorated of homes. As a prominent figure in the arts and music, Howard Swimmer wanted the new reef aquarium in his tasteful home in Pittsburgh to complement the surroundings while making a statement. His goal was to have the captivating animals within the tank itself be the focal point, with the system itself meant to be unobtrusive.

To fit the aquarium into the modern architecture and interior design of his home, Howard had his tank stand and canopy custom designed and built. Wanting the latest in filtration techniques as well as a minimalist approach to equipment, Howard decided to utilize an Ecosystem refugium. By eliminating the need for a protein skimmer (with its pumps and plumbing) and other technology, Howard was able to have his reef tank fit neatly into the decor of the family room without having a bank of filtration equipment to be seen and heard.

The aquarium itself is simply a standard rectangular 120-gallon tank, but in slightly more than two years the corals have demonstrated impressive growth and have given the aquascape a full, mature look. The system is primarily stocked with soft corals and large polyped stony corals that have rapidly developed from rather ordinary looking specimens to outstanding show pieces. As impressive as their size is the overall health of the animals in this aquarium. Virtually all of the coral polyps are beautifully extended when the lights are on, adding tremendous interest to the reef.

Hidden beneath the live rock is an open framework of PVC pipe that

*Relatively easy-to-keep corals and fishes have made this reef a pleasure to maintain, says Howard, who relies on a Caulerpa-filled refugium for nutrient control.*

supports the reef, while allowing for an extraordinary amount of open space under the rockwork. Howard says that this prevents the type of rock-on-rock detritus accumulation that is seen frequently in many tanks. This has several advantages: first, the detritus can readily be siphoned out from this area, as there are no dead spots under the rock. Second, the cavernlike open space under the rock provides shelter where fishes can hide and feel safe. Third, this design requires much less live rock than is typically called for in a tank this size. Interestingly, the presence of the PCV pipe is apparent only from the rear of the tank, owing both to Howard's meticulous placement of live rock over the structure and the rapid growth of the corals over the live rock and the PVC.

The operation of this tank is interesting in its simplicity. A modified 30-gallon sump rests beneath the main display tank and houses an Ecosystem mud filter. The entire volume of system water passes through this filter approximately seven times per hour and is pumped back into the main tank where it is dispersed in random fashion through the use of Sea Swirl rotating water returns. A small amount of carbon and ozone are used monthly to keep the water crystal-clear and free of any yellowing compounds that may be released by the *Caulerpa* growing in the refugium. An Aquadyne Octopus controller runs the lights and fan as well as a UV sterilizer used to reduce the risk of any disease outbreaks.

While Howard has not populated the tank with really exotic corals, his choice of fishes is unusual—if not unconventional. The fishes include a small Clown Triggerfish, a small school of blue Hippo Tangs, and a trio of different fairy wrasses. These are particularly beautiful in that they include a Red Sea Exquisite Wrasse, an Australian Scott's Fairy Wrasse, and a coveted Lineatus Wrasse. This last wrasse, *Cirrhilabrus lineatus,* is arguably the most brilliantly colored and patterned of all of the fairy wrasses. In addition there is a pair of

## FILTRATION

**UV STERILIZER:** Rainbow Lifeguard 40 watts.

**OZONIZER:** MoreZone. Runs 24 hours 1 day per month.

**CARBON:** 10 ounces, left in sump for one week per month.

**BIOLOGICAL FILTER:** Ecosystem 30 gallons sump serving as filter and refugium with densely packed *Caulerpa* on a 2-inch-deep mud bed. Water enters sump through a chamber filled with bio-balls and then flows into the mud section and out through another section of Bio-Balls.

**REFUGIUM:** Ecosystem doubles as a refugium. Heavily populated with copepods and various shrimp, worms, and tiny invertebrates.

**LIVE ROCK IN DISPLAY TANK:** Fiji live rock, approximately 100 lbs.

**SAND/SUBSTRATE IN DISPLAY:** CaribSea Oolitic sand.

**SAND/SUBSTRATE IN SUMP/REFUGIUM:** 2 inches of Miracle Mud.

## LIGHTING

**FLUORESCENT BULBS:** CustomSeaLife PowerCompact Fluorescents: two Ultra Daylight 96 watts 6,700 K each, and two Ultra-Actinic 96 watts each. Lights are mounted on hood approximately 6 inches above water.

**PHOTOPERIOD:** Actinics on for 11 hours. Daylight bulbs on simultaneously for 9 hours, creating simulated sunrise and sunset each day.

**HOW OFTEN REPLACED:** Replaced every nine months.

**OTHER BULBS:** Two 18-inch Gro-lux bulbs over sump for *Caulerpa* growth; on 24 hours a day.

**NATURAL LIGHT:** Excellent natural light in room.

**LIGHTING CONTROLLER(S):** Aquadyne Octopus 3000.

## SYSTEM PARAMETERS & CHEMISTRY

**WATER TEMPERATURE:** 75.8 to 78.2°F.

**SPECIFIC GRAVITY:** 1.023.

**PH:** 8.32-8.45.

**ALKALINITY:** 3.2.

**CALCIUM:** 450.

**PHOSPHATE:** 0 ppm.

**WATER SUPPLY:** Municipal; Allegheny County water, Pittsburgh, PA.

**DEIONIZATION:** SpectraPure RO/DI unit for all makeup water.

**SALT USED:** Instant Ocean Reef Crystals.

**WATER CHANGE SCHEDULE:** 12 gallons every two weeks.

**ADDITIVES OR SUPPLEMENTS USED:** Kalkwasser for all make-up water, dosed 24 hours a day. Bio-Calc 10 cc once a week, Strontium 10 cc twice a week, Lugol's Iodine 4 drops once a week, Ecosystem additive daily, Seachem Buffer added once every three weeks. Strontium added on Monday and Thursday, Iodine added on Friday, Kalkwasser added daily.

**MONITORING EQUIPMENT:** Aquadyne Octopus 3000.

*The worlds of music culture and tropical nature meet in Howard's family room, with modern art sharing space with the neatly contained reef. Lighting consists of four 96-watt PowerCompact fluorescent bulbs, and there is no skimmer on the system.*

**DOSING EQUIPMENT USED:** SpectraPure Liter Meter.

**MAINTENANCE SCHEDULE:** Regular water changes every other week. Clean glass every few days, clean lights every two weeks, clean pump every six months.

## LIVESTOCK

**FISHES:** 25.
**STONY CORALS:** 20.
**SOFT CORALS:** 20.
**OTHER LIVESTOCK:** Two *Tridacna maxima* clams, *T. derasa* clam, *T. gigas* clam, sea urchins, Blue *Linckia* starfish, several serpent starfish, several brittlestars, 3 sea cucumbers.
**NOTEWORTHY SPECIMENS:** Long-lived red *Dendronephthya* sp. coral. Lineatus

Flame Hawkfish, a Mystery Wrasse, an Obliquelined Dottyback (*Pseudochromis mccullochi*), and a Green Mandarinfish. This mandarin has not only survived, but has almost doubled in size since arriving. This appears to be the result of healthy breeding populations of various microfauna supported by the Ecosystem refugium and constant foraging opportunities for smaller fishes.

The stability of this system, coupled with Howard's attention to maintenance details, makes it both a biological success and the focal point in a room filled with beautiful objects. For many guests, the show put on by live corals undulating in the currents and glorious reef fishes weaving in and out of the reef are far more eye-catching than any of the man-made objects in the vicinity. This system succeeds in making the statement Howard intended, a living display of some of nature's most spectacular and fascinating underwater designs.

*A trio of active Palette Surgeonfish or Pacific Blue Tangs (Paracanthurus hepatus)(1) provides constant movement in the aquascape. Note Clown Triggerfish (Balistoides conspicillum) (2), generally regarded as unsafe in a peaceful reef aquarium.*

Wrasse (*Cirrhilabrus lineatus*), Comet (Marine Betta), Scott's Fairy Wrasse, mated pair Flame Hawkfish, Clown Triggerfish (as of this date has not bothered or destroyed anything), Mystery Wrasse, Green Mandarinfish, Exquisite Wrasse, Copperbanded Butterflyfish, Obliquelined Dottyback.

**SPAWNING EVENTS:** Kenya tree coral and purple tonga mushrooms, as well as all other mushrooms in tank, produce daughter colonies regularly.

## FEEDING

**REGIMEN FOR FISHES:** Feed six days a week, approximately two times a day—something different at every meal, such as *Mysis* shrimp, plankton, nori, fresh shrimp, squid, various flake foods, Vibra-Grow, glassworms, bloodworms, Formula One, Formula Two, *Spirulina*.

**REGIMEN FOR CORALS/INVERTS:** DT's Liquid Phytoplankton dosed daily.

## NOTES

**PROBLEMS OVERCOME WITH THIS SYSTEM:** Elevated pH to 8.6 as a result of low buffer capacity. Seachem buffer added to regulate problem. During this fluctuation I lost three *Tridacna crocea* first-grade clams.

**BEST ABOUT THIS SYSTEM:** Leng Sy's mud system has proved to be exceptionally stable, with virtually all corals extending their polyps every day. The number of fishes able to be kept in this system seems to be infinite with no apparent stress on the biological load.

**FAVORITE COMMENTS BY OTHERS:** "Howard, this tank is so clean you could give birth in there."

**OVERALL POSITIVES:**
1. Great conversation piece.
2. Most stable tank I have ever set up.
3. Large capacity for fishes and corals as a result of the Leng system.

**OVERALL NEGATIVES:**
1. I wish it were about a thousand gallons bigger.
2. Because it is so healthy, corals grow very quickly and have to be moved around frequently. Disrupting the aquascape always frustrates me.

# Well-Calculated Success

*Careful planning and very intense lighting helped Steve Weast's 500-gallon reef develop into a showpiece in less than a year.*

## AQUARIUM PROFILE

**OWNER & DESIGNER:** Steve Weast.
**LOCATION:** Portland, OR.
**DATE ESTABLISHED:** February 2001.
**DATE PHOTOGRAPHED:** December 2001.

### TANK
**CONFIGURATION:** Rectangular.
**DISPLAY TANK VOLUME:** 500 gallons.
**DISPLAY TANK DIMENSIONS:** 72" X 30" X 48".
**DISPLAY TANK MATERIAL:** Acrylic.
**SUMP VOLUME:** 125 gallons.
**LOCATION (ROOM):** Aquarium in garage (mechanical room), facing into a study.
**CABINETRY:** Cherry wood, picture-framed.

### CIRCULATION
**MAIN SYSTEM PUMP(S):** Dolphin Amp Master 3000, 3,000 gph.
**WATER RETURNS:** Two 1-inch return lines.
**ADDITIONAL PUMPS:** Twelve Tunze 3000 powerheads 792 gph each, operated continuously.
**CONTROLLERS:** Aquadyne Octopus 3000.

### TEMPERATURE CONTROLS
**FANS:** Eight 4-inch computer fans in light hood.

THE FIRST YEAR AFTER A REEF TANK IS SET UP is generally thought to be the most difficult time for the tank. The bacterial beds for biological filtration need to become established, kinks in the plumbing and equipment need to be worked out, the fish and corals must become acclimated to a captive environment, and myriad other things need time to settle into place. Steve Weast appears to have found a shortcut with his 500-gallon system, which reached the look of a well-established reef well within the one-year anniversary date.

An ample budget helped, but the primary credit for the success of this system must go to Steve and the fact that he planned this tank out to the tiniest detail before he began setting it up. Once started, he kept to his plan. A first step for Steve was to determine optimal conditions for a successful reef tank, after which he set out to assemble the equipment that would allow these parameters to be met.

The most obvious attribute of his mechanical choices is how strikingly bright the tank is. It's been said that you can't overilluminate a reef tank, and Steve wanted to create as much light as possible for his charges. There are 4,200 watts of light above this tank, or more than eight watts per gallon. As the tank is only 30 inches deep, the corals and anemones at the bottom are illuminated almost as well as the corals at the top. The lighting scheme uses eight 400-watt 10,000 K metal halides lamps plus six actinic fluorescent lamps. This combination produces a blue-white light that is both pleasing to the human eye, as well having a high PAR (photosynthetically active radiation)

*Aggressive water circulation—more than 12,500 gallons of total movement through the system each hour—may help explain Steve's success with anemones, including the impressive rose anemone (Entacmaea quadricolor) that is thriving front and center.*

*A complex aquascape includes Tridacna clams, bright green star polyps, sea anemones, large-polyped stony corals, and numerous small-polyped stony corals.*

**HEATERS:** Two 1,000-watt flow-through.
**CHILLER:** 3/4 hp flow-through.

### FILTRATION
**SKIMMER:** Four Precision Marine Bullet 3's.
**MECHANICAL FILTER:** Prefilter pad in each of the two overflows.
**UV STERILIZER:** 120-watt unit.
**OZONIZER:** 200 mg per hour.
**CARBON:** 2 liters, changed every 8 weeks.
**BIOLOGICAL FILTER:** 1,200 lbs. live rock.
**REFUGIUM:** 125 gallons with 50 lbs. live rock, 2 inches live sand, some *Caulerpa* (4 species). No livestock yet.
**LIVE ROCK IN DISPLAY TANK:** 1,200 lbs. Fiji and Marshall Islands rock.
**LIVE ROCK IN SUMP:** 50 lbs. Fiji rock.
**SAND/SUBSTRATE IN DISPLAY:** 2 inches of aragonite.
**SAND/SUBSTRATE IN SUMP/REFUGIUM:** 2 inches of aragonite.

### LIGHTING
**FLUORESCENT BULBS:** Six 165-watt VHO actinics from Hamilton.
**PHOTOPERIOD:** 12 hours.
**HOW OFTEN REPLACED:** Once every 8 months.
**METAL HALIDE BULBS:** Eight 400-watt 10,000 K PFO ballast from Hamilton.
**PHOTOPERIOD:** 10 hours.
**HOW OFTEN REPLACED:** Once every 8 months.
**HEIGHT ABOVE WATER SURFACE:** 8 inches.
**LIGHTING CONTROLLER(S):** Aquadyne Octopus 3000 controller.

*Ingeniously keeping the mechanical side of the system out of the house, Steve designed this neatly organized unit to support the tank in the garage, where lights, pumps, calcium reactors, Caulerpa-filled refugium, sump, and skimmers are located.*

## SYSTEM PARAMETERS & CHEMISTRY

**WATER TEMPERATURE:** 77.5 to 78.5°F, a set point of 78°F.

**SPECIFIC GRAVITY:** 35 ppt or 1.026.

**PH:** low of 8.1 high of 8.3.

**ALKALINITY:** 10 dKH.

**CALCIUM:** 450 ppm.

**NITRATE:** Less than 0.25 ppm $NO_3$-N LaMotte Test Kit.

**PHOSPHATE:** Undetectable with LaMotte Test Kit.

**RESINS OR DEVICES USED TO REDUCE NITRATE OR PHOSPHATE:** Marc Weiss Phosphate Remover.

**MUNICIPAL WATER SUPPLY:** Yes.

**REVERSE OSMOSIS:** Yes.

**DEIONIZATION:** Yes.

rating to promote coral growth. The lights are mounted only 8 inches above the surface of the tank to maximize illumination.

The aggressiveness of Steve's water motion approach also really stands out. A 3,000-gallon per hour pump provides circulation through the 125-gallon sump/refugium and skimmers. In addition, Steve uses 12 powerheads that move approximately 9,500 additional gallons per hour. This volume of water movement prevents any dead spots from developing and keeps virtually all detritus in suspension long enough so that it is either removed by mechanical filtration or by the protein skimmers.

As with everything else in this system, Steve has planned and designed the filtration to maximize what it is supposed to do, in this case is to expedite nutrient export. Water in this system is first prefiltered via pads in the two overflows. These act to trap most detritus before it gets to either the sump or

*Although replete with technology, this system also displays an owner providing good husbandry, true attention to detail, and high maintenance standards.*

**SALT USED:** Kent.
**WATER CHANGE SCHEDULE:** 150 gallons each month.
**ADDITIVES OR SUPPLEMENTS USED:** Kent Iodine added to maintain 0.06 ppm.
**MONITORING EQUIPMENT:** Octopus 3000. pH, Redox, Temperature, Conductivity.
**DOSING EQUIPMENT USED:** SpectraPure Litermeter for iodine additions.
**MAINTENANCE SCHEDULE:** Clean viewing panel every 3 days, vacuum sand once a week.

## LIVESTOCK
**FISHES:** 20.
**STONY CORALS:** 40.
**SOFT CORALS:** 15.
**OTHER LIVESTOCK:** 4 rose anemones, 1 blue Haddon's carpet anemone.
**SPAWNING EVENTS:** Rose anemone has split.

## FEEDING
**REGIMEN FOR FISHES:** Every other day, various frozen brine, *Mysis* shrimp, squid, and plankton.
**REGIMEN FOR CORALS/INVERTS:** None, other than what the fish get.

## NOTES
**PROBLEMS OVERCOME WITH THIS SYSTEM:** Size and weight of the system, along with trying to achieve a clean built-in look.
**THINGS THE OWNER WOULD LIKE TO CHANGE:** Nothing really.
**THINGS OWNER LIKES BEST ABOUT THIS SYSTEM:** The 48-inch depth makes interesting aquascaping possible.
**SPECIAL ABOUT THIS SYSTEM:** The mechanical space under the tank and the sliding light hood assembly.
**FAVORITE COMMENTS BY OTHERS:** The depth of the tank along with the mechanical room is what impresses most.
**OVERALL POSITIVES:**
1. The lighting system.
2. The depth of the tank.
3. The mechanical room.
**OVERALL NEGATIVES (OR THINGS TO DO DIFFERENTLY NEXT TIME):** I spent a lot of time pre-planning. I really don't think I would change a thing.

refugium or the skimmers. One third of the water coming down from the tank moves into the refugium that contains a live sand bed coupled with live rock and *Caulerpa* where detritus can settle out and be consumed by the inhabitants of the sand bed. The remaining two-thirds of the water, after moving through the heater and chiller units, flows into the sump from where it can be skimmed by one of four protein skimmers before being pumped back into the tank. This bare-bottom sump acts as a settling tank, where much of the detritus from the tank can settle out and be removed later.

Ozone is employed full time to remove any additional waste from the water, as is carbon. This keeps the water free of yellowing compounds as well as the deleterious compounds produced by soft corals in the tank. This multi-pronged filtration approach produces water that is low in nitrate, phosphate, and other nutrients despite the heavy bioload.

The tank's 4-foot width (front to back) allows for some interesting aquascaping. Instead of the traditional reef-face look, the tank is aquascaped so that there are multi-levels and a slope downward toward the middle rather than toward the front. In addition, there are caves facing the front so that even the cryptic inhabitants can be readily viewed. While the health and size of the corals are readily apparent, the animals that steal the show in this tank are the anemones. A blue Haddon's (saddle carpet) sea anemone and four rose (bubble-tip) anemones stand out, both with their brilliant colors and the swaying movement of their tentacles in the strong surge. The rose anemones have already split into daughter colonies and continue to grow quite rapidly, suggesting that they will continue to divide on a regular basis. Steve's uncommon success with these anemones more than anything else shows what can be accomplished with dedication and careful planning to replicate the conditions of a wild reef as closely as contemporary equipment allows.

# Down Home Coral Farm

*One of a handful of stony coral pioneers, Bob Mankin continues to grow impressive corals from fragments and small colonies.*

## AQUARIUM PROFILE

**OWNER:** Bob Mankin (www.coralfarms.com).
**LOCATION:** Cupertino, CA.
**DATE ESTABLISHED:** April 1995.
**DATE PHOTOGRAPHED:** October 1998.

### TANK

**CONFIGURATION:** Rectangular.
**DISPLAY TANK VOLUME:** 187 gallons.
**DISPLAY TANK DIMENSIONS:** 60" x 30" x 24".
**DISPLAY TANK MATERIAL:** Plexiglas.
**SUMP VOLUME:** 40 gallons.
**LOCATION:** Family room.
**CABINETRY/ARCHITECTURAL DETAILS:** 36 inch tall black washed oak stand with Euro style doors for full access.

### CIRCULATION

**MAIN SYSTEM PUMP(S):** MAK 4 and Iwaki 55 RLT used over the years for main pump.
**WATER RETURNS:** Full-length spray bar located low in the back of the tank behind the rockwork.
**ADDITIONAL PUMPS:** Three Gemini pumps used for circulation.
**WAVEMAKING DEVICES:** BlueLine Tsunami.

### CONTROLLERS

**TEMPERATURE CONTROLS:** AquaController.

TIME AND PRESSURE combine to make one of the world's most precious gems—diamonds from insignificant pieces of carbon. For Bob Mankin, time and proper husbandry work together to produce stony corals as beautiful as any gems, starting with modest little colony fragments. As one of the first importers of wild-propagated colonies just a few inches tall from the Solomon Islands, Bob has been able to acquire and grow some of the most-coveted stony corals in the reefkeeping world. Rare colonies of blue, pink, and purple corals were the base from which Bob started his tank. These initial colonies were mostly less than 2 inches in height or diameter when placed in the home display tank for coralfarms.com, Mankin's small company.

Only through meticulous care has Bob been able to grow them out into full-sized colonies that retain both the colors and the normal growth patterns of wild colonies. Remarkably, these corals have grown and filled Mankin's tank with color and a live aquascape relatively quickly. The system conforms to the classic Berlin method, with some slight modifications. It is Bob's meticulous attention to detail that sets this 187-gallon tank apart.

The tank itself is in the family room next to the television. Bob says this is his attempt to keep television viewing to a minimum, and the beauty and activity going on in the tank is a definite distraction for anyone trying to watch anything less than the most riveting program. Filtration is provided by a modified downdraft skimmer, along with approximately 150 pounds of Pacific live rock. Carbon is used continuously to keep any yellowing from the water and to allow maximum light penetration. Water clarity is critical, as Bob has

*This mated pair of Percula Clowns (Amphiprion percula) puts on a regular display of reproductive behaviors, spawning frequently. Note orange serpent star arm (1).*

*Bob credits the use of a calcium reactor of his own design for the results seen in his calcium-hungry system, which is heavily stocked with fast-growing Acropora corals.*

**HEATERS:** 300-watt Ebo-Jager to keep up during colder months. Not used during the summer.
**CHILLER:** Aqua Logic 1/3 hp.

### FILTRATION
**SKIMMER:** ETS Model 1000 driven with a GRI 520.
**CARBON:** Approximately 2 lbs. used continuously in a Magnum canister filter; changed every 6-8 weeks.
**BIOLOGICAL FILTER:** Basic Berlin style.
**LIVE ROCK IN DISPLAY TANK:** Approximately 100 lbs. of Fiji premium with some 30-40 lbs. of Hawaiian (pre-ban).
**SAND/SUBSTRATE IN DISPLAY:** Approximately 2-3 inches Caribbean live sand.

### LIGHTING
**METAL HALIDE BULBS:** Two 400-watt 20,000 K bulbs. (Various Kelvin temps tried over the years including 20,000 K, 10,000 K, and for a short period of time 6,500 K—"I didn't care for the color look without actinics.")
**PHOTOPERIOD:** Approximately 13 hours.
**HOW OFTEN REPLACED:** 12-16 months.
**HEIGHT OF LIGHTS ABOVE WATER SURFACE:** About 5 inches.
**LIGHTING CONTROLLER(S):** Aquacontroller.

### SYSTEM PARAMETERS & CHEMISTRY:
**WATER TEMPERATURE:** 79.5 to 80.5°F.
**PH:** 8.25-8.4.
**ALKALINITY:** ~12 dKH.
**CALCIUM:** 375-400 ppm.
**NITRATE:** 0.
**PHOSPHATE:** 0.

### WATER:
**WATER SOURCE:** Tapwater.
**REVERSE OSMOSIS:** Yes.
**DEIONIZATION:** Yes.
**SALT USED:** Instant Ocean.
**WATER CHANGE SCHEDULE:** About 30 gallons every 6-8 weeks.
**MAINTENANCE SCHEDULE:** Two hours per week, doing routine stuff like cleaning the glass and checking everything.

### LIVESTOCK
**FISHES:** 19.
**STONY CORALS:** 50.
**SOFT CORALS:** 20.
**NOTEWORTHY SPECIMENS:** Mated pair of *A. percula* that I've had for 5+ yrs., a trio of Purple Tangs that were acquired when approximately 50-cent size. Mated pair of Swissguard Basslets, pair of Golden Angels, and a trio of Sunburst Anthias.
**SPAWNING EVENTS:** Mated pair of Solomon Island *A. percula* were spawning regularly before inexplicable loss of female.

### FEEDING:
**REGIMEN FOR FISHES:** Twice per day mixed frozen and flake foods.
**REGIMEN FOR CORALS/INVERTS:** No special feeding directed at corals initially. Started using planktonic foods later (ESV spray dried and live sources).

**THINGS THE OWNER WOULD LIKE TO CHANGE:**

1. Bigger tank! At 30 inches deep, this was deeper than any tank I had worked with previously, but I would have welcomed even more depth.
2. Heat management is a concern during summer months. Tank located in a smallish room with marginal air circulation.

**THINGS OWNER LIKES BEST ABOUT THIS SYSTEM:** Phenomenal SPS growth via the use of a calcium reactor. I had several of the faster-growing SPS species go from 2 inch or less to 18-inch monsters in less than 20 months.

**OVERALL POSITIVES:**

1. Many of the most dramatic display corals were grown from fragments, with some rare species of stony corals included. Rockwork was built over a PVC framework for dramatic affect, rather than the typical "pile of rocks." I was one of the first to use this method in the U.S, to my knowledge.
2. Extremely low maintenance system once it was set up. You could almost call it neglected.
3. Fairly low-tech lighting solution using relatively inexpensive hydroponic light fixtures. Too many reefkeepers get hung up in the "ultimate Kelvin rating/light fixture" debate. Pick a bulb, any bulb, above 6,500 K, 400 watt for SPS corals that suits your viewing pleasure and be done with it!

**OVERALL NEGATIVES (OR THINGS TO DO DIFFERENTLY NEXT TIME):**

1. Learn patience to plant small SPS fragments further apart and allow the reef to "grow in" over a 12-18 month period.
2. Spray bar held up and performed well for approx 3 years, after which buildup within the pipes necessitated it be cut out and a simpler return be put in its place.
3. Design stronger circulation into the system. While initially it might seem too strong, coral growth will quickly impact this and slow it down as will pump aging and debris buildup (slime, calcium deposits, etc.).

corals and clams in the tank at all depths, from the bottom substrate to the surface. Two 400-watt 20,000 K bulbs, without supplemental fluorescent lighting, provide illumination for the tank. Bob has experimented with various color temperature metal halide lamps over the years and has settled on the 20,000 K lamps, believing that they provide the most natural and brightest colored corals without the need for additional lights. These lights are mounted just 5 inches above the water's surface and without the usual acrylic shields. Although some would argue that this poses a hazard if one of the bulbs were to burst, Bob says that the configuration allows corals to be placed even in the lowest recesses of the tank and still receive adequate light.

Strong lighting is only part of the explanation for the bright coloration of the corals and their vigorous growth. Bob has experimented with calcium supplementation for years and has designed his own calcium reactor, which he now sells. He has found that optimal coral growth in his corals occurs not just as a function of adequate calcium levels being present, but also only when alkalinity levels (with their provision of carbon in the form of carbonate) are high as well. With constant attention to both alkalinity and calcium levels, Bob is able to grow some coral species from small fragments less than 2 inches in size to colonies that measure more than 18 inches in less than 20 months. Having seen this phenomenal growth, he says if he were to do it again he would start off with only a small number of prize coral fragments and let them grow up to fill the tank in a year, rather than crowding the tank with too many colonies or trying to acclimate any large wild colonies.

The aquascaping of the reef, now disappearing under a cover a of live coral, is somewhat unusual. Rather than a construction created by stacking live rock alone, as is done in most tanks, Bob has carefully arranged his live rock base on a hidden framework of PVC pipe. This makes for an aquascape that is much more open than conventional aquascapes and one that allows for much easier removal of any detritus that accumulates within the hollow reef structure. This method also reduces the need for live rock to about half the amount usually required to fill the same amount of space.

While Bob is well-known in the reefkeeping community for his coral nurturing skills, the fishes in his home system are also uncommon and interesting. Not only is there a pair of Percula Clownfish spawning regularly, but the system also houses a trio of Sunburst Anthias and a trio of Purple Tangs that were raised from the size of 50 cent pieces. Even more spectacular are the pairs of Swissguard Basslets and Golden Angelfish. These cryptic fishes typically hide in most tanks or disappear into the rocks and die. Perhaps because of the construction of the tank with its many accessible hiding places, these shy fish thrive and are seen regularly out in the open.

Other than better control over heat during the summer, the only thing Bob would like to change is to make the tank bigger. Judging by how well the fishes and corals have done in his current system, it is fun to speculate about what Bob and his husbandry techniques could do with a really large system. Until that day comes, the current reef will stand as an inspiration for anyone who doubts that spectacular, gemlike stony corals can be grown from humble fragments in a matter of months rather than years.

*Unseen in a reefscape that is increasingly encrusted with coral, this system has a hidden framework of PVC pipe beneath the live rock. This approach calls for the use of much less rock initially, while allowing active water circulation throughout the tank.*

# Penn State Reef

*"Is it alive?"* is the most common question heard around this awesome 500-gallon reef in Penn State University's student union.

## AQUARIUM PROFILE

**OWNER:** Penn State University.
**DESIGNERS:** Sanjay Joshi and Robert Minard.
**LOCATION:** State College, PA.
**DATE ESTABLISHED:** November 1999.
**DATE PHOTOGRAPHED:** July 2001.

### TANK
**CONFIGURATION:** Rectangular.
**DISPLAY TANK VOLUME:** 500 gallons.
**DISPLAY TANK DIMENSIONS:** 8' X 3.5' X 2.5'.
**DISPLAY TANK MATERIAL:** Glass.
**SUMP VOLUME:** 100 gallons.
**LOCATION (ROOM):** Student Union Building.
**CABINETRY:** Built into a wall.

### CIRCULATION
**MAIN SYSTEM PUMP(S):** Iwaki 100 RLT.
**WATER RETURNS:** Two returns from main pump, one on each side of tank directed toward the tank center.
**ADDITIONAL PUMPS:** Three Iwaki 70 RLT pumps for circulation.

**B**RING TOGETHER THE BEST AND BRIGHTEST students from the biology, chemistry, and engineering departments of a major university to work together on a 500-gallon reef tank, and the results might look like the stunning system that graces the student union building at Penn State University in State College, Pennsylvania.

Designed by Professor Sanjay Joshi and Robert Minard, the aquarium gives many students their first look at live corals and, for those who help maintain it, an opportunity to learn about the proper conditions to keep the marine creatures thriving in a system hundreds of miles from the nearest coast. Filled with nature's unbelievable colors and casting a welcoming glow, the reef has become a focal point for the busiest building on the Penn State campus.

Funded by a Class Gift to the university, the tank was designed to provide optimal conditions for corals and other animals. An efficient downdraft skimmer is utilized for primary filtration. In addition, a refugium was designed into part of the sump where a deep sand bed and *Caulerpa* are located. The refugium provides a site for denitrification and extraction of nutrients from the water, while also serving as a source of microfauna, such as amphipods and copepods, that reproduce freely there. The only other means of nutrient export

is a 50-gallon water change carried out every two weeks. A custom-designed calcium carbonate reactor is used to meet the calcium and alkalinity demands of the corals in the tank. No trace elements or other additives are added to this system.

Lighting is provided by four 400-watt 10,000 K metal halide lamps fired with standard metal halide ballasts. These lamps are housed in large Diamond light reflectors and are about 8 inches from the water surface to maximize the amount of light reaching the corals. The reflectors are designed so that 16 facets within the reflector focus the light down into the tank. The effectiveness of the reflector design can be seen by the fact that the room housing the tank can be dark while the interior of the aquarium is brightly lit.

Using this reflector, Sanjay estimates that more than 40% of the light that would normally be lost is reflected down into the tank. As a result, no additional supplemental lighting is required. Thanks in part to this lighting configuration, the tank's corals are putting on a show of exceptional coloration and rapid growth. Most of the colonies in this tank were taken from cuttings in Sanjay's home reef.

There is no lack of water motion in this tank. A 2,000-gallon per hour

**WAVEMAKING DEVICES:** X-10 controllers used with the Neptune AquaController.

## CONTROLLERS
**HEATERS:** One 200-watt heater (only used in winter).
**CHILLER:** Chilled water system with Titanium heat exchanger.

## FILTRATION
**SKIMMER:** ETS 1200.
**UV STERILIZER:** Yes.
**REFUGIUM:** About 70 gallons, with live rock, 6-inch sand bed, algae, and shrimp.
**LIVE ROCK IN DISPLAY TANK:** 300 lbs. Fiji live rock.
**LIVE ROCK IN SUMP:** 50 lbs. Fiji live rock.
**SAND/SUBSTRATE IN DISPLAY:** 2-3 inches Florida Keys live sand.
**SAND/SUBSTRATE IN SUMP/REFUGIUM:** 5-6 inches live sand and CaribSea Aragamax combined.

## LIGHTING
**METAL HALIDE BULBS:** Four 400-watt 10,000 K Ushio.

*An overhead view reveals the tiered, whorling growth of a large colony of red Montipora capricornis.*

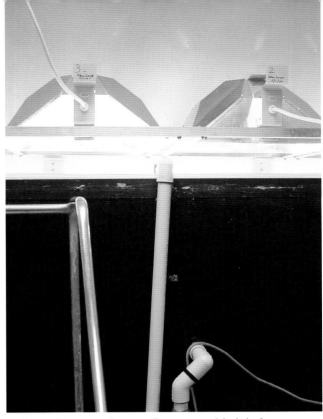

*Industrial Diamond-type reflectors/metal halide fixtures provide a superior light dispersion pattern over the tank.*

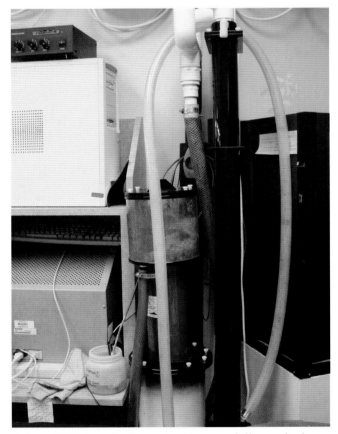

*A large ETS downdraft protein skimmer, chiller, and other equipment are located in a utility room behind the tank.*

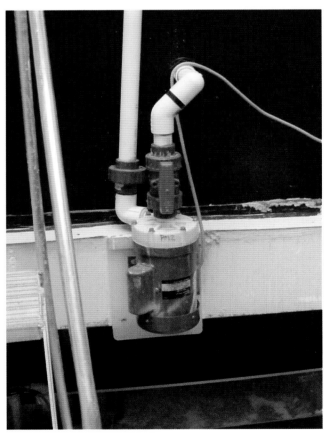

*The closed-loop circulation plan for three external water pumps uses water intakes in the back wall of the aquarium.*

*Faculty member and avid aquarist Sanjay Joshi says that this reef gives thousands of students and visitors their first glimpse of living reef fishes and corals.*

**PHOTOPERIOD:** 12 hours.
**HOW OFTEN REPLACED:** 9-12 months.
**HEIGHT ABOVE WATER:** 8 inches.
**LIGHTING CONTROLLER(S):** X-10 controlled by the Neptune AquaController.

## SYSTEM PARAMETERS & CHEMISTRY

**PH:** 8.0-8.2.
**ALKALINITY:** 6-9 dKH.
**CALCIUM:** 300-400 ppm.
**NITRATE:** 0.1 ppm $NO_3$.
**PHOSPHATE:** 0.02 ppm.
**MUNICIPAL WATER SUPPLY:** Yes.
**REVERSE OSMOSIS:** Yes.
**DEIONIZATION:** No.
**SALT USED:** Instant Ocean.
**WATER CHANGE SCHEDULE:** 50 gallons every other week.
**MONITORING EQUIPMENT:** Neptune AquaController and AquaNotes, with pH probe, ORP probe, and temperature probe.
**DOSING EQUIPMENT USED:** ReefFiller.
**MAINTENANCE SCHEDULE:** 1.5 hours per week, cleaning glass and skimmer.

## LIVESTOCK

**FISHES:** 25.
**STONY CORALS:** 70.
**SOFT CORALS:** 6.
**OTHER LIVESTOCK:** Starfishes, snails, crabs, shrimps, sea cucumber.

## FEEDING

**REGIMEN FOR FISHES:** Three times a day: nori, flake food, brine shrimp, and frozen food.
**REGIMEN FOR CORALS/INVERTS:** Same as above.

## NOTES

**PROBLEMS OVERCOME WITH THIS SYSTEM:** Accidental overheating of tank, cyanobacteria.
**THINGS OWNER LIKES BEST ABOUT THIS SYSTEM:** Very low maintenance.
**SPECIAL ABOUT THIS SYSTEM:** Tank serves as a beautiful public display as well as providing education and outreach activities to schools in central Pennsylvania. A great educational tool.
**FAVORITE COMMENTS BY OTHERS ABOUT THIS AQUARIUM:**
  1. "Is it alive?"
  2. "One of the best Class gifts."
**OVERALL POSITIVES:**
  1. Great aquascaping.
  2. Lots of circulation and strong water movement.
  3. Corals thrive.

pump moves water from the tank through the sump and skimmer, and three additional 1,500-gallon-per-hour pumps circulate water constantly throughout the tank via Sea Swirl oscillating devices. The tank's total volume is circulated approximately 11 times per hour. Very little detritus is allowed to settle within the tank, and this increases the skimmer's ability to remove waste.

The tank was also aquascaped with two views in mind. The first is from directly in front, where the rock structure resembles a reef mount with a large island in the center of the tank and open spaces surrounding it. The other view is from the left end, where a large dining area for students is located. The rockscape is lowest on this end, and gradually rises up toward the far end. This allows for some of the reef to be seen even by those seated far away and allows more students to enjoy the reef while seated than would be the case with a conventional layout of rock.

Sanjay has chosen myriad interesting fishes and other animals to be housed with the corals, adding greatly to the level of interest that this reef generates. This includes several pairs of different species of clownfishes that not only live in different areas of the tank but also put on spawning shows on a regular basis. One clown even uses a giant clam as a replacement for its anemone. A giant sea cucumber constantly sifts through the sand, and numerous starfishes, crabs, and shrimps occupy every vacant niche.

This glorious system not only brings some uncommon beauty into the student union, but it also provides insight into the living treasures and biological complexity of a natural reef. For the throngs of students and faculty who are exposed to a world-class reef tank for the first time, it is exactly the educational tool its donors hoped it would be.

# Surge Reef Tank

*Back-and-forth wave action gives this 150-gallon Los Angeles-area reef designed by Jim Stime an unusual element of realism.*

## AQUARIUM PROFILE

**OWNER:** Craig Polisky.
**DESIGNER:** Jim Stime/Aquarium Design
www.aquarium-design.com
**LOCATION:** Agoura Hills, CA.
**DATE ESTABLISHED:** December 1997.
**DATE PHOTOGRAPHED:** July 1998.

### TANK

**CONFIGURATION:** Rectangular.
**DISPLAY TANK VOLUME:** 150 gallons.
**DISPLAY TANK DIMENSIONS:** 60" X 24" X 30".
**DISPLAY TANK MATERIAL:** Acrylic.
**SUMP VOLUME:** 35 gallons.
**LOCATION:** Dayroom.
**CABINETRY/ARCHITECTURAL DETAILS:** The aquarium is positioned on a platform that supports the tank and allows only the face to penetrate beyond the wall into the room. The sump, chiller, and protein skimmer all sit alongside the platform. Two surge reservoirs are placed on a shelf above the tank.

### CIRCULATION

**MAIN SYSTEM PUMP(S):** Iwaki 40 RLT for filter circulation, 750 gph; Iwaki 40 RLXT for internal circulation, 1,200 gph.
**WATER RETURNS:** The system pump returns via a spray bar positioned under the live

WATER MOTION ON CORAL REEFS is immensely powerful, multi-directional, and very difficult—if not impossible—to replicate in a small marine aquarium. When Jim Stime set out to design a new 150-gallon tank for Craig Polisky, he wanted to mimic the conditions on a reef as closely as possible. Realizing that he could not match the strength of ocean water movements across the corals, he nevertheless tried to create conditions as close to those of a natural reef as possible in a small-scale system.

Having ready access to the Pacific, he started out using clean natural seawater both for the initial filling of the tank and for the 10-gallon bimonthly water changes. The use of natural seawater has allowed this tank to thrive without the addition of trace elements or other additives. Even without supplements, the calcium level has remained at a steady 430 ppm and the alkalinity at 9 dKH.

The steady state of important chemical parameters is complemented by the tank's overall stability. It has been set up for more than four years, and very few changes have needed to be made. Algae has never been a problem, and for the most part, the corals are the same specimens bought to stock the system at the outset. Over time, these corals have grown significantly, and Jim attributes much of the robust success of this system to the strong water motion surging within the tank.

Two external nonsubmersible pumps are used to provide circulation at over 1,900 gallons-per hour. One provides circulation through the sump and skimmer, while the other provides circulation via a closed loop. (The water

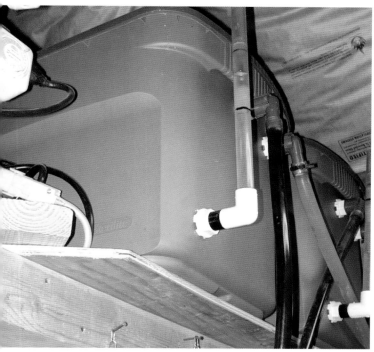

*Hidden from view, two 15-gallon elevated reservoirs provide alternating flushes of water to the display tank. Dubbed the "Carlson Surge Device," this type of unit is filled by a water pump but empties itself automatically.*

*Plumbed by an experienced hand, the back of this acrylic tank has various ports connected to the surge devices, which depend on gravity and siphon effects for their automatic triggering and their forceful return of water to the aquarium.*

*A strong flush of water from the Carlson Surge Device floods back into the display tank, producing a positive effect on the system's inhabitants, such as this mushroom leather coral (Sarcophyton sp.). Many corals—and even fishes—seem to do better with strong currents, which provide oxygenation, waste removal, dispersal of food items, and other benefits.*

rock and blows debris out from under the live rock. The circulation pump returns its water at two points opposite each other in the upper rear corners of the tank.

**ADDITIONAL PUMPS:** Two Rio 2500 powerheads used to fill the surge units.

**WAVEMAKING DEVICES:** Two Carlson surge makers, 15 gallons each, dispensing at opposite ends of the tank.

## CONTROLLERS

**TEMPERATURE CONTROLS:** Chiller thermostat.

**HEATERS:** Ebo-Jager 300 watt.

**CHILLER:** West Coast Aquatics.

**SKIMMER:** 4-foot venturi-driven unit.

**MECHANICAL FILTER:** Prefilter pad.

**CARBON:** 10 ounces, changed every 3-4 months.

## FILTRATION

**BIOLOGICAL FILTER:** This tank utilizes the Berlin method, which eliminates a dedicated biological filter and in turn relies on the bacterial population within the live rock and live sand.

**LIVE ROCK IN DISPLAY TANK:** Approximately 200 lbs. of Marshall Islands branching live rock.

**SAND/SUBSTRATE IN DISPLAY:** 100 lbs. of live sand, approximately 2 inches deep.

## LIGHTING

**FLUORESCENT BULBS:** Two 40-watt actinic 03.

**PHOTOPERIOD:** 9 hours.

**HOW OFTEN REPLACED:** Once a year.

**METAL HALIDE BULBS:** Three 250-watt, 10,000 K Coralife.

**PHOTOPERIOD:** 8 hours.

**HOW OFTEN REPLACED:** Once a year.

**HEIGHT ABOVE WATER SURFACE:** 8 inches.

**LIGHTING CONTROLLER(S):** Hardware store analog timers.

## SYSTEM PARAMETERS & CHEMISTRY:

**WATER TEMPERATURE:** 76 to 79°F.

**SPECIFIC GRAVITY:** 1.022.

**PH:** 8.1.

**ALKALINITY:** 9 dKH.

**CALCIUM:** 430.

**NITRATE:** 20 ppm.

**NATURAL SEA WATER:** Yes.

**WATER CHANGE SCHEDULE:** 10 gallons bi-monthly.

**ADDITIVES OR SUPPLEMENTS USED:** None.

**MONITORING EQUIPMENT:** pH and temperature.

**MAINTENANCE SCHEDULE:** Bi-monthly, 1 hour allows time to clean algae from the front panel, clean protein skimmer, and change 10 gallons of water.

## LIVESTOCK

**FISHES:** 22.

**STONY CORALS:** 13.

**SOFT CORALS:** 10.

## FEEDING

**REGIMEN FOR FISHES:** Frozen *Mysis* shrimp every other day.

*Presenting a glowing face within owner Craig Polisky's day room, the reef is framed into a dividing wall, with all mechanical components kept behind the scenes.*

intake of the pump is fed directly from the tank, reducing noise and the amount of water that must flow through the sump.) The returning currents from these pumps are directed across each other as well as having some of the output move through a spray bar behind the live rock. Most interesting, however, is the effect of two 15-gallon Carlson Surge Devices that mimic the effects of waves periodically rushing through the reef. Custom built to a design originated by Dr. Bruce Carlson, former director of the Waikiki Aquarium, these surge devices are filled by medium-sized powerhead pumps, but otherwise operate by gravity and siphon effects, providing realistic surges of water throughout the tank.

In total, the circulation plan maximizes the randomness of the water currents and yields many positive effects that are at least partly responsible for the good health and growth of the corals. Strong flows keep detritus from accumulating, and dead spots that trap nutrients have never developed. As a result, algae growth has never been a problem, nor has cyanobacteria. Vigorous circulation also keeps the water supersaturated with oxygen with no temperature or chemical gradients able to develop as can happen in systems with poor water flow. Chaotic currents keep the corals constantly bathed with clean water and cleansed of any waste they may generate, just as this process occurs on the reef. Strong currents also contribute to the health of the fishes, as

they need to swim strongly to maintain themselves in this current. As a result they have not gotten fat or developed fatty livers, which can be a problem in tanks with minimal water movement.

This system has more than 5 watts per gallon of mixed light above it, with both fluorescent and metal halide lamps being utilized to support the photosynthetic activities of the soft- and large-polyped stony corals that fill the tank. A 4-foot venturi skimmer and 200 pounds of live rock provide filtration. A small filter pad is utilized for mechanical filtration, and 10 ounces of carbon provides chemical filtration and polishes the water. Remarkably, maintenance is minimal—just two hours per month for regular chores.

The tank houses 23 coral colonies and 22 fishes, with the corals dominating the aquascape and quickly filling in any available empty spaces within the tank. The surging currents add a realistic dimension to the scene, and the placement of the tank, through a wall, gives the impression of a framed scene of a live reef hanging in a family room. Proper planning and execution are the secrets behind this biological mirage, which is both beautiful and easy to maintain—the twin, elusive goals of most reefkeepers.

## NOTES

**PROBLEMS OVERCOME WITH THIS SYSTEM:** No algae problems: the surge units create an always-changing water flow.

**THINGS THE OWNER WOULD LIKE TO CHANGE:** Increase the diameter of the surge siphon tubes, which would allow for a much stronger surge within the tank.

**THINGS OWNER LIKES BEST ABOUT THIS SYSTEM:** The size of the individual corals, attributable to the strong current.

**FAVORITE COMMENTS BY OTHERS:** "Check out the water movement."

**OVERALL POSITIVES:**
1. The ability to turn over the water within the tank quickly.
2. Accessibility to equipment, in a room behind the tank.
3. Various colors of the living corals and their successful growth.

**OVERALL NEGATIVES (OR THINGS TO DO DIFFERENTLY NEXT TIME):**
1. Poor choice in protein skimmer design (square unit).
2. Eliminate spray bar behind live rock.
3. Use a much higher volume water pump for internal circulation.

# Hidden Reef

*Lovely display of large soft corals and large-polyped stony corals is a noted landmark for Philadelphia area marine enthusiasts.*

## AQUARIUM PROFILE

**OWNER:** George Kunz/Siegfried "Ziggy" Gutekunst
www.thehiddenreef.com.
**DESIGNER:** Siegfried Gutekunst.
**LOCATION:** Philadelphia, PA.
**DATE ESTABLISHED:** January 1996.
**DATE PHOTOGRAPHED:** August 2001.

### TANK
**CONFIGURATION:** Rectangular.
**DISPLAY TANK VOLUME:** Oceanic 180-gallon Reef Ready, Modern Oak.
**DISPLAY TANK DIMENSIONS:** 72" X 24" X 25".
**DISPLAY TANK MATERIAL:** Glass.
**SUMP VOLUME:** Total volume is 42 gallons, half-filled with water.
**LOCATION (ROOM):** Retail store.
**CABINETRY:** Oak stand.

### CIRCULATION
**MAIN SYSTEM PUMP(S):** Two Gen-X pumps with 1,190 gph flow and one Iwaki 70 RLT 1,536 gph flow.
**WATER RETURNS:** Iwaki 70 RLT returns the water back into the tank via Sea Swirl.
**WAVEMAKING DEVICES:** Tsunami Junior that switches back and forth between the two Gen-X pumps.

SELDOM DO LARGE-POLYP STONY CORALS dominate contemporary reef aquariums, but in Siegfried "Ziggy" Gutekunst's system they are the scene stealers in a noteworthy system that displays specimens that the public failed to snap up for their own tanks. Constantly in the public eye at Philadelphia's Hidden Reef aquarium shop, this standard 180-gallon tank has now been in operation for several years and the showpiece LPS corals have all grown from small colonies plucked out of the store's available-for-purchase displays.

Their large sizes, bright colors, and vitality really make these corals stand out in a tank full of very nice small-polyp stony and soft corals. The large-polyp corals are not the easiest to keep, and most aquarists relegate them to the role of the supporting actors. In this tank they are the stars. Among the interesting LPS colonies, Ziggy has bright red, yellow orange, and green *Lobophyllias*, a red *Echinophyllia*, a lime green and a red and green *Trachyphyllia*, a cherry red *Cynarina*, a green *Symphyllia,* and a *Wellsophyllia* just to name a few. There are also large colonies of *Sarcophyton* leather corals and *Sinularias*, bright examples of *Acropora* and even a colony of *Goniopora*. All of these are interspersed with bunches of calcareous *Halimeda* algae that provides an interesting green contrast to various corals.

In Ziggy's hands, colony losses have been minimal, and most of these happened when the corals were moved from an older 120-gallon tank to their present location. Because the tank is in a store, Ziggy and his employees like to stay on top of maintenance, but at busy times the tank tends to fend for itself.

*Ziggy's unusual red Echinophyllia aspera has a mounding skeleton, warty corallites, and a tendency to extend stinging sweeper tentacles at night.*

*Green bubble coral (Plerogyra sinuosa) is a very hardy species that makes a curious display specimen with its water-filled vesicles that emerge only during the day.*

The only maintenance that Ziggy feels is absolutely essential is a regular 20% monthly water change to prevent the growth of nuisance algae. The design of the system and routine chores that are automated allow the tank to run well even when some of the day-to-day maintenance is skipped.

The tank is set up in the traditional Berlin manner, with a large downdraft skimmer for filtration and some mechanical filtration to remove large particulates from the water. There is also a one-inch-deep sand bed and a denitrator in use to keep the nutrient levels low. The use of this device, plus the frequent water changes, has kept nutrient levels very low and problem algae in check.

## CONTROLLERS
**TEMPERATURE CONTROLS:** Neptune AquaController for chiller/heater.
**FANS:** Two 4-inch computer fans on Hamilton lighting fixtures.
**HEATERS:** 300-watt Aquarium Systems.
**CHILLER:** Aquanetics inline.

## FILTRATION
**SKIMMER:** ETS dual stack runs with 4 MDQ-SC pump.
**MECHANICAL FILTER:** Two bag-type fine-mesh filters that are in Berlin sump.
**BIOLOGICAL FILTER:** 160 lbs. live rock.
**LIVE ROCK IN DISPLAY TANK:** 160 lbs. of mixed Fiji, Indonesia, Vanuatu, and Tonga.
**SAND/SUBSTRATE IN DISPLAY:** CaribSea Seaflor Reef Sand 60 lbs., to 1 inch just in front.

## LIGHTING
**FLUORESCENT BULBS:** Two 160-watt VHO URI actinic bulbs.
**PHOTOPERIOD:** 11 hours 15 minutes.
**HOW OFTEN REPLACED:** 9 months.
**METAL HALIDE BULBS:** Three 250-watt Iwasaki 6,500 K.
**PHOTOPERIOD:** 5-7 hours.
**HOW OFTEN REPLACED:** 9 months.
**HEIGHT OF LIGHTS ABOVE WATER:** 2 inches.
**LIGHTING CONTROLLER(S):** Neptune.

## SYSTEM PARAMETERS & CHEMISTRY
**WATER TEMPERATURE:** Winter 74°F; summer 75 to 78°F.
**SPECIFIC GRAVITY:** 1.023.
**PH:** 8.3-8.4.
**ALKALINITY:** 2.7.
**CALCIUM:** 405 ppm through use of calcium reactor.
**RESINS OR DEVICES USED TO REDUCE NITRATE OR PHOSPHATE:** AquaMedic Denitrator.
**REDOX:** 425-450.
**REVERSE OSMOSIS:** Kent RO 650 gpd.
**SALT USED:** Mostly Marine Enterprise Crystal Sea.
**WATER CHANGE SCHEDULE:** 20% per month.
**ADDITIVES OR SUPPLEMENTS USED:** Kent Strontium/Molybdenum (3 teaspoons every week), Kent Lugol's Iodine (6 drops once per week), Kent dKH Buffer (when needed).
**DOSING EQUIPMENT USED:** Calcium reactor with PinPoint Marine pH controller, 20 lb. $CO_2$ tank, and Coralith media.
**MAINTENANCE SCHEDULE:** 2 hours once per month for water changes and a good cleaning, 15 minutes per week for glass cleaning.

## LIVESTOCK
**FISHES:** 14.
**STONY CORALS:** 29.
**SOFT CORALS:** 12.
**OTHER LIVESTOCK:** *Tridacna derasa* clam, brittle starfish, serpent starfish, mated pair banded coral shrimp.
**NOTEWORTHY SPECIMENS:** All starfishes, a Black Tang, and a Chevron Tang about 13 years old (from old tank).

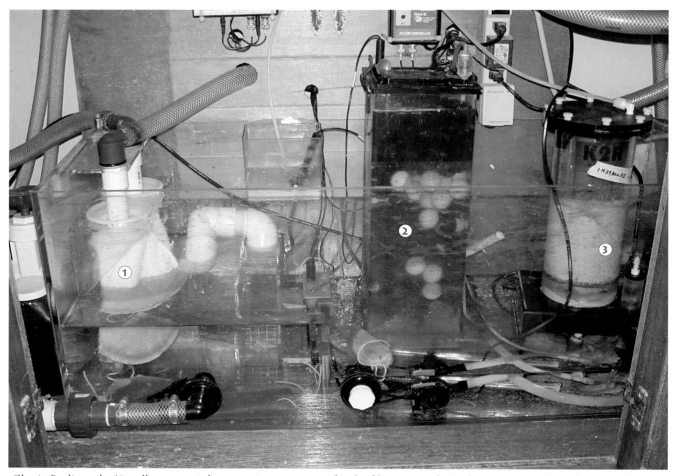

*Classic Berlin-style 42-gallon sump is bare, serving as a nexus for the filtration and circulation systems. Note fine mesh bag that filters particulate matter from incoming tank water (1). An AquaMedic denitrator unit is used (2), as is a calcium reactor (3).*

## FEEDING

**REGIMEN FOR FISHES:** Once every other day. Flake food first and then a little while later frozen foods: bloodworms, brine shrimp, CombiSan Full Spectrum Marine Supplement, Algae Plus, Formula One and Two.

## NOTES

**PROBLEMS OVERCOME WITH THIS SYSTEM:** Bubble algae and planaria.

**THINGS THE OWNER WOULD LIKE TO CHANGE:** More lights next time, three 400-watt metal halides.

**SPECIAL ABOUT THIS SYSTEM:** Since it is our store we don't always have the time to keep up with it, but only add the additives and do 20% water changes once per month. We clean filter bags every day and try to clean the glass twice per week.

**OVERALL POSITIVES:** Low maintenance. Only lost about 7 pieces in 5 years, the rest are original pieces.

**OVERALL NEGATIVES:** When we don't stay on top of our water changes we get algae after two months.

Light is provided by three 250-watt 6,500 K bulbs and two 160-watt actinic bulbs that are almost resting on the water's surface. The conventional wisdom often says that LPS corals prefer weak to moderate light. By providing them with brighter light, Ziggy has shown that they can be much more interesting and beautiful animals than is customarily thought. By providing them with the intensity needed for productive photosynthesis, Ziggy says that he is able to avoid feeding these LPS corals directly. While the corals randomly receive some food that the fishes do not consume, they have thrived, grown, and turned into exceptional specimens without the intentional feeding that is usually recommended. In addition, Ziggy uses a calcium reactor to maintain adequate alkalinity and calcium levels to keep the heavy skeletons of these LPS corals as thick as when they were originally brought in from the wild.

Obviously, anyone having access to weekly incoming boxes of corals has access to some rare and wonderful specimens. The policy at the Hidden Reef is to offer a new coral for public purchase for at least a week, after which it may be moved to the display reef. It is a tribute to Ziggy's determination that the these corals in this tank are never sold, but kept to show what can be achieved over time with corals that are bought small: given the right conditions, they will blossom into highly coveted living treasures.

*Stocked with corals that are overlooked by customers in the Hidden Reef shop, this system is a testament to the virtue of patience—letting small or seemingly common corals acclimate and then grow into noteworthy specimens over time.*

*Housed in a standard Oceanic 180-gallon Reef Ready tank and wooden stand, this system uses readily available stock equipment, partly as a demonstration to beginning aquarists of what can be accomplished without custom components.*

# Perfectionist in Action

*An exceptional collection of stony corals and Tridacna clams fills Wayne Shang's relatively new 700-gallon reef in Fremont, CA.*

## AQUARIUM PROFILE

**OWNER:** Wayne Shang
www.underseadiscovery.net.
**LOCATION:** Fremont, CA.
**DATE ESTABLISHED:** July 2001. (Combined a 6-year-old 300-gallon tank with a 2-year-old 180-gallon tank.)
**DATE PHOTOGRAPHED:** October 1999, June 2000, August 2001.

### TANK

**DISPLAY TANK VOLUME:** 700 gallons.
**DISPLAY TANK DIMENSIONS:** 96" X 48" X 36".
**DISPLAY TANK MATERIAL:** Starfire glass.
**SUMP VOLUME:** 200 gallons.
**LOCATION:** Garage.
**CABINETRY:** Custom wood stand.

### CIRCULATION

**MAIN SYSTEM PUMP(S):** Two Dolphin Amp-Master (3,000 gph each).
**WATER RETURNS:** Two 1-inch Sea Swirls.
**ADDITIONAL PUMPS:** Six Tunze Turbelle 2002 (600 gph each) and two ATK 6560 (1,700 gph each).

### CONTROLLERS

**TIMER:** Tunze Power Timer.
**TEMPERATURE CONTROLS:** Octopus controller.

STILL IN ITS INFANCY, the cultivation of corals in captivity has made tremendous advances in just a few years. Many of the corals themselves, however, are not fooled and aquarium specimens often assume shapes and colors seldom, if ever, seen in nature. World-renowned Australian coral scientist Dr. Charles Veron, in fact, says he is often amazed by the ability of North American hobbyists to keep these animals alive—even if he finds it impossible to identify them because their domesticated forms have morphed from their familiar wild appearances.

But the 700-gallon reef tank of Wayne Shang is an exception, with stony coral specimens that look as if they had been plucked from the pages of Dr. Veron's definitive work, *Corals of the World*. As in the book, Wayne's corals are robust, perfectly shapely, vibrantly pigmented, and as impressive as any collection of live corals in the reef aquarium world. Even though this tank is packed with corals and other invertebrates, there is little evidence of destructive competition between the corals and no signs of bleaching or other health problems or oddly grown skeletons.

This captive reef represents the accumulation of success that Wayne has had with smaller tanks in the past. This relatively new 700-gallon display has been stocked almost entirely from Wayne's previous 300-gallon and 180-gallon reefs without having to add much in the way of live rock or corals. By virtue of their age, some of these corals are very large in size, at least by home aquarium standards, with some of the colonies being one to two feet across. Having both scale and intense color, Wayne's prize specimens have the ability to render first-

*Framed by pink and green table Acroporas, a robust colony of Bali green staghorn coral (Acropora yongei) is one of many specimens transferred from one of Wayne's earlier systems. His corals display the strong, natural growth forms seen on wild reefs.*

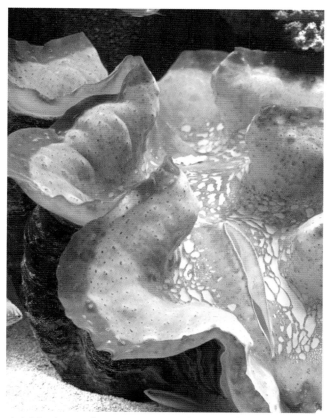

*A 16-inch—and growing—giant clam (Tridacna gigas), solidly anchors its own corner of the reefscape.*

*Stunning colors abound, as in this purple Acropora nobilis staghorn coral (1) and turquoise Tridacna clam (2).*

*Considered one of the most outstanding home reef tanks ever created, Wayne's corals are the envy of many experts. Note green and purple colonies of Seriatopora hystrix (1 and 2), large purple Acropora nobilis (3), lavender Stylophora pistillata (4).*

**CHILLER:** 3/4 hp Power Cooler.

## FILTRATION
**SKIMMER:** Sander Helgaland.
**LIVE ROCK IN DISPLAY TANK:** Approximately 600 lbs. Tonga and Fiji.
**LIVE ROCK IN SUMP:** About 250 lbs. Fiji.
**SAND/SUBSTRATE IN DISPLAY:** 3 inches CaribSea aragonite.
**SAND/SUBSTRATE IN SUMP/REFUGIUM:** 2 inches CaribSea aragonite.

## LIGHTING
**FLUORESCENT BULBS:** Four 36-inch actinic-03 (30 watts each), two 60-inch actinic-03 (60 watts each).
**PHOTOPERIOD:** 14 hours.
**HOW OFTEN REPLACED:** Every 6 months.
**METAL HALIDE BULBS:** Four 400-watt 14,000 K and four 250-watt 14,000 K German HQI.
**PHOTOPERIOD:** 10 hours.
**HOW OFTEN REPLACED:** Every 12 months.
**HEIGHT ABOVE WATER SURFACE:** 8 inches.
**OTHER BULBS:** Six 100-watt Halogen with blue filter (Blue Moon Light).
**LIGHTING CONTROLLER(S):** Electronic timers.

## SYSTEM PARAMETERS & CHEMISTRY
**WATER TEMPERATURE:** Winter 78 to 79°F, summer 80 to 82°F.
**SPECIFIC GRAVITY:** 1.022-1.024.
**PH:** 8.0 to 8.2.

time visitors incredulous.

The lush growth of corals makes it very difficult to see any of the underlying reef structure, despite there being approximately 600 pounds of Tonga and Fiji live rock in this tank. There is no sign of algae growing anywhere, although the glass is cleaned daily to remove any thin films that appear.

As with most outstanding tanks, there is no single, magical secret to Wayne's success. Success seems to come from his mastery of well-established Berlin methodology and his attention to detail. Lighting is provided by a combination of metal halide and standard actinic fluorescent lights. Surprisingly, the total illumination amounts to a relatively modest four watts per gallon. Extremely intense lighting is sometimes credited with bringing out the best colors in small-polyped stony corals, but in this case the results may come from good lighting coupled with great water quality. Nutrient levels are so low that the golden-brown zooxanxthellae within the corals do not predominate and the bright colors of the pigments within the coral tissue shine through.

Nutrient export is accomplished by a very large skimmer that sits beside the tank, along with a 10% monthly water change. If all of this seems unremarkable, water movement with the tank is far beyond the usual hobbyist range. Two 3,000-gallon per hour external pumps and eight powerheads producing approximately 7,000-gallons per hour of current are used in this system. This total of 13,000 gallons per hour of internal circulation prevents dead spots from forming and keeps virtually all detritus in suspension until it is

*Wayne's centerpiece Acropora nobilis thrives. The "secrets" here are simple enough: intense metal halide lighting and actinic fluorescent lighting, chaotic water movement (the system volume turns over 14 times per hour), and pristine water quality.*

skimmed off. All of this strong, chaotic water movement also serves to ensure that dissolved oxygen levels stay high throughout the tank. Adding in the additional 200 gallons of water in the sump, the entire system is turned over approximately 14 times per hour.

In addition to beautiful show colonies of purple *Acropora nobilis*, green *Seriatopora hystrix,* and pink *Stylophora pistillata*, Wayne has collected an astonishing array of *Tridacna* clams. Blue, green, and purple *Tridacna maxima* and *T. crocea* clams are scattered throughout the tank. A huge *Tridacna gigas* clam occupies the lower left front portion of the tank and is at least 16 inches across. Numerous soft corals also occupy the lower tier of the tank, along with a colony of red *Goniopora* that completes the total aquascape. Fishes are also part of this system, with a glittering school of Blue Green Chromis and a mixed school of anthias providing realistic visual interest. Various tangs, wrasses, and *Genicanthus* angels weave in and out among the coral branches.

Despite having moved his corals and fishes from smaller tanks—always a risky ordeal—Wayne has managed to keep his livestock healthy and thriving. This tank is proof that it is not necessary to reinvent the wheel in order to create a world-class reef aquarium. Success can come by following time-tested methods that work, being unstinting in providing light, circulation, and excellent water conditions, and by correcting small problems before they become major ones. It also helps if you are as meticulous and conscientious as Wayne Shang, truly a reef perfectionist.

**ALKALINITY:** 12-14 dKH (Tropic Marin Test Kit).

**CALCIUM:** 450-500 ppm (LaMotte Test Kit).

**NITRATE & PHOSPHATE:** Undetectable (LaMotte Test Kit).

**OTHER READINGS:** Magnesium: 1,400 ppm (Salifert Test Kit).

**REVERSE OSMOSIS:** 6-stage RO/DI system.

**SALT USED:** Tropic Marin.

**WATER CHANGE SCHEDULE:** 10% every 4-6 weeks (from fish-only tank, page 84).

**ADDITIVES OR SUPPLEMENTS USED:** All evaporated water is replaced with Kalkwasser (calcium hydroxide).

**DOSING EQUIPMENT USED:** AquaTune doser for topping off evaporated water (Kalkwasser).

### LIVESTOCK
**SPAWNING EVENTS:** Clams (*Tridacna maxima* and *T. crocea*) spawn every 3 to 4 months, normally a few days after the full moon.

### FEEDING
**REGIMEN FOR FISHES:** Fishes are fed once or twice a day with frozen *Mysis*, krill, and brine shrimp.

### NOTES
**FAVORITE COMMENTS BY OTHERS:** "Wow!"

**OVERALL NEGATIVES:** Energy cost in California.

# Clownfish & Anemone Reef

*With more than 50 sea anemones and five pairs of clownfishes, this 2,000-gallon public exhibit mimics a Pacific patch reef.*

## AQUARIUM PROFILE

**OWNER:** Atlantis Marine World
www.atlantismarineworld.com.
**AQUARIST:** Matt Gannon.
**DESIGNER:** Joseph Yaiullo.
**LOCATION:** Riverhead, NY.
**DATE ESTABLISHED:** June 2000.
**DATE PHOTOGRAPHED:** June 2001.
**PHOTOGRAPHER:** Charles Glatzer.

### TANK
**CONFIGURATION:** Rectangular.
**DISPLAY TANK VOLUME:** 2,000 gallons.
**DISPLAY TANK DIMENSIONS:** 8.5' X 6.5' X 6.5'.
**DISPLAY TANK MATERIAL:** Fiberglass with viewing windows (7.5' X 5.5').
**SUMP VOLUME:** 200 gallons.
**LOCATION:** Public aquarium display at Atlantis Marine World along with three other exhibits the same size (Piranha, Shipwreck, and Malawi Cichlids).

A CLOWNFISH DARTING IN AND OUT OF AN ANEMONE may get more hobbyists involved in setting up a saltwater tank than any other single motivation. The sight of a colorful little reef fish lolling within a mass of poison-tipped tentacles is one of nature's more fascinating displays of symbiotic behavior, and the 2,000-gallon anemone display maintained by Matt Gannon is one of its most popular displays at Atlantis Marine World. The size of this system allows Matt to keep not just a single pair of clownfish, as in most home tanks, but rather five pairs of clownfishes representing three different species. This tank also houses more than 50 anemones of five different species.

Seeing these clownfishes move through these different anemones is a real attention grabber. The tank is aquascaped in such a manner that it tries to mimic a patch reef with all of the live rock in the center of the tank and open space surrounding the live rock and anemones. The rockwork is artfully arranged to create many small caves and holes into which the anemones can place their rubbery "feet" and establish secure footings. As a result, much of the rock cannot even be seen as the anemones are now growing and covering much of the rock structure. After a relatively short time in operation, this display has come to resemble the areas in the wild where large aggregations of anemones occur. It is easy to see how in a few years none of the live rock will be visible at all. The anemones also occupy different levels within the structure and this further adds to the look of a natural patch reef.

Certain areas of the structure have come to be preferred by the anemones, while other areas are shunned. As a result, Matt and Joe Yaiullo, who designed the system (see page 58), are now placing soft and stony corals in these non-preferred areas not only to fill them in, but also to give the structure a more natural appearance as anemones rarely settle where there are no corals. At present this placement is working out well, as the corals are thriving in the areas that are free of anemones. However there is some worry that over time, as the corals and anemones both grow and reproduce, more chemical battles between these animals will occur.

Lighting for this tank is very intense—for the sake of both the anemones and the corals. Because most of the animals are in the center of the tank, the light is concentrated there, producing an alluring, dramatic effect, with the fringes of the display much darker and the shadows much sharper. To accomplish this, a 1,000-watt lamp hangs over the center of the reef structure and two 400-watt lamps are offset from this. In addition, four 96-watt power compact actinic fluorescent lamps are used to augment the colors. These fluorescent lamps are also used to simulate dawn and dusk.

The tank is filtered with two downdraft-style skimmers as well as a swimming pool sand-media filter that is backwashed weekly. Carbon is used to remove any chemical contaminants and is changed every 2 to 3 months. A 5% water change made with filtered seawater is performed every week. Even though just 11 fishes are housed in this tank, the anemones are fed at least twice weekly, making this filtration necessary. To limit problems with algae, a large number of active herbivores are kept in this tank as well. Matt refers to them as his maintenance crew: 500 blue-leg hermit crabs, 1,500 *Astraea* snails, 100 Mexican true *Turbo* snails, about 200 serpent stars and brittle stars, about 50 Caribbean sea cucumbers, and 50 bumble bee snails.

Because Matt is so conscientious about the appearance of this tank and the health of its residents, he takes a weekly scuba dive onto the captive reef. During this excursion he adjusts the rockwork and corals and checks the underwater equipment. He also stirs up the sand to make the removal of any detritus easier. This is the most time-consuming part of the maintenance that he has to perform on the tank.

This aquarium represents the largest anemone display in the U.S. and demonstrates that, given the right conditions and enough space, a thriving anemone community can be replicated in a closed system. One interesting aspect of this tank is how the anemones have come to place themselves as they would on a natural reef. Long-tentacled Anemones have chosen spots on the bottom in the sand, while the bubble tips are at every depth and the *H. magnificas* are all at the top of the reef structure. This natural dispersion is only possible in a tank this size and shows how far we have come in replicating a natural environment. It will be interesting to observe these animals over time to see how well they reproduce, given the optimal conditions they now have. Once reproduction occurs on a regular basis, it may then be possible to set up other systems for the express purpose of reproducing these much-desired animals.

## CIRCULATION

**MAIN SYSTEM PUMPS:** Two Hayward pool pumps. One 1 hp, one 3/4 hp.
**WATER RETURNS:** Six returns, one in each corner and two centered on the side walls.
**WAVEMAKING DEVICES:** The two returns on the side walls are hooked up to 1 inch Sea Swirls which sweep 180° over the center of the display. A third return is planned for one corner.

## CONTROLLERS

**TEMPERATURE CONTROLS:** The main room with all of the exhibits is kept at 70 to 72°F. To keep it cool, all of the Atlantis Marine World exhibits are plumbed into the Geo Therm line provided by our local power authority.

## FILTRATION

**SKIMMER:** Two MTC 1000 downdraft skimmers.
**MECHANICAL FILTER:** One Purex-Triton TR60 High Rate sand filter (pool). The nice thing about all of the sand filters at AMW is that they all have 8,000 gallons of freshwater available to them (3 large vats that are gravity-fed and are plumbed to each system via a loop around the whole park) for backwashing, so you don't have to rely on doing a large water change on the system to backwash them well. Especially good in a reef where you want to be able to clean the mechanical filtration often.
**OZONIZER:** Coming soon.
**CARBON:** About 3 lbs. every 2-3 months.
**BIOLOGICAL FILTER:** Live rock, base rock, sand bed.
**REFUGIUM:** Coming soon.
**LIVE ROCK IN DISPLAY TANK:** Quarry limestone base called holy boulder, approximately one ton—perhaps more. Tonga slab rock, 250 lbs. Fiji South Pacific rock, about 100 lbs. Tonga Finger rock, about 100 lbs.
**SAND/SUBSTRATE IN DISPLAY:** 3-4 inches superfine aragonite, 50 lbs. of Caribbean live sand.

## LIGHTING

**FLUORESCENT BULBS:** Four 96-watt Actinic power compacts.
**PHOTOPERIOD:** 13 hours.
**HOW OFTEN REPLACED:** 8-10 months.
**HEIGHT OF LIGHTS ABOVE WATER SURFACE:** 6 inches.
**METAL HALIDE BULBS:** Two 400-watt Iwasaki 6,500 K, one 1,000-watt Sunmaster.
**PHOTOPERIOD:** 11 hours for 400-watt, 8 hours for 1,000-watt.
**HOW OFTEN REPLACED:** 10-12 months.
**HEIGHT OF LIGHTS ABOVE WATER SURFACE:** 15 inches for 400-watt, 6 inches for 1000-watt.
**LIGHTING CONTROLLER(S):** Electronic timers.

## SYSTEM PARAMETERS & CHEMISTRY

**WATER TEMPERATURE:** 77 to 79°F.
**SPECIFIC GRAVITY:** 1.023.
**PH:** 8.2.

*In a classic display of symbiotic behavior, a pair of Clark's Clownfish (Amphiprion clarkii) nestles into its long-tentacle sea anemone (Macrodactyla doreensis) host. Current theory is that both fish and anemone derive protective benefits from each other.*

**ALKALINITY:** 3.2-3.8 meg.

**CALCIUM:** 380-400.

**NITRATE:** <2 ppm.

**PHOSPHATE:** <0.1.

**RESINS OR DEVICES USED TO REDUCE NITRATE OR PHOSPHATE:** Ultralife phosphate remover used when algae seems to be growing.

**WATER SOURCE:** Natural seawater, cold sterile for top off. Not happy with that so we will be going back to R.O./D.I. (Cold sterile not removing enough phosphate even with activated alumina.)

**CALCIUM:** 380-400.

**MAGNESIUM:** 1,200-1,300.

**IODINE:** 0.04.

**SALT USED:** Natural seawater.

**WATER CHANGE SCHEDULE:** 20% every 4-6 weeks or as necessary.

**ADDITIVES OR SUPPLEMENTS USED:** CaO added with evaporated water 5 out of 7 days. Sodium bicarb and CaCl as necessary (not often). Magnesium as necessary—about every 2 weeks daily until reading of 1,200-1,300 is reached. Iodine added about once every 2 months.

**MONITORING EQUIPMENT:** PinPoint pH monitor, Rainbow Lifeguard temperature monitor.

**MAINTENANCE SCHEDULE:** The CaO drip is manually started each day. Regular glass cleaning every other day. Backwash high-rate sand filter 1-2 times weekly. Open up sand filter once per month to pressure hose the sand to keep it from clumping together. 5% water change every week with natural filtered seawater which has the alkalinity, Ca, Mg, and temp adjusted before adding to system. Alkalinity and Ca are tested every other day. Mg is tested weekly. Iodine about once a month. Salinity stays consistent and

temp is monitored daily.

Using scuba with a regulator and 30-foot hose, the inside of the viewing window is cleaned with an acrylic scraper, and coralline that grows on the side walls is removed with a stainless-steel scraper (we're trying to keep the side walls free of growth to make the reef look like a patch reef in an endless ocean).

Any detritus is fanned out of from the rocks every few days. 5-10 hours a week are spent maintaining the reef.

## LIVESTOCK

**FISHES:** 3 Pink Skunk Clowns, 3 pairs of tank-raised Clark's Clowns, 1 pair of Saddleback Clowns, and 1 gold stripe Maroon Clown.

**STONY CORALS:** About 24.

**SOFT CORALS:** 5 *Swiftia exserta* (orange gorgonian from the Caribbean), yellow polyps, green stars, gorgeous multi-color button polyps.

**ANEMONES:** 4 ritteri (*Heteractis magnifica*), 8 assorted colored long tentacled anemones (*Macrodactyla doreensis*), about 40 asst. bubble tips (*Entacmaea quadricolor*), 2 *Heteractis crispa*, 1 *Stichodactyla haddoni*.

**OTHER LIVESTOCK:** Maintenance crew (blue leg hermits, *Astraea* snails, Mexican true Turbo snails, serpent and brittle stars, Caribbean sea cucumbers, bumble bee snails).

**NOTEWORTHY SPECIMENS:** Huge bubbletip anemones.

**SPAWNING EVENTS:** Clownfishes spawn regularly. Sometime in the future we'll look into capturing and raising the fry.

## FEEDING

**REGIMEN FOR FISHES:** 3-4 times weekly. Clowns get fed mysid shrimp, chopped clams, flake food, and Cyclop-eeze.

**REGIMEN FOR CORALS/ANEMONES:** Corals get freeze-dried phytoplankton and Cyclop-eeze 4-5 times per week. Anemones get chopped silversides and clams' tongue fed to them as required, 1-2 times a week. (Ritteris get the most, about twice a week.)

## NOTES

**PROBLEMS OVERCOME IN THE SYSTEM:** Had trouble with ritteri and carpets in the beginning, now we dip them in Doxycycline for 48 hours upon arrival. They do much better now, the system being more established might have something to do with that.

**THINGS THE OWNER WOULD CHANGE:**

1. The acrylic window scratches too easily. Glass might have been better, but we might have lost clarity at 2.5 inches thick.
2. We will be adding a Ca reactor, ozone, a refugium, and another Sea Swirl.

**THINGS THE AQUARIST LIKES BEST ABOUT THE SYSTEM:**

1. The reef is in the center only. I like being able to access all four walls.
2. As far as livestock goes, I really like the way our 2 ritteris are up top on branches resembling pom poms and are surrounded by stag-type *Acroporas* perched at the tips of finger rock. They will look phenomenal when they grow in (as long as we can keep the anemones away from them). I also really like the orange gorgonian down low and plan to get several more.
3. The viewing window is really nice because it is 7.5 feet long x 5.5 feet high.

# Piece of the Reef

*An ambitious combination of stony corals and large fishes, including some 33 surgeonfishes and tangs, in a 650-gallon tank.*

Bugs Bunny used to joke about going to Cucamonga. For California reef aficionados this is now home to the widely known reef tank of Bill Schroer in his Piece of the Reef shop in Rancho Cucamonga—and anything but a cartoon destination. By bringing together an interesting blend of more than 130 fishes, some 250 colonies of corals and many other invertebrates, Bill has attempted to establish a realistic ecosystem rather than simply a collection of corals.

Among the many gloriously colored and healthy fishes housed in this tank are a large selection of tangs and surgeonfishes, which help keep algae growth to a minimum. These include a small school of Blue Hippo Tangs, a Powder Blue Tang, a Dussumieri Tang, an Orange-Shouldered Tang, and a Sailfin Tang. Several hard-to-keep tangs also thrive in this system, including a Gold-Rimmed Tang, two Lined Surgeonfish (Clown Tangs) and a beautiful polka-dotted Vlamingi Tang. This tank is also home to several fishes not normally thought of as reef friendly. These include a Goldflake Angel, an 8-inch Crosshatch Triggerfish, a solid red Flame Angel, a Clown Triggerfish, and a Moorish Idol.

Competing with the fishes for the visitor's eye are myriad soft and stony corals, many as intensely colored as ever seen in captive systems. To achieve these levels of bright coral coloration, Bill says he started off with beautifully colored colonies and has tried to come as close as possible to mimicking the amount of light striking a reef. The light used not only has an intensity much

## AQUARIUM PROFILE

**OWNER:** William Schroer.
**LOCATION:** Rancho Cucamonga, CA.
**DATE ESTABLISHED:** January 2000.
**DATE PHOTOGRAPHED:** June 2001.

### TANK
**DISPLAY TANK VOLUME:** 650 gallons.
**DISPLAY TANK DIMENSIONS:** 130" X 37" X 32".
**DISPLAY TANK MATERIAL:** Glass.
**SUMP VOLUME:** 150 gallons.
**LOCATION:** Showroom floor.

### CIRCULATION
**MAIN SYSTEM PUMP:** 3 hp Sequence pump producing 9,600 gph flow.
**WATER RETURNS:** Two 2-inch returns on each side of tank; five 1-inch returns on back of tank.
**ADDITIONAL PUMPS:** Two Asynchronous motored pumps at 900 gph.
**WAVEMAKING DEVICES:** 2 inch 3-way ball valve and 1 inch Sea Swirl.
**CONTROLLERS:** Digital controller for chiller.

### TEMPERATURE CONTROLS
**FANS:** Pancake fans in hood.

**CHILLER:** West Coast Aquatics Chiller.

## FILTRATION
**MECHANICAL FILTER:** Three sock filters for large detritus.
**UV STERILIZER:** 80-watt Aqua UV.
**OZONIZER:** Sanders 200 variable rate.
**CARBON:** Two quarts changed every 2-4 weeks.
**BIOLOGICAL FILTER:** Live rock and live sand.
**LIVE ROCK IN DISPLAY TANK:** Fiji, Aquacultured Florida, Marshall Island, Tonga branch, Tonga plate, Jakarta.
**SAND/SUBSTRATE IN DISPLAY:** Florida and Fiji live sand 3-6 inches deep.

## LIGHTING
**METAL HALIDE BULBS:** Four 400-watt 20,000 K Osram HQI, two 1,000-watt 20,000 K Radium and one 1,000-watt 10,000 K Aqualine Buschke.
**PHOTOPERIOD:** 400-watt bulbs: 12-14 hours; 1,000-watt bulbs: 1.5 hours.
**HOW OFTEN REPLACED:** 400-watt bulbs every 4-6 months and 1000 watt bulbs every 1.5-2.5 years.
**HEIGHT OF LIGHTS ABOVE WATER SURFACE:** 12-14 inches.
**NATURAL LIGHT:** Morning sunlight.
**LIGHTING CONTROLLER(S):** Digital timers.

## SYSTEM PARAMETERS & CHEMISTRY
**WATER TEMPERATURE:** 77 to 80°F.
**SPECIFIC GRAVITY:** 1.027.
**PH:** 8.4.
**ALKALINITY:** 11.
**CALCIUM:** 420.
**NITRATE:** less than 10.
**PHOSPHATE:** 0.05.
**MUNICIPAL WATER SUPPLY:** Yes.
**REVERSE OSMOSIS:** Yes.
**DEIONIZATION:** Sometimes.
**SALT USED:** Kent Marine.
**WATER CHANGE SCHEDULE:** 40 gallons every other week.
**ADDITIVES OR SUPPLEMENTS USED:** Lugol's iodine: 4 dropperfuls a week.
**DOSING EQUIPMENT USED:** Dosing pump makeup water, 5-7 gallons per day.
**MAINTENANCE SCHEDULE:** Routine maintenance done as needed.

## LIVESTOCK
**FISHES:** 33 tangs and surgeonfishes, 100 small assorted other fishes.
**STONY CORALS:** 75 colonies, 150 fragments.
**SOFT CORALS:** 25 colonies.
**OTHER LIVESTOCK:** 25 pistol shrimps, 9 shrimp gobies, 15 starfishes, 350 *Astraea* snails, 400 hermit crabs.
**NOTEWORTHY SPECIMENS:** Goldflake Angel, solid red Flame Angel, 8-inch Cross Hatch Trigger (male), two Blue-spotted Jawfish.

## FEEDING
**REGIMEN FOR FISHES:** 1 to 2 feedings per day; flake food, Omega Sea, frozen Super shrimp, Lifeline foods.

greater than that found over most tanks, but it also has a photoperiod that closely mimics that seen on most reefs. The tank is well lit for 12 hours of effective daylight, but with an extremely intense period of only a couple of hours, mimicking the midday sunlight peak in the tropics with very powerful metal halide lamps. To achieve the desired results, Bill uses four 400-watt 20,000 K bulbs that are on for 12 hours and an additional three 1,000-watt bulbs of either 10,000 or 20,000 K that come on for an additional 90 minutes in the middle of each day. This is all enhanced by the fact that the tank also receives some direct morning sunlight.

Coral growth and colors are nothing short of spectacular. The bright green or pink *Montipora capricornis* stand out as numerous colonies have populated the aquascape. Baby blue and red colonies of *Acropora* contrast markedly with the brown colonies of *Acropora* encountered in many other tanks. Bill believes that these colors show what intense lighting of the proper spectrum can produce. Carbon and ozone are employed to keep any yellowing agents out of the water and to allow the light's full intensity to reach the corals. Lastly, the 400-watt 20,000 K bulbs are changed every six months to maximize their intensity and spectrum. Growth rates have also been outstanding, with many colonies reaching the impressive scale seen in the accompanying photographs in less than 18 months.

Light, of course, isn't everything, and the system also has very strong water motion. The entire tank's volume is turned over approximately 15 times per hour, and a great deal of turbulence is always present—a major benefit to both corals and fishes. The water has low levels of phosphate and dissolved organics, despite the large fish load. This is the result of an efficient protein skimmer and frequent large water changes. Lastly, the corals are fed directly with plankton or microvert food to support their health and growth.

Having achieved results that are envy of all who make the pilgrimage to Rancho Cucamonga, Bill says that he is already dreaming of making this tank bigger. This is no surprise, and after seeing how fast the corals have outgrown their 650-gallon aquarium, one wonders what tank will ever be big enough to match Bill's skills. For anyone who takes the old Bugs Bunny route— "Anaheim, Azusa, and Cucamonga"—seeing this tank is worth the trip.

*Glowing with vivid pigmentation, a small colony of purple branching Acropora was started as a fragment attached to the live rock substrate.*

*A spectacular scene by any measure, Bill Schroer's reef is graced with about 75 colonies of stony coral with more than 125 fragments scattered throughout the aquascape. Among the 133 fishes are a number of large and hard-to-keep species.*

**REGIMEN FOR CORALS/INVERTS:** Very irregular but in large amounts: Plankton and microvert.

## NOTES

**PROBLEMS OVERCOME WITH THIS SYSTEM:** Maintaining constant temperature.

**THINGS THE OWNER WOULD LIKE TO CHANGE:** Would not put in as many hermit crabs.

**THINGS OWNER LIKES BEST ABOUT THIS SYSTEM:** It has been a complete success, as the fishes have thrived and the corals are brilliantly colored.

**SPECIAL ABOUT THIS SYSTEM:** It has lots of fishes and is completely packed with corals. Runs very well with great color.

The rock is put together with stainless steel pins.

**FAVORITE COMMENTS BY OTHERS:** "Wow, That is the best looking tank that I have ever seen."

**OVERALL POSITIVES:** It's large, efficient, and the corals grow beautifully with minimal maintenance.

**OVERALL NEGATIVES (OR THINGS TO DO DIFFERENTLY NEXT TIME):**
1. Bigger sump.
2. Bigger tank.
3. More efficient pumps.

# Window to a Reef

*The "entertainment center" in Bob and Debbie James's Toronto-area home: a 350-gallon reef aquarium started in 1989.*

## AQUARIUM PROFILE

**OWNERS:** Bob & Debbie James.
**LOCATION:** Thornhill, Ontario, Canada.
**DESIGNER:** Bob James.
**ESTABLISHED:** Early 1989.
**PHOTOGRAPHED:** May 2001.

### TANK

**DISPLAY TANK:** 350 gallons, glass.
**DISPLAY TANK DIMENSIONS:** 90" X 30" X 30".
**SUMP:** 45 gallons, 30" X 12" X 30".
**LOCATION:** Ground-floor den, on a concrete floor (townhouse with no basement).
**CABINETRY/ARCHITECTURAL DETAILS:** Built into a cedar wall, only the front shows from the viewing area. The last 6 inches of the tank is the overflow area and is behind the front wall.

### CIRCULATION

**MAIN SYSTEM PUMP(S):**
  (a) Iwaki MD 100 RLT.
  (b) Iwaki MD 55 RLT.
  (c) Iwaki WMD 40 RLT.
**WATER RETURNS:**
Pump (a) main return is through bottom of tank, at the rear right-hand corner, directed at 45° to the front and 45° to horizontal. A smaller return is at left-hand rear of tank, just below water level.

IN MOST HOMES, the family room has come to be the home of the television and the audio-visual component cabinet. In the case of Bob and Debbie James, their townhouse entertainment center is actually a dramatic, thriving 350-gallon reef aquarium.

The tank appears even bigger than it is because of the profusion of life within: there are no spaces within the tank that do not contain thriving colonies of animals. In addition, none of the equipment necessary to run a tank of this size and with this population density is visible. The tank itself is viewed from a ground floor den, but actually sits behind a wall in an adjoining room, and this keeps the equipment from being seen.

Bob's engineering background is apparent in the physical design of the system, which follows the classic Berlin approach, but attention to marine husbandry principles is also evident. Bob took a long-term view on how the tank would fill in over time and it clearly has. Unlike most hobbyists with large new systems who can't resist adding large colonies of corals at the beginning, Bob used small cuttings or fragments of stony corals and allowed them lots of room to grow. The corals appear to have filled the space naturally, spending their energy on growth rather than on competition with other introduced colonies.

This has produced some rather interesting results. The tank has an 11-year-old carpet anemone that has grown so large that it looks like a huge leather coral. The health and size of the anemone are amazing enough, but just as interesting is that a colony of *Montipora digitata* looks to be growing up through the anemone. What has actually happened is that two lobes of the

*This 11-year-old giant carpet anemone (Stichodactyla gigantea) has grown to more than 24 inches in diameter and hosts a very territorial adult Tomato Clownfish.*

*Many corals were started as gift fragments from marine luminaries given to the Jameses—themselves active leaders in North American marine society circles.*

Pump (b) return is via a spray bar that runs along the bottom rear of the tank.

Pump (c) pushes the water through a chiller. The return is at the back left, directed toward the front of the tank.

**ADDITIONAL PUMPS:** An Iwaki WMD 30 RLT feeds the two skimmers. It draws water from the sump, which returns to the sump downstream from the input. A small power-head adds some additional circulation to the display tank.

**WAVEMAKING DEVICES:** None.

**CONTROLLERS:** None.

**FANS:** One fan blows air over the metal halide lights and runs continuously.

**HEATERS:** None.

**CHILLER:** 1/2 hp Universal Marine Industries Inc. (UMI). Probe in tank controls temperature.

## FILTRATION

**SKIMMER:** Two skimmers, both Aquarien Technik Klaes 8-inch outside diameter, 6.9 feet tall (including cup).

**MECHANICAL FILTER:** Just some batting, to stop fish going over the overflow.

**UV STERILIZER:** None.

**OZONIZER:** None.

**CARBON:** None.

**BIOLOGICAL FILTER:** None, used to have large wet-dry with Bio-Balls. Dismantled a long time ago, with no obvious benefit or detriment.

**REFUGIUM:** None.

**LIVE ROCK IN DISPLAY TANK:** 500 lbs. of base rock from Florida, poor quality, not very porous; 500 lbs. of quality live rock, hand selected by Jeff Turner and Julian Sprung, then of Exotic Aquaria.

**LIVE ROCK IN SUMP:** Just a few bits, temporary surplus from display tank.

**SAND/SUBSTRATE IN DISPLAY:** None.

**SAND/SUBSTRATE IN SUMP/REFUGIUM:** None.

**PLENUM:** None.

## LIGHTING

**FLUORESCENT BULBS:** 2 VHO actinics 140 watts each (Phillips 03).

**HOW OFTEN REPLACED:** Approx. every 8 months.

**METAL HALIDE BULBS:** 4 double ended, 250 watts each, Osram.

**HOW OFTEN REPLACED:** Approx. every 16 months.

**PHOTOPERIOD:** 9 hours per day.

**OTHER BULBS:** 15-watt incandescent "moonlight" (provides one hour of "dawn," before VHO actinics come on, and one hour of "dusk," after actinics go off).

**NATURAL LIGHT:** Essentially none.

**LIGHTING CONTROLLER(S):** All lights on timers.

## SYSTEM PARAMETERS & CHEMISTRY:

**WATER TEMPERATURE:** 75.5 to 76.5°F.

**SPECIFIC GRAVITY:** 1.024.

**PH:** Not measured since 1997.

**ALKALINITY:** Not measured since 1997, usually ~ 5 dKH.

**CALCIUM:** Not measured since 1997, usually about 420 ppm.

**NITRATE:** Not measured since 1997, was always less than 1 ppm.

**PHOSPHATE:** Not measured since 1997, always undetectable.

**RESINS OR DEVICES USED TO REDUCE NITRATE OR PHOSPHATE:** None.

**WATER SOURCE:** Municipal tap water.

**REVERSE OSMOSIS:** Yes.

**DEIONIZATION:** Yes.

**SALT:** Aquarium Systems Reef Crystals.

**WATER CHANGE SCHEDULE:** 12 gallons per week.

**ADDITIVES OR SUPPLEMENTS USED:** Calcium chloride and buffer added daily to maintain calcium saturation. Strontium chloride and iodine added once a week.

**MONITORING EQUIPMENT:** None.

**MAINTENANCE SCHEDULE:** Daily (15 minutes): feed fish, add CaCl and buffer, add makeup water to compensate for evaporation. Weekly (3 to 4 hours): check specific gravity, change water, add strontium and iodine, remove algae, clean skimmers, mediate coral territorial disputes.

## LIVESTOCK

**FISHES:** 18 fishes.

**STONY CORALS:** 20+ different species, multiple specimens of many.

**SOFT CORALS:** 10+ different species, multiple specimens of many.

**LIVESTOCK GROWTH:** The carpet anemone (*Stichodactyla gigantea*) has grown from about 8 inches in diameter to about 24 inches in approximately 11 years. It has not been fed since 1991.

The clam (*Tridacna derasa*) has grown from 4 to 15 inches end-to-end, in about 11 years.

Elegance coral (*Catalaphyllia jardinei*) (Sept. 1991) has grown substantially, now 14 inches across.

Bubble coral (*Physogyra lichtensteini*) (Oct. 1992) has grown substantially, now 8" X 12".

Pink-tipped (*Seriatopora* sp.) (Jan. 1996) has grown substantially.

Table coral (*Acropora* sp.) (May 1996) was originally 4" diameter, now 12" X 20".

Green whirl (*Montipora* sp.) (Dec. 1996) was originally 1" flake, now 6 layers deep and 8" across.

Joe's coral (*Acropora* sp.) (Jun. 1995) has grown from tiny fragment to 9" tall.

**SPAWNING EVENTS:** A pair of *Amphiprion frenatus* has spawned 87 times (confirmed observations—probably actually more).

## FEEDING

**REGIMEN FOR FISHES:** Daily (very occasionally twice per day)—lots of variety: romaine lettuce leaf or nori or occasionally zucchini. Scallop or shrimp or frozen brine shrimp or flakes or food pellets.

**REGIMEN FOR CORALS/INVERTS:** None, except juices from fish foods.

*A spreading colony of velvet finger coral (Montipora digitata) (1) grows up in close proximity to the huge carpet anemone (2), which thrives without direct feeding.*

*Tucked into the realistically crowded reefscape is a giant derasa clam (Tridacna derasa) that has grown in length from about 4 inches to 15 inches in 11 years.*

anemone are wrapped around the branching coral, and the *Montipora* is continuing to grow above the anemone. Another indication of the overall health of the system is that numerous impressively large colonies of *Acropora* sp. corals grow throughout the tank. This in itself is not remarkable, except that all of the colonies have developed from small fragments placed in the tank only a few years ago. A sizable *Tridacna derasa* is another example of how time is the friend of a successful reefkeeper. This clam has grown from 4 inches to 15 inches over the past 11 years.

One of the basic tenets of reef keeping is that you cannot successfully house soft corals and stony corals in close proximity to each other. The reasoning behind this is that chemicals produced by the soft corals are deleterious or inhibitory to stony corals. Indeed, many hobbyists who have tried to keep stony corals in a tank containing predominantly soft corals have seen the stony corals fail over time. The James's Toronto system is an exception to this rule.

Not only do the stony corals survive with the soft corals, they have actually thrived and grown as well as they might have in the wild or in a tank devoted only to stony corals. A possible explanation is the use of two large, very efficient skimmers that are employed to remove not only the waste in the tank, but also any chemicals produced by the soft corals. Despite recent discussions about potentially overskimming a tank, this system may illustrate the advantages of aggressive skimming when soft and stony corals are housed together.

If health and growth of the many corals are an obvious indication of Bob and Debbie's success, the fishes are further evidence of how well this system succeeds. The Powder Blue Tang is a perfect example of what this difficult-to-keep fish should look like in captivity. Its full belly and bright colors attest to how well it is doing. Other species also look as vibrant and as healthy as any found on the reef. Relatively recent additions include a Harlequin Tuskfish and a Regal Angelfish, the latter a delicate species and neither particularly common in tanks filled with corals. The longevity of both fishes and invertebrates in this system is both a credit to the owners and proof that reef animals can lead long, healthy lives in the aquarium.

The James's love and enjoyment of the hobby is also shown by the many years that they have been involved in the Marine Aquarium Society of Toronto (MAST). Both have been on the executive committee of the society for many years, with Bob serving as president and Debbie as secretary-treasurer. They have been responsible for organizing two MACNA conferences in Toronto as well as bringing numerous speakers to help their members keep up with the latest developments in marine aquarium keeping. Both Bob and Debbie credit their reef with bringing them into contact with a wide circle of friends.

"Most of the coral fragments placed in our systems have come from luminaries in the marine aquarium field and/or close friends, so the tank evokes many happy memories of good times spent together," they say. "The aquarium brought us into contact with the Marine Aquarium Society of Toronto, and several members of MAST have become good friends, as fellow aquarium hobbyists, mountain bikers, and lovers of fine food and wine. The tank thus enriches our lives in many ways. It also fulfills our vision of being a "Window to a Reef," although we recognize it is but a very modest representation of the real thing."

## NOTES

**PROBLEMS OVERCOME:** The biggest design flaw was that water returns go through the bottom of the tank. They relied upon non-return valves actually working and not letting the whole tank drain onto the floor. After a just-prevented tragedy, the sump was raised to the level of the tank. Now, during a power outage, the display tank and sump levels equalize just a bit below the normal tank level.

**THINGS THE OWNER WOULD LIKE TO CHANGE:** If money were no object, we would have a tank much bigger in size. That would allow more innovative aquascaping. We would like Starfire (ultra-clear, colorless) glass for the front panel. (It is hard to find in some areas and is expensive.) A surge system would be nice. The water top-up and chemical additions should be automated. Additional sound proofing would be advantageous.

**SUCCESSES:** We are often told the tank is "so natural looking," with no equipment seen from the viewing area, and with an appealing balance of healthy, thriving hard and soft corals and fishes.

**THINGS SPECIAL ABOUT THIS SYSTEM:**
1. It was not assembled: it was grown. Most corals have grown from small fragments, and have developed in a natural looking way that could not be achieved by any amount of dollars and epoxy resin.
2. Several of the stony corals are quite rare, at least here in Canada. Most of the fragments have come from luminaries in the marine aquarium field and/or close personal friends, so the tank evokes many happy memories of good times spent together.
3. The aquarium brought us into contact with the Marine Aquarium Society of Toronto and benefited from the wealth of knowledge of Society members and guest speakers. (www.MASTCanada.org)

**FAVORITE COMMENTS BY OTHERS:**
1. A non-aquarist just back from a submarine sightseeing trip: "The Hawaiian reef was disappointing; I expected it to be like your tank."
2. A major U.S. coral importer: "This is in the top ten tanks that I have seen, and I have seen a *lot* of tanks."
3. An experienced aquarist: "It was so beautiful, I cried."

**OVERALL POSITIVES:**
1. It works and it's paid for!
2. We have acquired some unusual corals, which are thriving.
3. The fish swim naturally in and out of the rock structure.

**OVERALL NEGATIVES:**
1. The persistent algae growth looks natural and may be good for the fishes, but it prompts high maintenance.
2. Water and chemical additions are not yet automated.
3. The system is a little noisy.

# Corals on High

*Perched 5 feet above the floor, Dave Wodecki's 360-gallon Ohio reef is an unorthodox but dramatic-looking system.*

## AQUARIUM PROFILE

**OWNER:** Dave Wodecki.
**DESIGNERS:** Dave Wodecki and Kurt Loos.
**LOCATION:** Willoughby, OH.
**DATE ESTABLISHED:** February 1996.
**DATE PHOTOGRAPHED:** 1996 to 1998.

### TANK

**DISPLAY TANK VOLUME:** 360 gallons.
**DISPLAY TANK DIMENSIONS:** 8' X 3' X 2'.
**DISPLAY TANK MATERIAL:** Glass.
**SUMP VOLUME:** 200 gallons.
**LOCATION (ROOM):** On steel I-beam scaffold
  in shop.
**CABINETRY/ARCHITECTURAL DETAILS:** Tank
  sits 5 feet above the ground so that
  bottom of tank is at eye level.

### CIRCULATION

**MAIN SYSTEM PUMP(S):** Jacuzzi pump.
**WATER RETURNS:** Four 1-inch returns at
  sides and back.

### CONTROLLERS

**HEATERS:** None.
**CHILLER:** 1 hp chiller.

### FILTRATION

**SKIMMER:** 5 foot custom-made downdraft
  skimmer.

WHEN ENTERING AN INDUSTRIAL SUPPLY STORE in Ohio, the last thing one might expect to see is a magnificent reef tank rising toward the ceiling. But pay a visit to Dave Wodecki and that is exactly what you see: a 360-gallon display tank on I-beam scaffolding 5 feet above the floor. This unorthodox positioning resulted from space considerations and the need to place the equipment in a readily accessible spot. The result places the bottom of the tank exactly at eye level.

To say the least, this is a rather dramatic perspective, and Dave has aquascaped the tank with this unusual view in mind. Tall, vertical corals such as a bright green branching *Acropora yongei* grow up the center right portion of the tank and dominate the view. The left hand side of the tank has a promontory of live rock that juts out from the reef face, on which grow other colonies of SPS corals. In all, the system is stocked with approximately 35 fishes, 100 stony corals, and some 20 colonies of soft coral.

While having all of the equipment directly under the tank provides excellent access, Dave says it has also provided some challenges. First, having the tank elevated so high requires a powerful pump to lift water for circulation. Second, the skimmer and plumbing had to be designed so that they would not overflow from the backpressure. Unfortunately, a winter storm knocked the power out for two days and caused the tank to drain down by 50%. All of the corals above the water line perished, while those that remained submerged managed to survive, despite cool temperatures, little light, and no water movement for almost 48 hours.

Having a tank this high also turns simple tasks such as cleaning the glass or moving a fallen coral into major undertakings performed on an 8-foot stepladder.

In addition to the oversized water pump, Dave also uses larger-scale equipment than usually seen on a tank of this size. This includes an industrial-sized 10-gallon Kalkwasser reactor, a 200-gallon sump, a 1-hp chiller, a custom-made 5-foot downdraft-style protein skimmer, and 3,200 watts of light. The lighting is most impressive, as the almost 10 watts per gallon of light provided by an equal number of 6,500 and 20,000 K metal halide lamps provide intense blue-white light that penetrates to the bottom of this 36-inch-deep tank. This intense light also produces dramatic shadows and glitter lines that contribute to its spectacular impression.

Excellent lighting, along with the fact that Dave started with mostly small colonies of SPS corals, has resulted in large colonies that have developed without the bleaching of lower branches seen in many systems. Good water conditions and lighting also appear to combine in supporting remarkably vivid coral colors. The acroporid corals display unusually long, brightly colored growth tips, evidence of rapid development that results from Dave keeping calcium and alkalinity levels high and feeding his corals with phytoplankton.

Despite having to climb a ladder every time he does anything, Dave manages to keep up with a 5-hour per week maintenance routine. Supplements of a two-part calcium/buffer additive are added daily to insure that these parameters are maintained at their proper levels. A 5% per week water change

*This bright green Acropora yongei is a showpiece coral, reaching toward the surface of the 36-inch-deep tank. Long growth tips (1), are evidence of good development.*

**MECHANICAL FILTER:** None.
**BIOLOGICAL FILTER:** Live rock.
**LIVE ROCK IN DISPLAY TANK:** 500 lbs. Fiji live rock.
**SAND/SUBSTRATE IN DISPLAY:** 2 inches live sand.

## LIGHTING
**FLUORESCENT BULBS:** Two 6-foot VHO actinic 03 bulbs.
**PHOTOPERIOD:** 10 hours.
**HOW OFTEN REPLACED:** Every 6 months.
**METAL HALIDE BULBS:** Four 400-watt 6,500 K Iwasaki and four 400-watt 20,000 K Radium bulbs.
**PHOTOPERIOD:** 8 hours.
**HOW OFTEN REPLACED:** Once per year.
**HEIGHT OF LIGHTS ABOVE WATER SURFACE:** 12 inches.
**LIGHTING CONTROLLER(S):** Electronic timers.

## SYSTEM PARAMETERS & CHEMISTRY
**WATER TEMPERATURE:** 77 to 81°F.
**SPECIFIC GRAVITY:** 1.024.
**PH:** 8.1-8.3.
**ALKALINITY:** 8 dKH.
**CALCIUM:** 350-400.
**NITRATE:** 0.
**PHOSPHATE:** 0.
**RESINS OR DEVICES USED TO REDUCE NITRATE OR PHOSPHATE:** None.
**WATER SOURCE:** Municipal.
**REVERSE OSMOSIS:** Use RO/DI unit.
**SALT USED:** Instant Ocean.
**WATER CHANGE SCHEDULE:** 5% per week.
**ADDITIVES OR SUPPLEMENTS USED:** ESV Bionic 3 gallons per week plus make-up water run through Kalkwasser reactor.
**MAINTENANCE SCHEDULE:** 5 hours per week doing water changes and cleaning the glass.

## LIVESTOCK
**FISHES:** 35.
**STONY CORALS:** 100 colonies.
**SOFT CORALS:** 20.
**OTHER LIVESTOCK:** Snails, hermit crabs, sea cucumbers, and brittle starfish.
**NOTEWORTHY SPECIMENS:** Colony of *Acropora yongei* grown from a fragment to a colony that extends from the bottom of the tank to the surface.

## FEEDING
**REGIMEN FOR FISHES:** 3 times per day—very mixed diet.
**REGIMEN FOR CORALS/INVERTS:** Occasional greenwater.

## NOTES
**PROBLEMS OVERCOME WITH THIS SYSTEM:**
1. Two-day power outage due to winter storms caused water level in tank to drop and corals above water line perished.
2. Maintaining the calcium and alkalinity levels.

**THINGS THE OWNER WOULD LIKE TO CHANGE:**
1. Difficult to work on tank so high up.
2. Depth of tank also makes it difficult to work in.

*Driving the coloration and growth of the corals are eight 400-watt metal halide lights and two 6-foot VHO fluorescent actinic bulbs. Dave does a 5% water change weekly and keeps calcium and alkalinity levels high with a two-part additive.*

3. Having all of the plumbing below the tank makes it difficult to get good flow.

**THINGS OWNER LIKES BEST ABOUT THIS SYSTEM:**
1. Wide diversity of organisms.
2. Having the tank at eye level really makes the tank stand out.
3. Great coloration in SPS corals.

**WHAT IS SPECIAL ABOUT THIS SYSTEM:** The size and wide variety of organisms that have grown well make it a really appealing tank.

**FAVORITE COMMENTS BY OTHERS:**
1. "How did you get the tank up that high?"
2. "This tank makes me want to set one up."

**OVERALL POSITIVES:**
1. Size of tank.
2. Easy to maintain.
3. Health of the corals.

**OVERALL NEGATIVES (OR THINGS TO DO DIFFERENTLY NEXT TIME):**
1. Make sure that if the power goes out for a long time, the tank won't drain by 50%.
2. Add a generator for the storm season in Ohio.
3. Start with fewer animals and let them grow.

schedule is closely adhered to, as is daily cleaning of the front glass and weekly water testing. By doing these small tasks on a regular basis, Dave feels that this tank is still a relatively easy tank to maintain. If he had it do over again, Dave would rethink the elevated position to make it easier to work in the tank. He would also incorporate failsafe devices for power outages, including a backup generator. Interestingly, he says he would also start with fewer animals, having never expected this tank to fill in as rapidly as it did—a problem that many aquarists wish they had in their tanks.

# Coral Garden

*A carefully selected array of colorful and less common Acropora and Montipora corals highlights Clayton Romie's 209-gallon reef.*

DETERMINED TO SUCCEED with small-polyp stony corals, Clayton Romie took the classic Berlin approach to setting up his new 209-gallon aquarium in 1995. He would depend on live rock and live sand for biological filtration, a large foam fractionator for nutrient export, and strong light and water movement to meet the demands of the corals. Finally, the SPS corals he planned to place in the tank would be the most brightly colored available—even if it meant starting them out as fragments from other people's tanks.

Today SPS corals literally fill every spot within the tank with a number of rare, difficult-to-keep, and highly coveted species included. Success did not come without problems and the need to overcome unexpected obstacles.

The first challenge was dealing with the glass aquarium he had chosen. He was unable find a workable solution to getting either the tank or his glass sump drilled, and a great deal of thought had to go into plumbing the system without in-tank overflows or external water pumps. First, a submersible pump moving 720 gallons of water per hour was used to return water from the sump. Second, two other 720-gallon per hour pumps located within the display aquarium were attached to Aquagates—devices that cause their output to move in a 90-degree arc across the tank. Although a bit unconventional for a system of this size, the arrangement achieved the water movement necessary to optimize the health of his corals.

Wanting to try the then-new 20,000 K metal halide bulbs, Clayton started with three 400-watt 20,000 K metal halide lamps, along with 80 watts of actinic fluorescent light. However, over time some of the corals began to

## AQUARIUM PROFILE

**OWNER:** Clayton Romie.
**LOCATION:** Studio City, CA.
**DATE ESTABLISHED:** March 1995.
**DATE PHOTOGRAPHED:** 1999.

### TANK
**DISPLAY TANK VOLUME:** 209 gallons.
**DISPLAY TANK DIMENSIONS:** 72" X 24" X 28".
**DISPLAY TANK MATERIAL:** Glass.
**SUMP VOLUME:** 20 gallons.
**LOCATION (ROOM):** Living room.

### CIRCULATION
**MAIN SYSTEM PUMP(S):** Rio 2500.
**WATER RETURNS:** One split-T.
**ADDITIONAL PUMPS:** Two Rio submersible pumps (720 gph each) with Aquagates.

### CONTROLLERS
**TEMPERATURE CONTROLS:** Medusa heater/chiller controller.
**FANS:** Two 90 cfm.
**HEATERS:** 250-watt Ebo-Jager.
**CHILLER:** 1/3 hp West Coast Aquatics.

### FILTRATION
**SKIMMER:** US Aquarium 6foot countercurrent.
**OZONIZER:** Three hours at night for water clarity.

**LIVE ROCK IN DISPLAY TANK:** 117 lbs. Haitian, 82 lbs. Marshall Island, 100 lbs. Gulf of Mexico, 100 lbs. Tonga, 35 lbs. Fiji.

**SAND/SUBSTRATE IN DISPLAY:** 1-2 inches of Fiji and Florida live sand, every 8-9 months additional Fiji live sand added to replace dissolved substrate.

## LIGHTING

**FLUORESCENT BULBS:** Two 40-watt 28-inch blue actinics.
**PHOTOPERIOD:** 12 hours.
**HOW OFTEN REPLACED:** When burned out.
**METAL HALIDE BULBS:** Five 400-watt 20,000 K Osram.
**PHOTOPERIOD:** 10 hours.
**HOW OFTEN REPLACED:** Every 3 months.
**HEIGHT OF LIGHTS ABOVE WATER SURFACE:** 8 inches.
**LIGHTING CONTROLLER(S):** Appliance timers.

## SYSTEM PARAMETERS & CHEMISTRY:

**WATER TEMPERATURE:** 76°F.
**SPECIFIC GRAVITY:** 1.024-1.025.
**PH:** 7.9-8.0.
**ALKALINITY:** 14-16 dKH.
**CALCIUM:** 400-550 ppm.
**NITRATE:** 0-10 ppm.
**PHOSPHATE:** Undetectable.
**STRONTIUM:** 8.02 mg/L.
**WATER SOURCE:** Municipal.
**NATURAL SEA WATER:** Catalina ocean water.
**REVERSE OSMOSIS:** Yes.
**WATER CHANGE SCHEDULE:** 25 gallons per month first year; after that 50 gallons per year or as needed.
**ADDITIVES OR SUPPLEMENTS USED:** B-Ionic when calcium reactor (Knop D model) could not keep up with growth.

## LIVESTOCK:

**FISHES:** 16.
**STONY CORALS:** 30 species not including fragments.
**SOFT CORALS:** 6 not including zoanthids or corallimorphs.
**NOTEWORTHY SPECIMENS:** *Acropora abrolhosensis*, blue *Acropora kirstyae*.
**SPAWNING EVENTS:** *Tridacna derasa* clam, *Astraea* snails, *Cladiella* coral.

## FEEDING

**REGIMEN FOR FISHES:** Rotifers when available.
**REGIMEN FOR CORALS:** 3 times per week.

## NOTES:

**THINGS THE OWNER WOULD LIKE TO CHANGE:** Get a larger tank.
**THINGS OWNER LIKES BEST ABOUT THIS SYSTEM:** A great device to monitor coral growth and fish behavior.
**WHAT IS SPECIAL ABOUT THIS SYSTEM:** Entire tank run by Rio pumps.
**OVERALL POSITIVES:**
1. Color.
2. Growth.
3. My cat used the chiller exhaust to keep herself warm.

overshadow other colonies lower in the tank, and Clayton has added two additional 400-watt lamps. More than 10 watts per gallon of intense bluish-white light were eventually located over the tank.

The protein skimmer used is a large countercurrent model utilizing limewood air stones and a powerful air pump—a throwback to earlier reefkeeping days, but a design some aquarists still swear by. The only other active filtration used is an ozone generator that switches on for three hours every night to maintain optimal clarity in the water. Five different types of live rock were used to build the reef's underlying structure and provide biological filtration. This broad mix of live rock also produced a great deal of biodiversity in the microfauna that populate the tank. Live sand from Florida and Fiji also helped to maintain the overall health of the system. Clayton found that this sand dissolved fairly quickly, and additional Fiji live sand is now added every 9 months or so in order to maintain the sand at a level of 1 to 2 inches.

Without an unlimited amount of space, Clayton restrained himself and tried to choose only the brightest and rarest coral species he could find. Some of the showpiece colonies found in this tank include a turquoise colony of *Acropora abrolhosensis*, a blue colony of *Acropora kirstyae* and a pink colony of *Acropora horrida*. In addition, there are multiple colonies of purple *Acropora humilis, Acropora samoensis,* as well as a rare green colony of *Montipora verrucosa* and other encrusting *Montipora* species.

The fishes that lend motion and interest to the scene are small, brightly colored species typical of European Berlin-style systems—small wrasses, hawkfishes, damsels, and dottybacks. The only real departure from the classic selection is a rather large pair of Tomato Clownfish that dominate the tank both visually and behaviorally.

To the casual visitor, this is simply a beautiful reef tank to behold. Coral fanatics are thrilled to encounter such vividly colored examples of rare species. Only veteran aquarists may recognize how much careful thought and planning has gone into this tank. It's a perfect example of a successful North American Berlin system and a credit to Clayton's constant vigilance, careful management, and ingenuity.

*With his corals jamming the reefscape, Clayton Romie has achieved a well-established look in his system—but now wishes it were much bigger.*

# Solar Success

*Michael Fontana's corals display phenomenal growth rates thanks to natural sunlight delivered via a "light chimney."*

ITTING NEXT TO THE FIREPLACE IN THE FAMILY ROOM of his cozy hillside home is the 200-gallon reef tank of Dr. Michael Fontana. This system owes its unique design to a Caribbean snorkeling trip when Michael realized that the amount of light above his home aquarium was nothing compared to the amount of light on a tropical reef. Neither fluorescent nor metal halide lighting would approximate the sun, he reasoned, no matter how many fixtures were placed above the tank. He didn't want to move his aquarium, and there was no nearby window to provide direct solar radiation. Michael decided to try a new technology and installed a light chimney above his tank.

This device brings in sunlight through the roof by using a set of mirrors that focus the energy down on one half of his tank. Even in western Pennsylvania, this device produces far more light than any conventional artificial light source.

By having the light chimney and fluorescent lighting on one half of the tank and metal halide and fluorescent lighting on the other half, Fontana says it was easy to see the effect of having sunlight, albeit at a reduced intensity, above the tank. The corals on the side of the tank with the light chimney literally grew to the surface of the water. However, it was not only the overall growth of the colonies that was impressive, it was also the form that the corals took. Most notably, a colony of *Euphyllia ancora* (hammer coral) grew from a palm-sized piece into a magnificent show colony 18 inches across in a little over a year. Even more impressive were the sizes of the individual polyps. Each

## AQUARIUM PROFILE

**OWNER:** Michael Fontana.
**LOCATION:** White Oak, PA.
**DATE ESTABLISHED:** March 1993.
**DATE PHOTOGRAPHED:** 1995, 1996, 1997.

### TANK
**CONFIGURATION:** Rectangular.
**DISPLAY TANK VOLUME:** 180 gallons
**DISPLAY TANK DIMENSIONS:** 6' X 2' X 2'.
**DISPLAY TANK MATERIAL:** Glass.
**SUMP VOLUME:** 40 gallons.
**LOCATION (ROOM):** Family room.
**CABINETRY:** Redwood trimmed in walnut.

### CIRCULATION
**MAIN SYSTEM PUMP(S):** Iwaki 70 RLT.
**WATER RETURNS:** Two 1-inch returns in corners.
**ADDITIONAL PUMPS:** 3 Rio powerheads.
**WAVEMAKING DEVICES:** Red Sea Wavemaster.
**CONTROLLERS:** Octopus controller.
**CHILLER:** Aquanetics.

### FILTRATION
**SKIMMER:** Downdraft type run by Iwaki 55 RLT.
**BIOLOGICAL FILTER:** Live rock.
**LIVE ROCK IN DISPLAY TANK:** 200 lbs. Fiji rock.

**SAND/SUBSTRATE IN DISPLAY:** 2 inches fine Oolitic sand.

### LIGHTING
**FLUORESCENT BULBS:** Four VHO, 2 actinic and 2 daylight.
**PHOTOPERIOD:** 8 hours.
**HOW OFTEN REPLACED:** Every 10 months.
**METAL HALIDE BULBS:** One 250 watt 6,500 K Iwasaki.
**PHOTOPERIOD:** 8 hours.
**HOW OFTEN REPLACED:** Once per year.
**HEIGHT OF LIGHTS ABOVE WATER SURFACE:** 12 inches.
**OTHER BULBS:** None.
**NATURAL LIGHT:** Light chimney located on right third of tank opposite from side with metal halide.
**LIGHTING CONTROLLER(S):** Octopus controller.

### SYSTEM PARAMETERS & CHEMISTRY
**WATER TEMPERATURE:** 77 to 79°F.
**SPECIFIC GRAVITY:** 1.025.
**PH:** 8.2-8.3.
**ALKALINITY:** 3 meq.
**CALCIUM:** 440.
**NITRATE:** 0.05.
**PHOSPHATE:** 0.01.
**REVERSE OSMOSIS:** SpectraPure RO/DI unit.
**SALT USED:** Instant Ocean.
**WATER CHANGE SCHEDULE:** 20 gallons per month.
**ADDITIVES OR SUPPLEMENTS USED:** Dosing pump for evaporation.
**MONITORING EQUIPMENT:** Octopus.
**MAINTENANCE SCHEDULE:** 8+ hours per week.

### LIVESTOCK
**FISHES:** 30.
**STONY CORALS:** 10.
**SOFT CORALS:** 30.
**NOTEWORTHY SPECIMENS:** An exceptionally large *Euphyllia ancora* and a *Hydnophora rigida* that has encrusted on the back glass.
**SPAWNING EVENTS:** Clownfish pair and budding of elegance coral.

### FEEDING
**REGIMEN FOR FISHES:** Frozen food 2 to 3 times per day.
**REGIMEN FOR CORALS/INVERTS:** None.

### NOTES
**PROBLEMS OVERCOME WITH THIS SYSTEM:** Hair algae and inadequate water flow.
**THINGS OWNER WOULD LIKE TO CHANGE:** More room to work in sump (I built the sides too high). Make it easier to work on plumbing as well.
**THINGS OWNER LIKES BEST ABOUT THIS SYSTEM:** Growth of coralline algae and growth of corals.
**SPECIAL ABOUT THIS SYSTEM:** Light chimney has produced phenomenal growth in the *Euphyllia* sp. and *Hydnophora* sp.
**FAVORITE COMMENTS BY OTHERS:**
1. "How did you get that hammer coral to grow so big?"
2. "What's your secret?"

*This hammer coral grew from a palm-sized piece to more than 18-inches in length in about a year under partial natural light.*

*Finding conditions to its liking, a horn coral (Hydnophora rigida) has become massive and is encrusting the rear panel of glass in Michael's system.*

hammer-shaped polyp was at least 1 inch across and in some instances 1 1/2 inches across. Polyps of this size are simply unheard of in aquariums—or even in wild colonies. In a similar demonstration of what strong light can do, a colony of *Hydnophora rigida* (green horn coral) grew from a 50-cent-piece-sized fragment into two sheets the size of dinner plates encrusting the live rock and the back wall of the tank in less than a year. The exposure of these corals to sunlight emanating from the light chimney is the only thing that can be credited with having caused this growth. Except for the light chimney, no other unique manipulations were done to this tank, which is in all other respects a normally equipped reef aquarium. In fact, the

*Soft corals dominate the side of the tank that does not receive direct illumination from the light chimney, and pink coralline algae (1) appear to grow more readily here.*

photoperiod for the other lights was actually quite short, at only eight hours per day. The growth of these corals, Michael and others believe, had to be a function of the intense light from the light chimney rather than from the other lights. The corals were not fed directly, nor were there excess nutrients in the tank. The fish population was not large enough to be a source of nutrition to produce exceptional growth. Eliminating these possibilities leaves the energy from the light chimney as the only possible explanation for the spectacular growth of the stony corals.

The corals and the fishes in this tank were otherwise commonly seen specimens—hammer corals, *Hydnophora* sp., elegance corals, star polyps, and brain corals predominated. But the corals directly under the light chimney grew vigorously to sizes not typically seen in corals in closed systems, except perhaps after many years of growth.

One other curious aspect of this tank was the coralline growth on the side opposite the light chimney. The growth here was remarkably thick and extensive, and it formed overlapping sheets of colorful calcareous algae that made for a rather unique visual display not seen in many other tanks.

Having natural sunlight reach our tanks is unfortunately not a viable option for most reef tank enthusiasts. However, by having sunlight penetrate a small section of his tank, Michael Fontana has demonstrated how important proper lighting is. It also suggests that, if we ever can get close to having light similar to sunlight filling our tanks in the future, the results may be truly amazing.

**OVERALL POSITIVES:**
1. Natural light.
2. Good circulation.

**OVERALL NEGATIVES (OR THINGS TO DO DIFFERENTLY NEXT TIME):**
1. Add plenum under sand.
2. Use a bigger and better chiller.

# Inventor's Reef

*Professor Sanjay Joshi's 180-gallon reef boasts a lighting system, skimmer, sump, and calcium reactors—all of his own design.*

## AQUARIUM PROFILE

**OWNER & DESIGNER:** Sanjay Joshi
www.personal.psu.edu/faculty/s/b/sbj4/
   aquarium/aquarium.html.
**LOCATION:** State College, PA.
**DATE ESTABLISHED:** March 1995.
**DATE PHOTOGRAPHED:** Various dates.

### TANK
**DISPLAY TANK VOLUME:** 180 gallons.
**DISPLAY TANK DIMENSIONS:** 6' X 2' X 2'.
**DISPLAY TANK MATERIAL:** Glass.
**SUMP VOLUME:** 50 gallons.
**LOCATION:** Basement.
**CABINETRY:** Built into the wall.

### CIRCULATION
**MAIN SYSTEM PUMP(S):** Little Giant 4-mdqx.
**WATER RETURNS:** Main pump 2 returns, one
   in each front corner of the tank, directed
   toward the tank center.
**ADDITIONAL PUMPS:** 2 Mag 7s, and 2
   Gemini powerheads.
**WAVEMAKING DEVICES:** Tsunami Wavemaker.

ONE OF THE COMMON CHARACTERISTICS among reefkeepers is an inherent urge to tinker and invent. A reef tank provides endless opportunities to exercise this drive, with new pieces of equipment and new techniques to ponder and adapt. Sanjay Joshi has carried this approach to an extreme, building just about everything involved with his 180-gallon tank in central Pennsylvania, except for the tank itself. His handiwork includes the lighting system and hood, the downdraft-style protein skimmer, the sump and refill system, and the calcium reactors. All of these have tweaks and improvements, which is what you might expect from a Penn State engineering professor. Some of Sanjay's own modifications include designing a special nozzle for the downdraft skimmer so that it does not require as large a pump as a skimmer of comparable size. The lights are mounted in a custom hood designed to provide the entire tank an equal amount of light. The overflow box is built so that if a fish gets caught in it, the fish can easily be removed.

All too often, such homemade equipment and ambitious tinkering creates unpredicted problems, but Sanjay's improvements have resulted in a tank where the SPS corals are growing to fill every available space. Most of these large coral colonies started as fragments or small colonies and have grown rapidly. These corals are not limited to common *Montipora* and *Acropora* corals,

## CONTROLLERS
**FANS:** Two fans in light hood.
**HEATERS:** 200-watt heater (used only in winter).

## FILTRATION
**SKIMMER:** DIY downdraft style.
**CARBON:** Two bags in the sump, changed at 2-to 3-month intervals.
**LIVE ROCK IN DISPLAY TANK:** 200 lbs. Florida Keys rock; 50 lbs. Tonga Branch rock.
**SAND/SUBSTRATE IN DISPLAY:** 2-3 inches Florida Keys live sand.

## LIGHTING
**FLUORESCENT BULBS:** Two HO Actinics.
**PHOTOPERIOD:** 12 hours.
**HOW OFTEN REPLACED:** Every 2 years or so.
**METAL HALIDE BULBS:** Three 400-watt Iwasaki 6,500 K.
**PHOTOPERIOD:** 10 hours.
**HOW OFTEN REPLACED:** Every 2 years.
**LIGHTING CONTROLLER(S):** Timers.

## SYSTEM PARAMETERS & CHEMISTRY
**PH:** 8.2-8.6.
**ALKALINITY:** 7-12 dKH.
**CALCIUM:** 350-440 ppm.
**NITRATE:** 0.2 ppm $NO_3$.
**PHOSPHATE:** 0.1 ppm.
**MUNICIPAL WATER SUPPLY:** Yes.
**REVERSE OSMOSIS:** Yes.
**SALT USED:** Instant Ocean.
**WATER CHANGE SCHEDULE:** Very infrequent.
**ADDITIVES OR SUPPLEMENTS USED:** None.
**MONITORING EQUIPMENT:** Pinpoint pH Meter.
**DOSING EQUIPMENT USED:** ReefFiller.
**MAINTENANCE SCHEDULE:** Clean glass and skimmer weekly.

## LIVESTOCK
**FISHES:** 6.
**STONY CORALS:** 35.
**SOFT CORALS:** 4.
**OTHER LIVESTOCK:** Starfish, snails, crabs, shrimp.
**NOTEWORTHY SPECIMENS:** Several large colonies of orange *Montipora capricornis*, green staghorn *Acropora* and corals well into 6th year in captivity.
**SPAWNING EVENTS:** Clams and snails.

## FEEDING
**REGIMEN FOR FISHES:** 2 inch square piece of homemade food per day.
**REGIMEN FOR CORALS/INVERTS:** Same as above.

## NOTES
**PROBLEMS OVERCOME WITH THIS SYSTEM:** Dinoflagellates, cyanobacteria, and other algae and diatoms.
**THINGS THE OWNER WOULD LIKE TO CHANGE:**
1. Drill back of the tank to allow closed-loop circulation pumps.
2. Lower the rock structure; the corals tend to reach the surface quickly.

but also less often seen *Merulina, Echinopora, Mycedium*, and many other eye-catching SPS corals.

The numerous colonies of orange *Montipora capricornis* are particularly striking and noteworthy, as they were all started from a single small fragment. In Sanjay's tank this often-delicate coral has come to dominate much of the aquascape.

In an attempt to keep nutrient levels low and to reduce maintenance, Sanjay keeps only a few fishes. These include tangs, anthias, clownfishes, and some of the other common species that are kept in reefs. The fishes are as healthy as the corals, as they are fed a custom-made food that Sanjay has formulated to maximize their growth and coloration. Sanjay was also one of the first hobbyists to realize the need to examine the nutritional needs of corals, and he has been experimenting with different food options for his corals for the past few years. He believes that improved nutrition and feeding of the corals has resulted in growth rates that exceed those on many reefs.

This increased feeding would have resulted in high nutrient levels in most tanks, but with Sanjay's efficient skimmer this is not a problem. Feeding also allows Sanjay to keep even some of the more difficult SPS corals, including the challenging, thick-branched *Acropora humilis* and *A. gemmifera*. Sanjay has also

*In a very elite class of stony coral aquariums, Sanjay's reef is biologically rich, visually spectacular, and highly productive, having provided "well over 1,000 coral fragments" that have gone to other marine aquariums around the country.*

**THINGS OWNER LIKES BEST ABOUT THIS SYSTEM:** Very low maintenance.

**SPECIAL ABOUT THIS SYSTEM:** Has provided well over 1,000 coral fragments to people all over the country, can trace at least 3-4 generations of captive corals to this system.

**FAVORITE COMMENTS BY OTHERS ABOUT THIS AQUARIUM:**
1. "One of best SPS tank I have seen."
2. "I didn't know corals could get that big in aquariums."

**OVERALL POSITIVES:**
1. All the circulation pumps are external to the system.
2. No overflow box taking up space inside the tank.
3. Corals thrive.

**OVERALL NEGATIVES (OR THINGS TO DO DIFFERENTLY NEXT TIME):**
1. Be quick to react to algae outbreaks.
2. Perform regular water changes even if the tank is looking fine.
3. Get a bigger tank.

observed and recorded some unusual behaviors among his fast-growing corals. Several of the *Acropora* colonies began to show table-like growth once they reached the surface of the water, even though this was not a typical growth pattern for these species. Also, despite not using high-temperature bulbs, Sanjay maintains coral colorations as intense as those seen in corals kept under bulbs with high Kelvin ratings. This may be the result of the close proximity of the bulbs to the water, along with the low nutrient levels and the feeding of the corals.

As a measure of this reef's productivity, Sanjay has already removed more than a thousand fragments for other hobbyists. He can now trace at least three generations of corals as having come from his system. Growth can also create problems, and Sanjay is considering reducing the underlying rock structure to give the corals more room. A better solution, says Sanjay, is when he gets his wish (shared by many hobbyists) for a bigger aquarium.

*Tiered colonies of plating Montipora capricornis (1) are prominent throughout the tank, all having started from one small fragment that has served as the source of many beautiful daughter colonies. Note the hard-to-keep Acropora gemmifera (2).*

*Having tested numerous lighting choices, Sanjay was running three 400-watt 6,500 K Iwasaki metal halide bulbs and two VHO fluorescent actinics over his system when these images were taken. (See pages 116-119 for another example of his work.)*

# Reef Redux

*The result of hard lessons learned, Earl Belden's 300-gallon Ohio reef is a successor to a 240-gallon tank that split at the seams.*

## AQUARIUM PROFILE

**OWNER:** Earl G. Belden.
**LOCATION:** Cleveland Heights, OH.
**DATE ESTABLISHED:** September 1999.
**DATE PHOTOGRAPHED:** April 2001.

### TANK
**DISPLAY TANK VOLUME:** 300 gallons.
**DISPLAY TANK DIMENSIONS:** 8' X 2' X 30".
**DISPLAY TANK MATERIAL:** Starfire glass.
**SUMP VOLUME:** 150 gallons.
**LOCATION (ROOM):** Dining room.
**CABINETRY/ARCHITECTURAL DETAILS:**
Custom-made stand and canopy.

### CIRCULATION
**MAIN SYSTEM PUMP(S):** Iwaki 100 RLT, 2,000 gph.
**WATER RETURNS:** Two 1-inch Sea Swirls.
**ADDITIONAL PUMPS:** Closed circuits: Two Iwaki 55 RLT. Two returns for each pump at bottom rear of tank.
**WAVEMAKING DEVICES:** Two Tsunamis controlling the Iwakis.

### CONTROLLERS
**FANS:** Two 4-inch circular fans going to 6-inch fan for exhaust to outdoors.
**CHILLER:** Aquanetics.

I N SETTING UP LARGER MARINE AQUARIUMS, second chances rarely come along. Given the investments involved and the size of the systems, bigger tanks tend to dictate that their owners live with any design mistakes. For Earl Belden, an unlikely second chance did come along when his 240-gallon acrylic reef tank failed due to a manufacturing flaw. Unhappily, his first tank split apart at the seams, but as he replaced it he was able to correct a number of configuration mistakes he had made in the original system and to design his dream tank.

Put together with the advice of Kurt Loos, a well-respected midwestern hobbyist, the first reef was successful in many ways. The corals grew very quickly and to large sizes in a short period of time, and the overall health of the system was excellent. Like most reefkeepers, Earl is a tinkerer, and he had learned enough with the first tank to know what he wanted to do differently. First, a leaking 8-foot-long box of water can be a frightening thing in a family dining room setting, so Earl had the second tank made from glass after his first unhappy experience with acrylic. He appreciated the clarity that acrylic had provided, though, so he had the replacement tank made from Starfire glass, which approximates that clarity. He also had the tank made 60 gallons larger, to 300 gallons, without having to change the size of the stand or the hood simply by making the tank 6 inches taller.

In the first tank, submersible powerheads were used for circulation. These added incrementally to an overheating problem in the original system, so they were replaced by two external water pumps that not only increased the flow

*Earl has elected to stock his system lightly to allow the 35 colonies of soft and stony corals space and time to grow and fill the aquascape naturally.*

within the tank, but did so without adding heat. The first tank had its temperature rise to an unacceptable 85 degrees in the summer, due in part to the presence of 12 metal halide lamps over the tank. Additionally, the water temperature of the 240-gallon tank tended to fluctuate over a much larger range than is generally considered optimal. Control of the temperature is now much better, as a 6-inch exhaust fan directs the heat generated by the metal halides outside, while a chiller keeps the temperature from going too high.

The large number of stony corals and their rapid rate of growth made maintaining proper calcium and alkalinity levels in the first tank a challenge. Initially a Kalkwasser reactor was used, through which all of the top-off water was added. However, even with this, the alkalinity levels still tended to fall over time. In the reconfigured system, a calcium reactor was added, and this has helped to keep the alkalinity levels constant and within the desired range.

Lastly, Earl did not restock the tank as heavily when he started over. The first tank contained 50 stony coral colonies and 20 soft coral colonies, while the new tank has but 30 stony corals and 5 soft corals. At first, the new tank had a comparatively bare look. However, Earl's new approach was quickly validated when the corals that had been given greater space simply grew faster than when they were placed in a crowded setting.

All these efforts produced a tank that looks more natural, a consequence of having been stocked with small colonies or fragments that have been allowed to grow unimpeded by the proximity of other corals. This differs from the more traditional route of placing large colonies that have been collected from the reef and then placed into tank conditions. The new growth on previously wild colonies often looks much different from the old growth that occurred on the reef, and these transplanted colonies often display odd forms suggestive of mutant corals.

Today Earl says that there is very little that he would like to change on the new tank. This tank is much easier to maintain and clean (removing algal growth from acrylic in a large system can be a laborious job, using soft scrapers rather than razor-sharp tools), and the growth and health of his corals is exceptionally good. The loss of most of his livestock when the first tank came apart might have driven a less dedicated aquarist to take up golf, but the success of this replacement system is a testament to Earl Belden's learning from past experiences and overcoming adversity to create a beautiful, thriving reef tank in his home.

## FILTRATION
**SKIMMER:** Two 6-foot countercurrent skimmers with 8" X 2" X 2" basswood airstones run with large air compressor.
**CARBON:** 1 quart. Used 3 days per month to remove discoloration from water.
**BIOLOGICAL FILTER:** Tonga rock at base, Fiji rock on top
**LIVE ROCK IN DISPLAY TANK:** 300 lbs. Fiji rock plus 75 lbs. of Tonga branch.
**SAND/SUBSTRATE IN DISPLAY:** Bio-Active Live Aragonite reef sand.

## LIGHTING
**FLUORESCENT BULBS:** Four 4-foot URI 120-watt Superactinic FR 40T12/03/VHS.
**PHOTOPERIOD:** 14 hours.
**HOW OFTEN REPLACED:** Every two years.
**METAL HALIDE BULBS:**
Four 175-watt 20,000 K Radium;
Four 250-watt 10,000 K Radium;
Four 250-watt 20,000 K Radium.
**PHOTOPERIOD:** 12 hours total; lights turned on two at a time at 60-minute intervals to simulate sunrise/sunset effect.
**HOW OFTEN REPLACED:** Once per year.
**HEIGHT ABOVE WATER SURFACE:** 12 inches.
**LIGHTING CONTROLLER(S):** 6 timers.

## SYSTEM PARAMETERS & CHEMISTRY
**WATER TEMPERATURE:** 77 to 81°F.
**SPECIFIC GRAVITY:** 1.023.
**PH:** 8.15-8.35.
**ALKALINITY:** 8.5-10 dKH.
**CALCIUM:** 460.
**NITRATE:** 0.
**PHOSPHATE:** 0.
**OTHER READINGS:** Magnesium 1200.
**MUNICIPAL WATER SUPPLY:** Cleveland.
**REVERSE OSMOSIS:** SpectraPure 25 gpd RO/DI autofeed unit with float switch
**SALT USED:** Reef Crystals.
**WATER CHANGE SCHEDULE:** 50 gallons per week.
**ADDITIVES OR SUPPLEMENTS USED:** Magnesium, strontium, Lugol's Iodine, Sera Marinevit, and Coral Vital.
**MONITORING EQUIPMENT:** Pinpoint pH, Pinpoint ORP.
**DOSING EQUIPMENT:** Calcium Reactor–Pro Cal.
**MAINTENANCE SCHEDULE:** Clean glass with a magnet daily. Scrape glass every two weeks.

## LIVESTOCK
**FISHES:** 13.
**STONY CORALS:** 30.
**SOFT CORALS:** 5.
**OTHER LIVESTOCK:** Hermits, snails, starfishes, and cucumbers.

## FEEDING
**REGIMEN FOR FISHES:** Daily Tetra ProCrisp, Frozen Ocean Nutrition Formula One and Two, brine shrimp, Omega 3/Selcon.
**REGIMEN FOR CORALS/INVERTS:** Marine snow and greenwater every other day.

## NOTES
**THINGS OWNER LIKES BEST ABOUT THIS SYSTEM:** Low upkeep and easy to clean.

# Inadvertent Reef

*Originally intended only for the culture of Xenia, Dave Lackland's New Jersey system has become a small-reef success.*

## AQUARIUM PROFILE

**OWNER:** David Lackland.
**LOCATION:** Pleasant Beach, NJ.
**DATE ESTABLISHED:** July 1999.
**DATE PHOTOGRAPHED:** June 2001.

### TANK

**CONFIGURATION:** Two 33-gallon tanks.
**DISPLAY TANK VOLUME:** 66 gallons.
**DISPLAY TANK DIMENSIONS:** 48" X 13" X 13".
**DISPLAY TANK MATERIAL:** Glass.
**SUMP VOLUME:** 30 gallons collectively.
**LOCATION (ROOM):** Living room.
**CABINETRY/ARCHITECTURAL DETAILS:** 2 X 4 and 2 X 6 construction.

### CIRCULATION

**MAIN SYSTEM PUMP(S):** Iwaki 20 RLXT.
**WATER RETURNS:** Two returns in the corners of each tank.
**ADDITIONAL PUMPS:** Iwaki 40 RLT for downdraft skimmer, four Hagen AquaClear 402 powerheads, two per tank.
**WAVEMAKING DEVICES:** Red Sea Wavemaster Pro.

### CONTROLLERS:

**TEMPERATURE CONTROLS:** Air-conditioned room.

SOMETIMES AQUARIUMS TAKE ON LIVES OF THEIR OWN. Such is the case for a pair of small tanks set up by Dave Lackland for *Xenia* propagation. The twin 33-gallon aquariums used a shared sump and minimal equipment. Over time, Dave began to add other organisms that had caught his eye, and the *Xenia* gradually gave way to a diverse collection of invertebrates. Eventually Dave discovered that several pieces of live rock in his tanks had small colonies of coral on them that were growing out nicely in the conditions of his system. This evolution into full-fledged reef tanks was all the more remarkable considering that Dave was using standard fluorescent lighting. Amazingly, even small-polyped stony corals are thriving with neither metal halides nor high-output fluorescent bulbs.

Each tank is lit with four 36-watt T-8 fluorescent tubes. By using these thinner tubes above the 33-gallon tanks, Dave is still able to get almost 5 watts of light per gallon over the corals. Because the tanks are only 13 inches tall, sufficient light is still able to reach even the bottom of each tank. These light conditions have proved acceptable to both mushroom anemones (*Actinodiscus*) and gorgonians that can thrive in subdued lighting, but also for small-polyped stony corals such as *Acropora, Montipora, Seriatopora,* and *Pocillopora*. Dave has even gotten two Caribbean corals (*Acropora prolifera* and *Eusmilia fastigiata*) to grow into colonies from just a few polyps that had attached to his cultured Caribbean live rock. The fluorescent bulbs are changed every three months to make sure that there is no dropoff in intensity or spectrum. Dave believes that this consistency helps in maintaining the coloration and vitality of the corals.

Good basic husbandry is also at work here. Dave is using a modified Berlin system combined with two small interconnected sumps that serve as refugiums that not only act as loci for microfauna reproduction but also help keep nutrient levels down. One of the sumps is a pure refugium with the entire bottom covered with live sand and live rocks with some *Caulerpa* to help reduce phosphate. The other sump contains a deep sand bed to help reduce nitrate. These sumps are connected to each other, and a series of baffles in the sump containing the deep sand bed allows water to pass over and through it without any of the substrate being drawn into the pump. These refugiums allow significant microfauna reproduction and this likely provides some of the nutritional requirements of the corals.

*Challenging to keep is this red-polyped gorgonian (Swiftia exserta), which has defied long-term survival in the tanks of many marine hobbyists.*

*Excellent polyp extension on his corals may be a result of Dave's feeding approach, which uses micropureed protein, Mysis shrimp, and phytoplankton.*

**HEATERS:** 200-watt Hagen Thermal Compact heater with remote Otto thermostat.

**FILTRATION**
**SKIMMER:** Custom-made downdraft skimmer with tweaked injector nozzle.
**MECHANICAL FILTER:** Foam blocks in sump.
**CARBON:** Changed every 6 months; amount changes every time.
**BIOLOGICAL FILTER:** Live rock, animals, and plants in refugiums.
**REFUGIUM:** Two-part sump with live rock, *Caulerpa* and, in one part, deep sand.
**LIVE ROCK IN DISPLAY TANK:** Combo of cultured Caribbean and wild-collected Indonesian.
**LIVE ROCK IN SUMP:** Cultured Caribbean.
**SAND/SUBSTRATE IN DISPLAY:** Pink Samoa sand, 2 inches in left tank and 4 inches in right tank.
**SAND/SUBSTRATE IN SUMP/REFUGIUM:** Approximately 5 inches.

**LIGHTING**
**FLUORESCENT BULBS:** Each tank lit by four 36-watt (T-8) bulbs housed in Phazer IV fixtures. Bulbs are two Sylvania Aquastar 10,000 K bulbs and two Sylvania Coralstar actinic bulbs.
**PHOTOPERIOD:** 13.5 hours.
**HOW OFTEN REPLACED:** Every 3 months.
**HEIGHT OF LIGHTS ABOVE WATER SURFACE:** 2 inches.
**OTHER BULBS:** Each sump has an 18 inch 15-watt Coralife 50/50, 10 inches above water surface. These are on 16 hours per day starting before main tank's lights go on and ending after main tank's lights go off.
**LIGHTING CONTROLLER(S):** Appliance timers.

**SYSTEM PARAMETERS & CHEMISTRY**
**WATER TEMPERATURE:** 77 to 78°F.
**SPECIFIC GRAVITY:** 1.024.
**PH:** 8.4.
**ALKALINITY:** 9-10 dKH.
**CALCIUM:** 440-460.
**NITRATE:** 0.044.
**PHOSPHATE:** 0.01.
**OTHER READINGS, IF AVAILABLE:** Mg 1320.
**MUNICIPAL WATER SUPPLY:** Yes.
**REVERSE OSMOSIS:** SpectraPure 24 gpd.
**DEIONIZATION:** Aquarium Pharmaceuticals Tapwater Purifier.
**SALT USED:** Instant Ocean.
**WATER CHANGE SCHEDULE:** 10 gallons, once per month.
**ADDITIVES OR SUPPLEMENTS USED:** ESV B-Ionic 56 ml of each daily, ESV Magnesium 60 ml 2 times per week.
**MONITORING EQUIPMENT:** EXS+A digital thermometer.
**DOSING EQUIPMENT USED:** Manual.
**MAINTENANCE SCHEDULE:** 3-5 hours per week not including viewing time, which I believe to be the most important time.

**LIVESTOCK**
**FISHES:** Left 15, right 16.
**STONY CORALS:** Left tank 24; right tank 15.
**SOFT CORALS:** Left 9, right 6.

*The paired 33-gallon reefs with connected, lighted sumps share a common downdraft skimmer (1) driven by a 750-gallon per hour pump. The left-hand sump is filled with live rock (2); its right-hand twin is filled with Caulerpa and a deep sand (3).*

**OTHER LIVESTOCK:** Large colonies of microfauna everywhere.

**NOTEWORTHY SPECIMENS:** *Eusmilia fastigiata* spreading into a nice colony that emerged from cultured Caribbean rock. A colony of *Acropora prolifera* has also emerged from only a few polyps on the live rock.

### FEEDING

**REGIMEN FOR FISHES:** *Spirulina* flake two times daily and freeze-dried krill once daily.

**REGIMEN FOR CORALS/INVERTS:** Frozen krill, brine shrimp, *Mysis*—all micropureed. Mixed with ESV Spray-Dried Marine Phytoplankton. This mixture is fed via 20-cc syringe and rigid air-line tubing.

### NOTES

**PROBLEMS OVERCOME WITH THIS SYSTEM:** Had to add bypass to skimmer returns, and the leveling pipes could not handle the volume of water coming through

**WHAT IS SPECIAL ABOUT THIS SYSTEM:** I have a one-foot strip of the ocean eight feet long and can grow just about anything—using just standard wattage.

**FAVORITE COMMENTS BY OTHERS:** "I can't believe you are doing what you are doing with only standard fluorescent lights."

**OVERALL POSITIVES:** Cheap, easy access to everything, and it works great!

**OVERALL NEGATIVES (OR THINGS TO DO DIFFERENTLY NEXT TIME):**
1. More light (this was originally designed as a *Xenia* propagation system).
2. No powerheads (they break down too frequently).

A homemade downdraft-style skimmer has a custom-designed nozzle and is powered by a 750-gallon per hour pump. Some aquarists fear that connecting such a large skimmer to a small tank might result in overskimming, but this has not appeared to be a problem here. Dave uses no trace element supplements, except through water changes, and the corals do not appear to be lacking in anything. Dave also feeds the corals a varied diet of micropureed high-protein foods and phytoplankton on a regular basis, and this very likely makes up for any shortages in trace elements. He adds calcium and maintains alkalinity via the use of a two-part supplement. As a result, both of these measures are well within the range found in normal seawater. These tanks also have significant water flow within them, as the water turns over approximately 10 times per hour in each tank.

In addition to having corals, including some demanding species, thrive, this system also appears to keep fishes in good health. In particular, Dave has a healthy Clown Surgeonfish that he has had since the tank started. This tang is typically one of the most difficult to keep, yet Dave has not only been able to keep it alive, but it has grown in size and kept its beautiful coloration—a real feat considering the size of the tank it inhabits.

Once the reef bug bit Dave, his goal was to devise a system that was inexpensive to set up and inexpensive to run. Although it evolved in some unexpected ways, his small reefs and refugiums are wonderful examples of what can be done with a minimum of expensive technology by taking advantage of the spirit of ingenuity and experimental husbandry.

# Home Office Tank

*Both profession and passion, this 120-gallon Berlin reef is Tony Nista's inspiration when working out of his home office.*

**M**OST OF US TRY NOT TO BRING OUR WORK home with us every day. For Tony Nista, a manager with Tetra Products, his livelihood and personal passion are the same: marine aquariums. Because he spends several days a week working out of his home office, he finds that the 120-gallon reef not only helps him to relax, but also keeps him connected with the same challenges faced by the hobbyists and store owners he encounters in his daily business.

His office system is set up in the traditional Berlin style, with a large counter-current protein skimmer serving as the cornerstone of the filtration scheme. Tony uses filter bags for mechanical filtration and a small UV sterilizer for disease control. Activated carbon is also used for a short period each month to maintain the water's clarity and optimize light penetration.

Having ample light is one of the concerns that Tony has had about this setup, despite having 570 watts of light over the tank, or about 4.5 watts of light per gallon. Despite his yearning for more intense lighting, the health and coloration of the corals appear to be near perfect. There are no signs of bleaching in the colonies and growth is quite impressive—thanks in part to the strong water movement within the tank. Using an external pump and three powerheads, Tony has arranged more than 2,000 gallons of water movement through this tank every hour. As a result, waste material is rapidly moved away from the corals, and oxygen and nutrients are always available. Tony says that many reefkeepers would see better results if they had stronger water circulation

## AQUARIUM PROFILE

**OWNER:** Tony Nista.
**LOCATION:** Madison, OH.
**DATE ESTABLISHED:** March 1992.
**DATE PHOTOGRAPHED:** July 2001.

### TANK
**DISPLAY TANK VOLUME:** 120 gallons.
**DISPLAY TANK DIMENSIONS:** 48" X 24" X 24".
**DISPLAY TANK MATERIAL:** Acrylic.
**SUMP VOLUME:** 30 gallons.
**LOCATION:** Home office.

### CIRCULATION
**MAIN SYSTEM PUMP(S):** Iwaki 30 RXT (1,140 gph).
**WATER RETURNS:** Two 1.25-inch bulkheads in upper rear corners, hard plumbed with PVC.
**ADDITIONAL PUMPS:** Two Maxi-Jet 1000, one Hagen AquaClear 802.
**WAVEMAKING DEVICES:** One Tsunami Wave Timer, one Natural Wavemaker by Aquarium Systems.

### TEMPERATURE CONTROLS
**FANS:** Two 120 mm in canopy.

*Robust coral growth, as in this large green plating Montipora (1), may be a consequence of strong, chaotic water circulation—approximately 2,000 gallons per hour, or almost 17 times the volume of the display tank. Note large-polyped trumpet coral (2).*

**CHILLER:** One 4 hp Universal Marine Industries Chiller with LCD control.

### FILTRATION
**SKIMMER:** 4-by-6 inch BS4 skimmer from Coral Connection.
**MECHANICAL FILTER:** Foam sponges in sump.
**UV STERILIZER:** Tetra UV3 sterilizer 36-watt power compact UV (used occasionally).
**CARBON:** Two cups used for 5 days every month.
**LIVE ROCK IN DISPLAY TANK:** 60 lbs. Fiji rock, 35 lbs. Florida rock, 20 lbs. Marshall Island rock, 25 lbs. Tonga rock.
**SAND/SUBSTRATE IN DISPLAY:** 25 lbs. CaribSea aragonite sand (1/8-inch particle size).

### LIGHTING
**FLUORESCENT BULBS:** Two 110-watt VHO URI actinics.
**PHOTOPERIOD:** 12 hours per day.
**HOW OFTEN REPLACED:** Every 4 months.
**METAL HALIDE BULBS:** Two 175-watt German 10,000 K.
**PHOTOPERIOD:** 10 hours per day.
**HOW OFTEN REPLACED:** Every 12 months.
**LIGHTING CONTROLLER(S):** Lamp timers.

### SYSTEM PARAMETERS & CHEMISTRY
**WATER TEMPERATURE:** 76°F.
**SPECIFIC GRAVITY:** 1.024.

in their tanks. One drawback to the current configuration, he says, is more noise from the system pump than he would like in an office setting.

Both large-polyped and small-polyped stony corals dominate the reefscape. Unlike most reef plans, where the SPS corals are all at the top and the LPS all at the bottom, these are intermingled in a more natural-looking arrangement. Large-polyped brain corals and candy cane corals grow with *Acropora* and *Montipora* corals right beside them. The SPS corals were all started from fragments or very young colonies and have grown into impressively large specimens over the past eight years—despite their being frequently harvested for fragments to give to other hobbyists. This massive growth has not been restricted to only the corals. A baby *Tridacna deresa* clam that was initially added to the tank at less than one inch in size has grown into an 11-inch beauty over the last seven years.

The fish population has been limited, as Tony believes that restricting the biomass of fishes and their resultant waste makes maintaining the tank and keeping it free of algae much easier—an important factor as his travel schedule often interferes with his routine aquarium chores. Although few in number, the fishes in this tank are interesting nonetheless. The Tomato Clownfish is more than 10 years old, and it—along with an Arabian Bluelined or Neon Dottyback (*Pseudochromis aldabraensis*)—dominate the tank. Another curious choice is the Flame Angelfish, a species that has a reputation for picking at LPS corals, such as Tony's orange *Cynarina* and his large green *Trachyphyllia* open brain coral. Fortunately this has not been the case. Tony attributes this to there always being a small amount of turf algae present on which the angel can browse as well as the daily feeding of vegetable-based flake food.

*Small-polyped Acroporas display strong skeletal growth. Tony uses a two-part calcium/alkalinity supplement twice weekly to keep his water parameters in line.*

*A large-polyped prize is this multi-colored lobed brain coral (Lobophyllia sp.) located on the bottom substrate of the tank. Note neighboring frogspawn coral (1).*

Overall, Tony regards this as a low-maintenance tank: "It's pretty self-sufficient, which is nice, because I travel for work." He's pleased with the growth rates of the corals, but would also like more light. He'd also prefer the mechanical components to be less noisy at times, and would arrange a more soundproof cabinet or a remote location for filtration equipment in a future redesign.

Tony has one major complaint about this system: the tank needs to be bigger. This may be the universal lament of all successful reefkeepers. For someone like Tony Nista, who is paid to work with marine organisms, wanting even more of them in his home office is a sure sign of the hold that saltwater has over so many aquarists, professional and amateur alike.

**PH:** 8.0 to 8.4.
**ALKALINITY:** 3.5 meq/L.
**CALCIUM:** 400 mg/L.
**NITRATE:** < 5 ppm.
**PHOSPHATE:** < 0.1 ppm.
**RESINS OR DEVICES USED TO REDUCE NITRATE OR PHOSPHATE:** Seachem phosphate remover (occasional use only).
**MUNICIPAL WATER SUPPLY:** Yes.
**REVERSE OSMOSIS:** Yes.
**DEIONIZATION:** Yes.
**SALT USED:** Instant Ocean.
**WATER CHANGE SCHEDULE:** 10% per month.
**ADDITIVES OR SUPPLEMENTS USED:** Sera Marinvit 60 ml twice/week. ESV B-Ionic 30 ml twice/ week. Strontium (Aquarium Systems) 20 ml two times per month.
**MONITORING EQUIPMENT:** PinPoint pH monitor; Rainbow Lifeguard Time or Temp.
**DOSING EQUIPMENT USED:** Vario Dosing Pump (Two Little Fishies).
**MAINTENANCE SCHEDULE:** 30 minutes per week.

## LIVESTOCK
**FISHES:** 8.
**STONY CORALS:** 45.
**SOFT CORALS:** 4.
**NOTEWORTHY SPECIMENS:** *Tridacna derasa* clam obtained in March 1994 at less than 1 inch, currently 11 inches.

## FEEDING
**REGIMEN FOR FISHES:** Tetra flake foods daily.
**REGIMEN FOR CORALS/INVERTS:** Occasional, *Artemia nauplii* and rotifers.

## NOTES
**PROBLEMS OVERCOME WITH THIS SYSTEM:** *Valonia.*
**THINGS THE OWNER WOULD LIKE TO CHANGE:** Bigger tank!
**THINGS OWNER LIKES BEST ABOUT THIS SYSTEM:**
1. Low maintenance.
2. High growth rates (especially SPS), self-sufficient (nice, because I travel for work).
**OVERALL NEGATIVES:**
1. Too small.
2. TOO NOISY (it's in my office).
3. Not enough light (is there ever?).

# Jewel Box Aquarium

*Although modest in size, Kurt Loos's lovely reef has yielded hundreds of coral fragments for fellow midwestern aquarists.*

## AQUARIUM PROFILE

**OWNER & DESIGNER:** Kurt Loos
www.bright.net/~fishboy/coral/coral.html.
**LOCATION:** Medina, OH.
**DATE ESTABLISHED:** 1994.
**DATE PHOTOGRAPHED:** 1995 to 1997.

### TANK
**DISPLAY TANK VOLUME:** 90 gallons.
**DISPLAY TANK DIMENSIONS:** 30" X 30" X 24".
**DISPLAY TANK MATERIAL:** Acrylic.
**SUMP VOLUME:** 120 gallons (with refugium).
**LOCATION:** Family room.
**CABINETRY/ARCHITECTURAL DETAILS:** Custom oak by owner.

### CIRCULATION
**MAIN SYSTEM PUMP(S):** Iwaki 40 RLT.
**WATER RETURNS:** Built-in internal overflow.
**ADDITIONAL PUMPS:** Tunze 1,000 gph.
**WAVEMAKING DEVICES:** Tunze pulser.

### CONTROLLERS
**TEMPERATURE CONTROLS:** Aquarium Systems heater.
**FANS:** One muffin fan.

### FILTRATION
**SKIMMER:** Homemade downdraft, 5 feet tall, Iwaki 55 RLT.
**OZONIZER:** Coralife 50 mg.

OUT IN THE FLAT OPEN SPACES in the middle of Ohio one feels a long way from any reef, but tucked behind Kurt Loos's easy chair at the back of the family room is a jewel box of color. Although modest in size, this 90-gallon tank shines with all the hallmarks of healthy small-polyp stony corals: bright coloration, good polyp extension, and rapid growth. This tank is not meant to display every SPS coral available, but rather to allow a few vividly colored specimens to grow to their full potential. Kurt's turquoise and purple colony of *Acropora aculeus* and blue colony of *A. millepora* have not only kept their beautiful coloration, but have grown fast enough provide hundreds of fragments for friends and members of the Cleveland Saltwater Aquarium Society.

The system incorporates a number of unusual features that reflect Kurt's experience as a reefkeeper. The sump is housed in the basement and it is larger than the display tank itself, at 120 gallons, including three separate compartments. This remote placement of the sump takes advantage of the cool basement temperatures to moderate the water temperature without the need for a dedicated chiller or other means of cooling. One portion of the sump complex is primarily involved in filtration by means of Kurt's homemade downdraft skimmer, while the other is a refugium for coral fragments and other animals that may one day make it upstairs into the display tank. This greater volume of water relative to the bioload gives the system greater stability than the size of the display aquarium suggests.

The tank avoids the conventional coral wall aquascape. Kurt has arranged the live rock in the center of the tank so that it resembles a small coral mount.

*A beautiful sight with its polyps extended, this thriving blue gorgonian is an uncommon sight in home aquariums but it can be propagated by cutting.*

This allows the fish to swim realistically around the live rock and coral rather than simply back and forth along the front glass. The density of coral growth adds to the authenticity of the scene, and the robustness of the colonies is likely the result of two things: strong water motion and strong lighting. Kurt has more than 10 times the tank's volume running through the display every hour. This has kept the corals from growing in a weak and spindly fashion that is too often the case where water motion is feeble. The light reaching the corals is also intense, with the bulbs almost touching the surface of the water and most of the corals growing near the surface where they retain their coloration.

Not only has Kurt been able to maintain the bright coloration of his SPS corals, but he has also succeeded in keeping some difficult species for extended periods of time. These include *Australogyra* as well as *Goniopora stokesi* and *G. lobata*—a true testament to the success of a system, as experienced coral keepers can attest. Kurt also has several *Tridacna maxima* clams in this tank, and these compete with the corals in the brilliance of their colors.

The fishes in this tank are not the primary focal point, but Kurt has found success with several difficult species. His trio of anthias (*Pseudanthias squamipinnis*) have put on a particularly interesting show. It is well known that when several anthias are introduced into a captive system, the dominant or largest anthias will often change sex and become a male. Kurt purchased one male and two female anthias, and a year later the male had reversed itself to become a female so a male anthias was no longer present in the tank. This reversal has previously not been reported in the literature.

One of the pleasing overall aspects of this system is the fact that it is plumbed to keep equipment and noise down below in the basement. This keeps all the gear and occasional messes out of sight, and also greatly reduces the risk of spills or disruptions in the living area. The lack of clutter is an aesthetic plus, allowing the full beauty of the tank to be enjoyed without the distraction of pumps and skimmers and other paraphernalia. It is a system worthy of note for many reefkeepers, using smart design and good husbandry to create a coral reefscape that glows with color and life.

**CARBON:** 8 ounces; changed monthly.
**BIOLOGICAL FILTER:** Live rock.
**REFUGIUM:** 60 gallons. Set up as reef tank, attached to main system. Located in basement.
**LIVE ROCK IN DISPLAY TANK:** 150 lbs. Florida, Indo, Fiji.

## LIGHTING
**FLUORESCENT BULBS:** Four URI actinic 03 24 inch 60-watt VHO (replaced every 3 to 6 months).
**PHOTOPERIOD:** 12 hours.
**HEIGHT OF LIGHTS ABOVE WATER SURFACE:** Approximately 4 inches.
**METAL HALIDE BULBS:** One 400-watt Ultralux 6,500 K (replaced every 9 to 12 months).
**PHOTOPERIOD:** 10 hours.
**NATURAL LIGHT:** Minimal.
**LIGHTING CONTROLLER(S):** Timer.

## SYSTEM PARAMETERS & CHEMISTRY
**WATER TEMPERATURE:** 80 to 84°F
**PH:** 8.4.
**ALKALINITY:** 3-4 meq/L.
**CALCIUM:** 400 ppm.
**NITRATE:** ~0.
**PHOSPHATE:** ~0.
**RESINS OR DEVICES USED TO REDUCE NITRATE OR PHOSPHATE:** None.
**SALT USED:** Reef Crystals.
**WATER CHANGE SCHEDULE:** 10% per month.
**ADDITIVES OR SUPPLEMENTS USED:** Strontium Chloride: 50 ml per week, 20% Lugol's Solution: 20 drops per week, 100% Sera Marinvit Plus: 50 ml per week.
**MONITORING EQUIPMENT:** American Marine pH monitor.
**DOSING EQUIPMENT USED:** Peristaltic pump.
**MAINTENANCE SCHEDULE:** 4 hours per week (scrape algae, water change, basic checks).

## LIVESTOCK
**FISHES:** 10.
**STONY CORALS:** 20.
**SOFT CORALS:** 7.
**NOTEWORTHY SPECIMENS:** *Australogyra*, budding *Goniopora stokesi* and *G. lobata*.
**SPAWNING EVENTS:** *Pocillopora damicornis*.

## FEEDING
**REGIMEN FOR FISHES:** Frozen mixtures, various brands, *Spirulina* flake, and nori. Feed 1-2 times per day.
**REGIMEN FOR CORALS/INVERTS:** None.

## NOTES
**THINGS THE OWNER WOULD LIKE TO CHANGE:** Add Ca/$CO_2$ reactor.
**THINGS OWNER LIKES BEST ABOUT THIS SYSTEM:** Tank shape (30" X 30").
**THINGS TO DO DIFFERENTLY NEXT TIME:**
1. More open top (hard to clean sides).
2. Direct water flow from the front instead of back.
3. Simplify basement plumbing (3 sumps and refugium).

# EcoSystem Model Reef

*Filled with rapidly growing soft corals, this system helped inventor Leng Sy demonstrate the effectiveness of his mud refugium.*

## AQUARIUM PROFILE

**OWNER:** Leng Sy
  www.ecosystemaquarium.com.
**LOCATION:** Irvine, CA.
**DATE ESTABLISHED:** August 1995.
**DATE PHOTOGRAPHED:** September 1998.

### TANK
**CONFIGURATION:** Rectangular.
**DISPLAY TANK VOLUME:** 120 gallons.
**DISPLAY TANK DIMENSIONS:** 48" X 24" X
  24".
**DISPLAY TANK MATERIAL:** Acrylic.
**SUMP VOLUME:** 30 gallons.
**LOCATION:** Lab.

### CIRCULATION
**MAIN SYSTEM PUMP(S):** Little Giant 4 mdq-
  sx (1,350 gph).
**WATER RETURNS:** Two 1 inch returns at the
  top.
**ADDITIONAL PUMPS:** None.
**WAVEMAKING DEVICES:** None.

### CONTROLLERS
**TEMPERATURE CONTROLS:** Air-conditioned
  room.
**FANS:** None.
**CHILLER:** None.

AMONG THE REBELS WHO HAVE URGED MARINE AQUARISTS to abandon their protein skimmers is a southern California inventor named Leng Sy who, for years, has eagerly invited skeptics to visit and see living proof of his unorthodox approach to nutrient control. In simplest terms, Leng uses an external tank that serves as a refugium for a lush crop of *Caulerpa* that grows under 24-hour-a-day lighting. The bottom of the algae tank is covered with a bed of soil-like mud, and water from the display tank is constantly circulated through the refugium. After a number of years' experimentation in his former aquarium shop and development in his current office, Leng has built a thriving business selling his invention as the EcoSystem Aquarium.

While most of the tanks at his lab would be considered experimental, for testing new ideas and demonstrating the positive effects of his husbandry on the health of marine animals, at least two aquariums serve as obvious examples of unusually successful reef systems. One, the 120-gallon soft coral tank, shown here, is uniquely devoid of the usual technology of Berlin method aquarists. Rather than having the usual skimmer or other mechanical devices, the modest 30-gallon refugium passively provides a setting for fronds of *Caulerpa* to extract nutrients from the water. Leng's patented Miracle Mud provides a locus for nutrient breakdown as well as a place to house numerous microfauna.

The result is a biologically healthy system that is far more stable than most and that has some distinct advantages. Leng performs very little maintenance on this tank, with no skimmer to clean and adjust, no activated carbon to replace, and virtually no nuisance algae to remove. The *Caulerpa* in the sump appears to absorb enough nutrients to starve out any microalgae in the display tank. The polyp extension on the soft corals, especially the leather corals, is exceptional. This may be a function of the constant supply of microfauna being introduced into the display tank from the sump. *Xenia* colonies have flourished—without crashing—in this tank for five years and need to be constantly harvested. The fishes in this tank are not only healthy, they display the same vivid coloration they showed when they were first imported. Not only are these corals healthy, but they are constantly spreading or being propagated. All of the leather corals in the tank are the offspring of a single colony. The same is true of the *Xenia* that now literally cover every bare spot in the tank, including much of the back and side glass.

This tank has undergone several incarnations as Leng has formulated and reformulated his Miracle Mud as well as the means for filtering the tank using it. His diligence (not to mention his refusal to bow to the skepticism of certain other "experts") has paid off in a system that has stabilized at near-optimal levels. Despite never using carbon or a protein skimmer, his nutrient levels are quite low, with nitrate at 0.04 ppm and phosphate at 0.01 ppm. His simple supplementation schedule of dosing calcium and buffer daily keeps these levels at a stable 400 ppm and 3 meq, respectively. The only nutrient export that is done on this system is a weekly 3 to 4 gallon water change, amounting to just 2 to 3% of the water volume. The filtration system he has devised does the rest.

As for fishes, Leng has been keeping two of the more difficult species in the aquarium trade alive and healthy for the past two years. These fishes, a Moorish Idol (*Zanclus cornutus*) and a Regal Angelfish (*Pygoplites diacanthus*), have kept their bright coloration and have grown considerably. Even more remarkable is the fact that they are thriving on a diet consisting exclusively of

*Closeup of leather coral (Sarcophyton) polyps illustrates one curious benefit of the EcoSystem approach: corals seem to display exceptional daytime polyp extension.*

## FILTRATION
**SKIMMER:** None.
**MECHANICAL FILTER:** None.
**UV STERILIZER:** None.
**OZONIZER:** None.
**CARBON:** None.
**BIOLOGICAL FILTER:** EcoSystem external refugium containing Miracle Mud and *Caulerpa.*
**REFUGIUM:** Two-thirds of the sump contains the EcoSystem filter which has a 2 inch layer of mud above which is a bed of *Caulerpa* of various species. The mud is full of microfauna and boring organisms including mollusks and worms.
**LIVE ROCK IN DISPLAY TANK:** 180 lbs. of Indonesian rock.
**SAND/SUBSTRATE IN SUMP/REFUGIUM:** 2 inches of owner's patented Miracle Mud.
**JAUBERT PLENUM:** No.

## LIGHTING
**FLUORESCENT BULBS:** None.
**PHOTOPERIOD:** None.
**HOW OFTEN REPLACED:** None.
**METAL HALIDE BULBS:** Two 175-watt 10,000 K metal halides.
**PHOTOPERIOD:** 10-12 hours.
**HOW OFTEN REPLACED:** Yearly.
**HEIGHT OF LIGHTS ABOVE WATER SURFACE:** 10 inches.
**LIGHTING CONTROLLER(S):** Timers.

## SYSTEM PARAMETERS & CHEMISTRY
**WATER TEMPERATURE:** 76 to 80°F.
**SPECIFIC GRAVITY:** 1.020-1.024.
**PH:** 8.0-8.3.
**ALKALINITY:** 3 meq.
**CALCIUM:** 400.
**NITRATE:** 0.04.
**PHOSPHATE:** 0.01.
**RESINS OR DEVICES USED TO REDUCE NITRATE OR PHOSPHATE:** None.
**MUNICIPAL WATER SUPPLY:** Yes.
**REVERSE OSMOSIS:** SpectraPure 60 gpd.
**SALT USED:** Instant Ocean.
**WATER CHANGE SCHEDULE:** 3-4 gallons weekly.
**ADDITIVES OR SUPPLEMENTS USED:** Calcium hydroxide and buffer added daily.
**MONITORING EQUIPMENT:** None.
**DOSING EQUIPMENT USED:** None.
**MAINTENANCE SCHEDULE:** 15-30 minutes weekly.

## LIVESTOCK
**FISHES:** 10.
**STONY CORALS:** 3.
**SOFT CORALS:** 40.
**NOTEWORTHY SPECIMENS:** Almost all of the leather corals in the tank as well as the *Xenia* are from single colonies that have reproduced. Two-year-old Regal Angelfish and Moorish Idol.
**SPAWNING EVENTS:** The clownfishes spawn regularly.

## FEEDING
**REGIMEN FOR FISHES:** Flake food 2-4 times daily.
**REGIMEN FOR CORALS/INVERTS:** None.

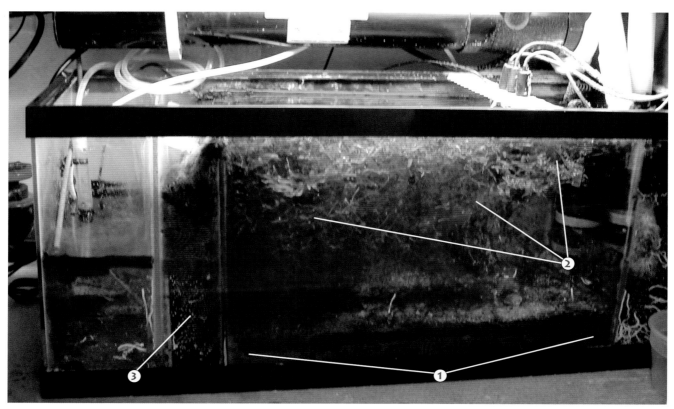

*The heart of an EcoSystem-type refugium is the main chamber with a bed of proprietary Miracle Mud (1) and a mass of green Caulerpa (2), that extracts nutrients from the water passing through. Bio-Balls (3) provide oxygenation and a bubble trap.*

## NOTES

**GOAL OF THIS SYSTEM:** To try and make the aquarium as simple and enjoyable as possible.

**THINGS THE OWNER WOULD LIKE TO CHANGE:** Better hood design to prevent fishes from jumping. The cooling system should be upgraded.

**THINGS OWNER LIKES BEST ABOUT THIS SYSTEM:** Simple to maintain with good coral stability.

**SPECIAL ABOUT THIS SYSTEM:** Amazing polyp extension and coral growth. Difficult-to-keep fishes are living for extended periods. Have been able to cure lateral-line disease.

**FAVORITE COMMENTS BY OTHERS:**
1. "How have you gotten your *Xenia* to grow so much without adding anything?"
2. "How do you keep your Moorish Idol so fat?"

**OVERALL POSITIVES:**
1. Simple and natural.
2. Low maintenance.
3. Overall healthy environment.

**OVERALL NEGATIVES (OR THINGS TO DO DIFFERENTLY NEXT TIME):**
1. This system takes a little longer to become established than does a traditional system.
2. Need to cure rock before placing it in system.

flake food—augmented by whatever natural food items they can forage in the aquarium. Leng asserts that his proprietary mud is slowly releasing key elements into the water, perhaps to be consumed by microalgae or microfauna that are then being consumed by the fishes and corals. Or it may be that since saltwater fish drink the water they are in that the nutrients from the mud are taken in that manner. He also claims that the EcoSystem method can prevent or even reverse head and lateral-line erosion (HLLE), a common malady of captive surgeonfishes.

After years of struggle, Leng is now seeing his idea gaining acceptance—and glowing testimonials—from a growing legion of aquarists willing to abandon their skimmers. Even if the full biological and chemical explanation of how this filtration method works is still shrouded in questions, the ever-enthusiastic Leng and his experimental aquariums are nonetheless an inspiration to many—a case of natural processes replacing mechanical devices.

# Coral Haven

*Ron Hunsiker's spectacular display of non-SPS corals includes a mammoth leather coral that tipped the scales at 120 pounds.*

CONSIDER RON HUNSIKER'S PROBLEM: a soft coral that has grown so large it had to be removed from his living room reef, a specimen that took two grown men to heft out of the aquarium, a homegrown *Sarcophyton* that tipped the scales at 120 pounds and measured almost 3 feet across!

While many contemporary reefkeepers are captivated by small-polyp stony corals, this aquarium is a demonstration of just how dazzling and successful an aquascape dominated by soft corals can be. In the hands of Ron Hunsiker, ordinary corals seem to reach extraordinary sizes resulting in a display that has made more than one fellow aquarist rethink his fixation with *Acropora* fragments.

Set up since 1991, this 265-gallon living room tank shows what can happen when a patient aquarist places a coral specimen in one place and leaves it alone to acclimate and grow. One example is a stunning hammer coral (*Euphyllia ancora*) that measures 18 inches by almost 30 inches. There is

## AQUARIUM PROFILE

**OWNER:** Ron Hunsiker
   www.bomani.com/saltwaterheaven.html.
**LOCATION:** Williamsport, PA.
**DATE ESTABLISHED:** March 1991.
**DATE PHOTOGRAPHED:** Various.
**PHOTOGRAPHER:** Keto Gyekis.

### TANK
**CONFIGURATION:** Rectangular.
**DISPLAY TANK VOLUME:** 265 gallons.
**DISPLAY TANK DIMENSIONS:** 7' X 2' X 31".
**DISPLAY TANK MATERIAL:** Glass.
**SUMP VOLUME:** 20 gallons.
**LOCATION (ROOM):** Living room.
**CABINETRY:** Oak stand.

### CIRCULATION
**MAIN SYSTEM PUMP:** Iwaki 70 RLT, 1,100 gph.

**WATER RETURNS:** 1-inch spray bar along bottom back of tank.
**ADDITIONAL PUMPS:** Two Iwaki 30 RLXT feeding 4 returns.
**WAVEMAKING DEVICES:** None.
**CONTROLLERS:** Redox controller for ozone.

## CONTROLLERS
**FANS:** Three 4-inch.
**HEATERS:** Two 200-watt.
**CHILLER:** Aquanetics.

## FILTRATION
**SKIMMER:** 3" X 4' tall homemade skimmer.
**MECHANICAL FILTER:** Quilted batting on overflows.
**UV STERILIZER:** 80-watt Rainbow.
**OZONIZER:** Sanders 100 mg.
**CARBON:** Four Chemi-pure bags changed every 3 months.
**BIOLOGICAL FILTER:** Live rock.
**LIVE ROCK IN DISPLAY TANK:** 390 lbs. from Fiji.
**SAND/SUBSTRATE IN DISPLAY:** Fiji live sand.

## LIGHTING
**FLUORESCENT BULBS:** Two VHO 6-inch daylight, four 40-watt actinic, two VHO 5-inch actinic, two 40-watt Ultralume.
**PHOTOPERIOD:** Approximately 12 hours with Ultralumes on for 4 hours.
**HOW OFTEN REPLACED:** 6 months.
**METAL HALIDE BULBS:** None.
**HEIGHT OF LIGHTS ABOVE WATER:** 4 inches.
**NATURAL LIGHT:** Morning sun in winter.
**LIGHTING CONTROLLER(S):** Timers.

## SYSTEM PARAMETERS & CHEMISTRY
**WATER TEMPERATURE:** 77 to 78°F.
**SPECIFIC GRAVITY:** 1.025.
**PH:** 8.1-8.5.
**ALKALINITY:** 15 dKH.
**CALCIUM:** 300.
**NITRATE:** 3 ppm.
**RESINS OR DEVICES USED TO REDUCE NITRATE OR PHOSPHATE:** Chemi-pure kept in powered Magnum canister filters with occasional use of Poly-Bio filters.

## WATER
**MUNICIPAL WATER SUPPLY:** Yes.
**REVERSE OSMOSIS:** SpectraPure.
**DEIONIZATION:** SpectraPure.
**SALT USED:** Reef Crystals.
**WATER CHANGE SCHEDULE:** 30 gallons per week.
**ADDITIVES OR SUPPLEMENTS USED:** Thiel Vital Gold 1 tbsp. every day, KSM Iodine 1 tbsp. every day, 6 ounces kH builder every week.
**MONITORING EQUIPMENT:** None.
**DOSING EQUIPMENT USED:** None.
**MAINTENANCE SCHEDULE:** Water change by pumping sump empty weekly, changing overflow sponges, and rinsing Chemi-pure in Magnum filters. Approximate time: 1 hour per week.

## LIVESTOCK
**FISHES:** 45.
**STONY CORALS:** 40.
**SOFT CORALS:** 41.

*An attention-grabbing elegance coral (Cataphyllia jardinei) had grown to more than a foot across at the time of this photograph.*

*This green-tipped hammer coral (Euphyllia ancora) measures 18 inches by 28 inches and is still growing under Ron's active care, including weekly water changes.*

virtually no indication within this tank that anything other than nature is present—no exposed surfaces or pieces of equipment are anywhere to be seen. Literally every space within the tank from the overflows to the tank's back and side glass walls are covered with life. Enlivening the massive display of corals and other inverts is a large fish population that swims through and around the corals. The impression is that someone has literally taken a small section from an actual reef and somehow managed to fit it into the confines of a glass box.

Ron's "secret" formula is simple: follow a few basic reefkeeping rules and perform a handful of routine maintenance tasks on a regular basis. The system is a standard Berlin method setup, kept perfectly tuned by Ron's adherence to performing all of the maintenance on a regular basis and keeping the tank's water parameters as stable as possible.

More than 390 pounds of live rock from Fiji serves as the biological filter. A custom-built protein skimmer is employed as the primary means of removing waste, assisted by quilted batting on the overflows for detritus

*Dwarfing a passing Lyretail Anthias, this domineering purple-tipped elegance coral is enough to cause some reef enthusiasts to rethink their single-minded pursuit of success with small-polyped stony corals. Corals are fed a mixed diet weekly.*

removal. In addition, ozone and bags of adsorbent Chemi-pure are used to keep the water crystal clear. Strong fluorescent light is one of the things to which Ron attributes the success of this tank. He has an array of ten fluorescent tubes over the tank, filling every available inch of the hood with mounted bulbs. These are on for approximately 12 hours per day. Nutrient levels are surprisingly low, considering the bioload in the tank, due in part to weekly 10% water changes. The calcium level is on the low side at only 300 ppm, while the alkalinity level is high at 15 dKH. Despite this, the growth of the corals has still been significant, even for the few stony corals that are included in this tank. The tank is supplemented daily with iodine and trace elements, and Ron believes that a small amount added daily is preferable to the usual once-a-week bolus dosing done in most tanks. The fishes require feeding three times per day, and the corals are fed once per week—just before the water change.

One measure of how well the animals within this tank have done is the centerpiece leather coral that measured 33 inches across when it was removed because it was threatening to dominate the entire aquascape. Similarly, *Xenia* needs to be harvested weekly as it covers the entire back and sidewalls of the tank as well as any live rock that is not covered with coral. The green-tipped hammer coral has grown to cover the bottom right quadrant of the tank, and the purple-tipped elegance coral has expanded to more than a foot across.

Just as impressive are the large number of fishes—anthias, tangs, damsels and angels—weaving between the corals and rock as they would on a natural reef. Their bright colors and full bellies are a testament to good husbandry, and the pair of Percula Clowns spawns every two weeks like clockwork. Amazingly, the system demands no more than an hour of care per week, and Ron says that the only problem now is that the tank is too small, with corals having literally overgrown every speck of available space.

**OTHER LIVESTOCK:** Shrimp, cucumbers, starfishes, and clams.
**NOTEWORTHY SPECIMENS:** Umbrella leather 33 inches across, hammer coral 18" X 28".
**SPAWNING EVENTS:** Percula Clownfish pair every 14 days.

**FEEDING**
**REGIMEN FOR FISHES:** 3 times per day, *Spirulina* with vitamins, homemade seafood, and brine shrimp.
**REGIMEN FOR CORALS/INVERTS:** Once per week before water change (phytoplankton, brine shrimp, and seafood mix).

**NOTES**
**THINGS THE OWNER WOULD LIKE TO CHANGE:** Bigger tank.
**SPECIAL ABOUT THIS SYSTEM:** Health and size of animals.
**FAVORITE COMMENTS BY OTHERS:**
1. "It's wild!"
2. "WOW!"
**OVERALL POSITIVES:**
1. Size of corals.
2. Health of fishes.

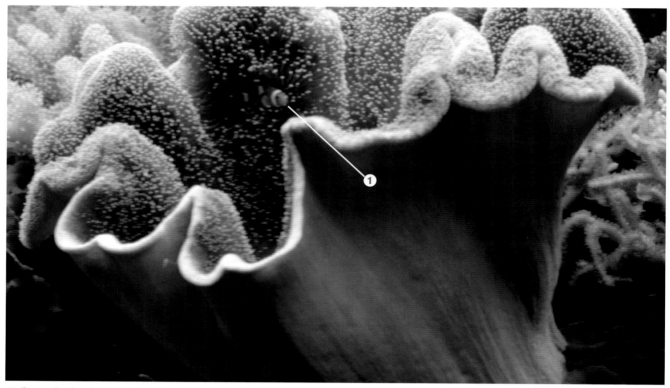

*Before it had to be moved, having totally outgrown its 265-gallon home, this leather coral (Sarcophyton) reached a diameter, when open, of 33 inches and needed two men to heft it out of the tank. Note clownfish (1) using the coral as a surrogate.*

*A Tomato Clownfish hovers near its anemone in the lower reaches of the tank. Elsewhere, a pair of smaller Percula Clownfish spawns regularly every two weeks. Note heavy encrustation of coralline algae in various hues of pink, lavender and purple (1).*

# Poseidon's Paradise

*Home of a spectacularly colorful coral collection, Tracy Gray's 200-gallon reef is housed in custom, owner-friendly cabinetry.*

**W**HEN UPGRADING A 100-GALLON dining room reef tank to 200-gallons, Tracy Gray set out to incorporate the best techniques of other aquarists—along with some unique ideas of his own. Unlike so many North American tanks that are tall and built on high stands, Tracy wanted his new display aquarium to be shallower and wider from front to back. He had the notion that the best view of a tank full of stony corals might actually be from the top, looking down at the water's surface, rather than peering in through the front glass. He intentionally built the cabinetry in which the tank is housed lower than normal to enhance top-down viewing. The results are considered by many to be nothing short of breathtaking—a world-class "look-down" view of captive-grown corals that rivals images from the healthiest of Indo-Pacific reefs.

Very little was left to chance when Tracy designed this system. Even his sump has been called better looking than most people's show tanks. A true testament to the success of this system is that one of the local fish stores, upon seeing Tracy's setup, redesigned the filtration on their store's marine tanks to mimic his system design. More than a few fellow hobbyists who have seen what Tracy has accomplished have gone home to start planning the reconfiguration of their own reef aquariums.

In truth, there is nothing totally new and different about Tracy's approach. The system is a hybrid, using typical Berlin methods with an efficient protein skimmer plus a sump that is divided in half to create a 30-gallon refugium area where *Caulerpa* is grown under lights. Filtration is provided by a custom-built

## AQUARIUM PROFILE

**OWNER & DESIGNER:** Tracy Gray
http://home.netcom.com/~mutagen/
pages/default.html.
**LOCATION:** Victorville, CA.
**DATE ESTABLISHED:** May 2000. Many specimens and rock transferred from a 3-year-old 100-gallon system.
**DATE PHOTOGRAPHED:** May 2001.

### TANK
**CONFIGURATION:** Rectangular.
**DISPLAY TANK VOLUME:** 200 gallons.
**DISPLAY TANK DIMENSIONS:** 60" X 36" X 24".
**DISPLAY TANK MATERIAL:** Glass.
**SUMP VOLUME:** 60 gallons, half is refugium.
**LOCATION:** Apartment dining room.

### CIRCULATION
**MAIN SYSTEM PUMP:** External pump is a Supreme Mag-Drive 1800.
**WATER RETURNS:** Water is returned through splitter box above and behind the tank. Water leaves the splitter box and returns at the back wall, one return on either side of the tank.
**ADDITIONAL PUMPS:** Internal circulation provided by two Supreme Mag-Drive 950s running two Ocean Current oscillators each (total of 4 oscillators).

*Acroporas galore populate Tracy's Berlin-plus-refugium reef, seen here looking down through the water's surface.*

*A plating Montipora sp. colony exhibits a highly sought-after color combination of bright green with purple rim.*

*Highly coveted Solomon Islands clove polyps (Clavularia sp.) glow blue and green under bright lighting.*

*A hard-to-keep Cleaner Wrasse (Labroides dimidiatus) grooms a Powder Blue Surgeonfish (Acanthurus leucosternon).*

*Designed for easy access, Tracy's system also allows viewing from three sides, as well as top-down, which gives an unusual perspective on the growing stony corals.*

6-foot aspirating skimmer, live rock, a deep sand bed, and the refugium.

A small amount of carbon is also used on a continuous basis to mitigate the suspected chemical warfare between the soft and stony corals in this system. The only other nutrient export is from the 10-gallon-per-week water change. Tracy reports that the *Caulerpa* in the refugium has not grown at a rate that has made harvest necessary, so nutrient export is minimal. Detritus is kept in suspension by the strong water movement within the tank. More than 3,700 gallons of water per hour are moved through the system by an external pump and two powerheads. The flow of water throughout the tank is made as random as possible by having each of the two powerheads connected to two oscillators.

While the exceptional health and color of the corals tends to grab the attention of most aquarists, Tracy's custom cabinetry adds to the beauty of the system. All of the equipment is tucked behind the tank, due to the low profile of the stand, which is just 18 inches high. This cabinet is open on the backside, allowing for easy access to the custom-built skimmer, calcium reactor, and sump/refugium. The refugium serves several purposes, housing macroalgae, breeding populations of microfauna, and holding fragments of corals as they are being grown out.

The canopy for the metal halide lamps is also designed to facilitate tank maintenance. The lights are supported in a canopy that covers the aquarium but leaves a 12 inch air gap between the top of the tank and the hood—a design that allows easy viewing of the water surface and excellent ventilation. The canopy can easily be lifted higher for easy access when doing maintenance, cutting coral fragments, or changing light bulbs. Tracy uses six metal halide

## CONTROLLERS

**FANS:** Two 4-inch fans over sump for cooling.
**HEATERS:** Two Ebo-Jagers (for occasional use only).
**CHILLER:** 1/3 hp chiller.

## FILTRATION

**SKIMMER:** Homemade unit 6 inch in diameter by 6 feet tall. Aspiration provided through suction side of a Supreme Mag-Drive 950 in a recirculation mode. Water throughput provided by Supreme Mag-Drive 350. Flow is from sump to sump.
**UV STERILIZER:** 40-watt system added after bleaching event during startup. No idea if it is helpful or not.
**CARBON:** One cup, changed and replaced every other week.
**BIOLOGICAL FILTER:** Live rock and 4-inch sand bed in tank.
**REFUGIUM:** 30 gallons of sump used as a refugium for *Caulerpa* and coral cuttings plus 4-inch sand bed. Splitter box for return water contains live rock with sponges. Approximately six species of *Caulerpa* and two or three of red algae are present. Feeding done on timer through splitter box so splitter box maintains a good population of mysid shrimp and "pods."
**LIVE ROCK IN DISPLAY TANK:** Combination of Fiji and homemade.
**SAND/SUBSTRATE IN DISPLAY:** 30% Fiji live sand with remainder aragonite to depth of 4 inches.
**SAND/SUBSTRATE IN SUMP/REFUGIUM:** Aragonite to depth of 4 inches.

## LIGHTING

**FLUORESCENT BULBS:** Power compact fluorescent over refugium on reverse daylight schedule. No fluorescents over main tank.
**PHOTOPERIOD:** 11 hours.
**HOW OFTEN REPLACED:** Once per year.
**METAL HALIDE BULBS:** Four 175-watt Ushio bulbs, one in each corner of the canopy pointing down and in toward the center. Two 400-watt 20,000 K bulbs are located in the center of canopy.
**PHOTOPERIOD:** 175s on for 11 hours, 400 watts on 5 hours with about 2 hours of overlap.
**HOW OFTEN REPLACED:** Replaced 175-watt bulbs at 9 months switching from 12,000 K to 10,000 K bulbs.
**HEIGHT OF LIGHTS ABOVE WATER SURFACE:** 12 inches.
**LIGHTING CONTROLLER(S):** Mechanical timers.

## SYSTEM PARAMETERS & CHEMISTRY

**WATER TEMPERATURE:** 78 to 79°F.
**SPECIFIC GRAVITY:** 1.026.
**PH:** 8.05-8.4 depending on time of day and evaporation rate.
**ALKALINITY:** 11 dKH.
**CALCIUM:** 450.
**NITRATE:** < 1 by LaMotte method.

**PHOSPHATE:** Nearly undetectable by LaMotte.

**OTHER READINGS:** Mg 1,350, but rarely checked.

**MUNICIPAL WATER SUPPLY:** Local water.

**REVERSE OSMOSIS:** Yes.

**DEIONIZATION:** Yes.

**SALT USED:** Instant Ocean and occasionally Kent.

**WATER CHANGE SCHEDULE:** 10 gallons per week or about 5%.

**ADDITIVES OR SUPPLEMENTS USED:** Reef Plus daily at 3 to 4 times recommended dosage. Soft corals seem to respond well. All makeup water is calcium hydroxide saturated.

**MAINTENANCE SCHEDULE:** Empty skimmer cup as needed. Scrape glass weekly. Fill makeup reservoir once per week. Remove *Dictyota* every three weeks. Occasionally kill a few *Aiptasia*, but they are not prolific in this tank. Totally clean skimmer twice a year.

## LIVESTOCK

**FISHES:** 4 tangs, 3 dwarf angels, two algae blennies, 5 anthias, one *Pseudochromis*, one Blackcap Basslet, one-year-old Cleaner Wrasse.

**STONY CORALS:** 30 to 40 SPS—some fragments and some large colonies.

**SOFT CORALS:** 100+ corallimorphs, some *Clavularia*, approximately 15 colonies of mixed zoanthids, a large stand of *Xenia*. One large green finger leather (*Sinularia*).

**NOTEWORTHY SPECIMENS:** Nothing special except a happy Powder Blue Tang.

**SPAWNING EVENTS:** None observed.

## FEEDING

**REGIMEN FOR FISHES:** Fishes are fed flake food twice per day from an automatic feeder, plus whatever the reef produces.

**REGIMEN FOR CORALS/INVERTS:** Corals are generally not fed, but the *Clavularia* seems to respond positively to target feeding of frozen phytoplankton.

## NOTES

**PROBLEMS OVERCOME WITH THIS SYSTEM:**

1. Salinity and pH stability have greatly improved by use of a 30-gallon reservoir for evaporation makeup. The reservoir gravity feeds the sump using a homemade float level controller. The float pinches silicon airline tubing closed to stop flow and opens when the sump level becomes low. In practice, a very constant level in the sump is maintained and a nice continuous feed of Kalkwasser is maintained.

2. The generally unsightly powerheads in the tank are hidden behind the overflow weir, which is not built into the side or back of the tank, but instead built about 4 inches off the back wall. The powerheads are still easily accessible when maintenance is required. The oscillators used for circulation are connected to the pumps with PVC, which is ugly

lamps for a total of 1,500 watts. The canopy is easily elevated after installation of new bulbs to prevent any bleaching of the corals due to changes in light intensity. The lights produce over 7 watts per gallon, enough to provide strong growth and bright coloration with no natural sunlight. However, Tracy says the high cost of electricity in California might motivate him to incorporate a light chimney into any future designs.

Of further note is Tracy's elegant solution to the constant problem of evaporation. In this case, intense lighting and dry desert air cause an evaporation rate of up to four gallons per day. Tracy's simple solution was to attach a float valve to a reservoir so that the water level would not vary by more than 1 to 2 liters per day. This markedly increased the stability of the tank's salinity. The novelty here is not in the fact that top-off water is supplied by gravity, but rather in the design of the top-off system. The valve simply uses silicone air-line tubing and a float attached to a lever that pinches the air-line tubing closed as the level rises. Tracy believes the slow, frequent addition of calcium-enriched water is a benefit to the health of the system.

All of this attention to detail has paid off in a tank that is beautiful to view from the customary front, but even more impressive from above. Looking down allows the observer to see the corals reflect light without a layer of glass to dim the colors, and the colonies are also seen arrayed without obstruction. The large colonies of pink *Seriatopora hystrix*, various *Montipora*s and *Acropora*s all literally glow when viewed from above. Tracy has even allowed and encouraged corallimorphs and zoanthids—banned by some other reefkeepers— to grow around the base of many of these corals so that there are no bare spots in the live rock. This further adds to the illusion that one is looking down on a robust patch of wild coral reef magically transported to an apartment dining room where all thought of dining was abandoned long ago.

*A coral-lover's dream: among too many others to note, red Montipora capricornis (1), green Acropora yongei (2), and purple Pocillopora damicornis (3),*

*Eye-level perspective of Tracy's California reef, with a complex aquascape of branching Acroporas (1), Montipora spumosa (2), deep purple bird's nest coral (Seriatopora hystrix) (3) and other corals reflected by the water's surface above.*

initially, but once covered in coralline algae the PVC is not so easily noticed. Having the overflow weir off the wall also gives four sides to the weir instead of the normal three. Increasing the overflow weir height has also decreased the level change in the tank when power fails, so the sump does not need to hold as much water in the case of a power outage.

3. The sump, refugium, skimmer, light ballasts, and makeup reservoir could not possibly fit below an 18-inch stand. They are all located behind the tank and enclosed in a bookshelf-like structure that also serves as a backdrop for the tank. Access to all the equipment is from the back of this structure.

**THINGS THE OWNER WOULD LIKE TO CHANGE:**

1. I plan to redesign the homemade calcium reactor to make it two-chambered rather than one. It will also be rectangular rather than circular to give more volume in the space where it will be positioned.

2. I would not allow *Dictyota* to become established. This would dramatically reduce the amount of work necessary to keep the tank thriving.

3. Would use only a few hermit crabs and preferably only scarlet hermits. The others roost in the SPS at night and sometimes do damage to the sensitive growing tips of the *Acropora*. They also leave feces in the low spots in *Montipora capricornis* and *Turbinaria*.

**OVERALL POSITIVES:**

1. Happy with the homemade float control system and the stability it provides. It is almost maintenance free and never plugs from the Kalkwasser going through it. Level control is superb from the valve.

2. The goals of easy access and top viewing with good light control were achieved.

3. Exceptional growth rates in *Montipora* sp. have been achieved, and good growth rates with some *Acropora*.

4. Fish are thriving with good coloration and no parasites.

**FAVORITE COMMENTS BY OTHERS:**

1. About the refugium/frag tank: "Your sump looks better than most people's show tank." This is an exaggeration to be sure, but I did appreciate the comment.

2. My favorite anecdote about the tank is that after the local aquarium store owners examined my system, they converted all their reef/salt water filtrations systems to mimic mine.

# A Pair of Reefs

*Looking for simplicity, Francesca Geertsma chose natural filtration for her 240-gallon (above) and 200-gallon linked reefs.*

## AQUARIUM PROFILE

**OWNER:** Francesca Geertsma.
**LOCATION:** Oakhurst, CA.
**DATE ESTABLISHED:** 200 gallon, April 1999;
  240 gallon, October 2000.
**DATE PHOTOGRAPHED:** June 2001.

### TANK

**DISPLAY TANKS VOLUME:** 200 gallons and
  240 gallons, glass.
**DISPLAY TANKS DIMENSIONS:** 200 gallon =
  8' X 2' X 20"; 240 gallon = 8' X 2' X 2'.
**SUMP VOLUME:** Photosynthetic Ecosystem
  refugiums, 55 and 40 gallons each;
  dark sump in basement (common), 150
  gallons.
**LOCATION:** Living room (both).
**CABINETRY/ARCHITECTURAL DETAILS:** Maple
  custom-built stands. Floor reinforced
  under each.

### CIRCULATION

**MAIN SYSTEM PUMP(S):** Dolphin Aqua Seas
  4700 X 2 (both in basement)/each with
  approx 3,000 gph outflow (taking head
  into account).
**WATER RETURNS:** 200 gallon = 2" X 1" PVC
  outlets; 240 gallon = 2 Sea Swirls.
**ADDITIONAL PUMPS:** 200 gallon = Rio 2100
  and Rio 2500; 240 gallon = Gemini and
  Penguin 1140.

IN HER POSITION as director of pediatric infectious disease in a California medical center, Dr. Francesca Geertsma is normally averse to taking chances. Surprisingly, in planning her two new reef aquariums, she was willing to try a relatively new and untested system for nutrient management and water-quality control. She chose the Ecosystem filtration method utilizing a refugium with a mud bottom with *Caulerpa* for several reasons.

Its simplicity appealed to her, as she has neither the time nor inclination to fiddle constantly with equipment. This system also does not require the addition of trace elements or additives, other than calcium, and she considered this a plus. Lastly, she felt that the refugium would help produce a supply of natural microfauna that would find its way into the tank. After running the system for approximately three years, she feels vindicated in her choice of a system that some still consider experimental at best.

The configuration of her 200- and 240-gallon tanks is also somewhat uncommon, in that a separate mud filter is employed for each tank, but these empty into a common sump. The presence of separate mud filters is the result of the two tanks having been set up at different times. The common sump was a way to increase the total tank volume by an additional 150 gallons. This sump also sits in a basement that is cooler than the rest of the house, a factor that assists the system chiller in operating with less energy use. (That the basement acts very efficiently to cool the tanks is indicated by the need to keep 2,000 watts of heaters present in the common sump for the cooler seasons of the year.)

A small colony of Acropora gemmifera (1) grows from its attachment point on the reef. Note purple-tipped colonies of Acropora secale (2) that have proliferated.

Stout branches on this healthy green Acropora formosa colony are indicative of the very good lighting, circulation, and chemical conditions in Francesca's reefs.

**WAVEMAKING DEVICES:** 200 gallon = one Osci-Wave with Rio 2100; 240 gallon = two 1-inch Sea Swirls.

**TEMPERATURE CONTROLS:** Cyclone drop-in chiller in common basement sump; 2,000 watts of heaters in common sump.

**FANS:** Two old computer fans in canopy of 200 gallon.

### FILTRATION

**CARBON:** Approx. 1 cup in canister filter attached to dark common sump.

**HOW OFTEN USED OR CHANGED:** Operated for 2 weeks every month.

**BIOLOGICAL FILTER:** Ecosystem mud filter with mixed *Caulerpa* bed and 24-hour light cycle.

**LIVE ROCK IN DISPLAY TANK:** In 200 gallon = 200 lbs. Tonga branch and Fiji. In 240 gallon = approx. 200 lbs. Tonga branch and Fiji.

**SAND/SUBSTRATE IN DISPLAY:** 200 gallon = bare; 240 gallon = approx. 1 cm aragonite.

**SAND/SUBSTRATE IN SUMP/REFUGIUM:** 1.5 inches Miracle Mud in photosynthetic sumps.

### LIGHTING

**FLUORESCENT BULBS:** In 200 gallon = two VHO 110 watt URI actinic; 240 gallon = two VHO 95 watt URI actinic; refugiums = 96 watt Sylvania power compact for each.

**PHOTOPERIOD:** 10 hours.

**HOW OFTEN REPLACED:** Once a year.

**METAL HALIDE BULBS:** 200 gallon = two 10,000 K 175 watt Red Sea; 240 gallon = two 10,000 K 400-watt Aqualine, three 20,000 K 400-watt Osram.

**PHOTOPERIOD:** 200 gallon = 8 hours; 240 gallon = 10,000 K's on 6 hours, 20,000 K's on 10 hours (since CA energy crisis).

**HOW OFTEN REPLACED:** Once per year.

### SYSTEM PARAMETERS & CHEMISTRY:

**WATER TEMPERATURE:** Winter 74 to 78°F; summer 76 to 80°F.

**SPECIFIC GRAVITY:** 1.023-1.025.

**PH:** 8.1-8.3.

**ALKALINITY:** 10-12 dKH.

**CALCIUM:** 425 ppm.

**RESINS OR DEVICES USED TO REDUCE NITRATE OR PHOSPHATE:** Knop PhosphatEx.

**WATER SUPPLY:** Well water.

**REVERSE OSMOSIS:** Yes.

**DEIONIZATION:** Yes.

**SALT USED:** Instant Ocean.

**WATER CHANGE SCHEDULE:** 30 gallons every 2 weeks.

**DOSING EQUIPMENT USED, IF ANY:** Pro Calcium calcium reactor.

**MAINTENANCE SCHEDULE:** 1 hour per week.

### LIVESTOCK

**FISHES:** Approx. 30 in both tanks.

**STONY CORALS:** 200 gallon = approx. 25; 240 gallon = approx. 65.

**SOFT CORALS:** 200 gallon = approx. 40; 240 gallon = none.

*The 200-gallon aquarium includes soft and stony corals dispersed over a rocky substrate with 200 pounds of Tonga branch and Fiji live rock. This tank empties into its own refugium, which then flows into a sump shared with the 240-gallon reef at right.*

**NOTEWORTHY SPECIMENS:** Asfur and Navarchus Angels kept for 7 years. Three-year-old rose anemone has undergone fission approx. 10 times.
**SPAWNING EVENTS:** Tomato Clownfish every 2 weeks; cleaner shrimp regularly.

**FEEDING**
**REGIMEN FOR FISHES:** Once per day. Nori and frozen raw seafood soaked in Selco.
**REGIMEN FOR CORALS/INVERTS:** None.

**NOTES**
**PROBLEMS OVERCOME WITH THIS SYSTEM:** I can finally grow SPS!
**THINGS THE OWNER WOULD LIKE TO CHANGE:** I hate my rock structures—they fall when I'm cleaning the tank.
**THINGS OWNER LIKES BEST ABOUT THIS SYSTEM:** Easy to maintain, polyp extension is awesome, and lots and lots of micro fauna and flora.
**WHAT IS SPECIAL ABOUT THIS SYSTEM:** Mud system for SPS somewhat unusual. Two level sump system is not typical either. I have common sump in basement to help with heat dissipation, so I only need one chiller.

This system does require the use of two large (3,000 gph) water pumps in the basement to provide adequate flow to the tanks. In addition, several powerheads are employed in each tank to generate current. The current created is random, due to the use of wavemaking and oscillating devices.

The two mud filters each contain approximately 1.5 inches of mud, with a healthy bed of *Caulerpa* that acts to keep the nitrate and phosphate levels low. Lighting is maintained over these beds 24 hours a day to maximize photosynthesis and to keep the *Caulerpa* from going into sexual production. As a precaution, a phosphate-lowering agent is also used. In order to keep any yellowing from occurring in the water, a small amount of carbon is employed for half of each month. Thirty gallons of water are changed every month, and no additional additives of any kind are added, while a calcium reactor maintains both the calcium and alkalinity levels.

Lighting is provided by a combination of fluorescent and metal halide lamps. The lamps chosen are 10,000 K and higher, and this has produced display tanks that are slightly bluer than most but still quite pleasing to view. The coloration of the corals has been maintained or even improved under these lamps and with this method of filtration.

Sixty-five coral colonies are housed in each tank with the 200-gallon tank housing both soft and stony corals, while the 240 houses stony corals

*Balancing corals and fishes, the 240-gallon reef has a spawning pair of Tomato Clowns (Amphiprion frenatus) (1), a large Asfur or Arabian Angel (Pomacanthus asfur), and a Bluegirdled or Navarchus Angel (Pomacanthus navarchus) (2).*

exclusively. It is interesting that without any protein skimming or ozone to break down the compounds produced by the soft corals, the stony corals have still thrived. A rose anemone in this system has split on 10 separate occasions, indicating the fundamental health of the system. Tomato Clownfish and cleaner shrimp also spawn on a regular basis. Dr. Geertsma has also been able to transfer two favorite large fishes, an Asfur Angel and a Navarchus Angel, to these tanks and has now successfully kept them both for over 7 years.

Despite the absence of skimmers, UV-sterilizers, ozonizers, and the like, this relatively uncomplicated system has paid off in the obvious health and coloration of the fishes and corals, as well as in the ease of upkeep. Dr. Geertsma says there is little she would change or improve, and the success of her tanks may be indicative of the increasing popularity of refugiums among aquarists seeking an improvement on the classic Berlin-method approach.

**FAVORITE COMMENTS BY OTHERS ABOUT THIS AQUARIUM:**
1. "It's the Oakhurst Aquarium!"
2. "You've come a long way."
3. "Are those things alive?"

**OVERALL POSITIVES:**
1. Ease of upkeep.
2. Health of corals and fishes.
3. Aesthetics of the tanks.

**OVERALL NEGATIVES (OR THINGS TO DO DIFFERENTLY NEXT TIME):**
1. Do a better job in securing my rockwork.
2. Build overflows and drains.
3. Find electronic ballast for metal halide that doesn't interfere with my controller.

# Beachside Reef

*Off to a flying start, Drew Wetherholt's 450-gallon Newport Beach reef combines good husbandry and excellent equipment.*

## AQUARIUM PROFILE

**OWNER:** Drew Wetherholt.
**LOCATION:** Newport Beach, CA.
**DATE ESTABLISHED:** February 2001.
**DATE PHOTOGRAPHED:** August 2001.

### TANK
**DISPLAY TANK VOLUME:** 450 gallons.
**DISPLAY TANK DIMENSIONS:** 120" X 30" X 30".
**DISPLAY TANK MATERIAL:** Glass with a central overflow.
**SUMP/REFUGIUM VOLUME:** Approximately 675 gallons.
**LOCATION (ROOM):** Family room.
**CABINETRY/ARCHITECTURAL DETAILS:** Free-standing; reinforced wood-frame/canopy stained deep blue.

### CIRCULATION
**MAIN SYSTEM PUMP(S):** Two main pumps Dolphin/4,800 gph; Sweetwater/4,400 gph.
**WATER RETURNS:** Two 2-inch returns, one in each back corner; seven 1-inch returns, 2 on each side, 3 on the back side.
**WAVEMAKING DEVICES:** 2-inch electric ball-valve controlled by a Tsunami Wavemaker. Creates a 10-minute surge in both directions across the tank.

I T IS GENERALLY BELIEVED that a reef tank needs a year or two to become established and to start living up to its potential. Drew Wetherholt, perhaps not knowing the rule, has shown that a new tank can look great in a relatively short time when set up properly. His 450-gallon tank, in a southern California beachside home, took little more than 6 months to look truly outstanding, and it is easy to see how he has achieved such exceptional results. He simply used the best technology available and implemented it properly from day one.

To begin with, he used a series of sumps and refugiums that contain 675 gallons of water—more than the display tank itself and a surefire method for increasing the water-quality stability of a system. The sump and refugium are separate, allowing the development of different habitats. For example, one is a refugium holding live sand and *Caulerpa* and various other animals that can thrive in isolation away from predatory fishes. In addition, instead of using a standard chiller, Drew designed a 250-gallon poly tank that is buried in the ground so that it acts like a heat exchanger. In this way, rather than having to use additional electricity, Drew is able to cool the tank naturally by pumping water through the cooling tank.

Because water movement is crucial for coral health, Drew uses two pumps circulating more than 9,000 gallons per hour throughout the tank. To spread and vary the currents and in an attempt to mimic natural water flow, he uses two 2-inch electronic ball valves powered by a wavemaker to change the direction of the flow within the tank every 10 minutes. This is done through

*Heavily stocked, Drew's system has live rock from Fiji, Tonga, Vanuatu, and Manono, live sand from Fiji, and dry sand from the Caribbean, more than 60 stony corals, 20-some soft corals, and 43 fishes, including many tangs and surgeonfishes.*

*A Powder Blue Surgeonfish (Acanthurus leucosternon) (1) swims over a bed of giant clams (Tridacna spp.) of different sizes clustered in an open spot on the reef floor.*

## CONTROLLERS

**CONTROLLERS:** Neptune AquaController.
**FANS:** Two 9-inch fans.
**HEATERS:** 200-watt Ebo-Jager heaters.
**CHILLER:** 250-gallon poly tank placed nearly 4 feet into the ground acting as a chiller. (The water table is high near the beach, allowing excess heat from the system to be tempered in the heat-exchange tank.)

## FILTRATION

**SKIMMER:** ETS 1400 Gemini.
**MECHANICAL FILTER:** Micron (50) filter bags where the water enters the sump.
**UV STERILIZER:** Aqua Ultraviolet 57 watt.
**OZONIZER:** Ozotech 250.
**CARBON:** Approximately 26 ounces every 3-4 weeks.
**BIOLOGICAL FILTER:** 75 and 125 gallons full of live rock with 4-inch sandbed.
**REFUGIUMS:** Two 75-gallon tanks (lighted) with 4-inch sandbeds full of macroalgae.
**LIVE ROCK IN DISPLAY TANK:** Fiji, Tonga, Vanuatu, Manono. Approximately 250 lbs. of each, many 24-30-inch pieces.
**LIVE ROCK IN SUMP:** Several hundred pounds.
**SAND IN DISPLAY:** 4-5 inches; 60% Fiji live, 40% Dry (CaribSea Select).
**SAND IN SUMP/REFUGIUM:** 4-5 inches sand both live and dry.

## LIGHTING

**FLUORESCENT BULBS:** Six 40-watt; on before and after metal halides come on/off; these lights act as dawn and dusk.

*Located in a tiled family room, the tank and lighting fixtures are enclosed in wooden cabinetry stained a deep blue. Mechanical systems are "remoted" to a well-thought-out enclosure attached to the back of the house (see right).*

**PHOTOPERIOD:** 1.5 hours each morning and evening.
**HOW OFTEN REPLACED:** Yearly.
**METAL HALIDE BULBS:** Three 400-watt Osram 20,000 K; two 400-watt German 10,000 K.
**PHOTOPERIOD:** 10 hours.
**HOW OFTEN REPLACED:** Yearly.
**HEIGHT OF LIGHTS ABOVE WATER SURFACE:** 12 inches (to be moved lower).
**LIGHTING CONTROLLER(S):** AquaController and separate timers.

## SYSTEM PARAMETERS & CHEMISTRY
**WATER TEMPERATURE:** 79 to 80.5°F.
**SPECIFIC GRAVITY:** Approximately 1.025.
**PH:** 8.3-8.4.
**ALKALINITY:** 10-12 dKH.
**CALCIUM:** Approx. 440-500 ppm Precision Marine Reactor and drip Kalkwasser.
**NITRATE:** Under 7 ppm.
**PHOSPHATE:** Extremely low; not detectable.
**MUNICIPAL WATER SUPPLY:** City of Newport Beach.
**REVERSE OSMOSIS:** Kent Marine.
**DEIONIZATION:** Kent Marine.
**SALT USED:** Kent Marine.
**WATER CHANGE SCHEDULE:** Approximately 50 gallons per week.

nine separate returns so that there is an almost constant change in the surge patterns coursing through the tank. The plumbing is sophisticated but not particularly hard to replicate, and the corals have responded with obvious health and growth.

Lighting is provided by 2,000 watts of metal halide lighting from both 10,000 and 20,000 K bulbs. In addition, standard fluorescent lighting is employed before and after the metal halide lamps come on to simulate dawn and dusk conditions so that the corals are not shocked by the light coming on or shutting down too abruptly.

The water is filtered by various means, including a large downdraft protein skimmer, activated carbon, ozone, and even micron filter bags to remove detritus mechanically. In addition, UV sterilization is employed to lower the risk of parasitic infections. To further expedite nutrient removal, 50 gallons of water are changed every week. Drew believes that aggressive nutrient removal is necessary to cope with the large number of fishes kept in the tank and the large amount of waste they produce. In addition, the corals are fed weekly as well. The no-holds-barred filtration plan keeps nutrient levels low (nitrate < 7ppm and phosphate undetectable), even though the tank has an extremely large bioload of both fishes and corals.

Approximately 80 colonies of coral, both soft and hard, are growing in this tank, along with more than 40 fishes. Interestingly, the fish population is

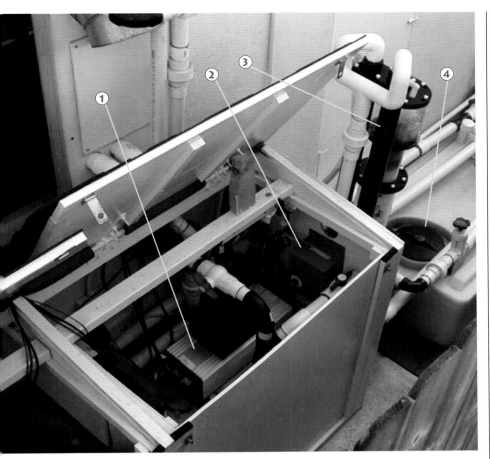

*Outdoor mechanical cluster includes lighting ballasts (1), ozonizer (2), skimmer (3), and 250-gallon inground poly sump (4) that moderates water temperatures.*

**ADDITIVES OR SUPPLEMENTS:** Kent Iodine and Kent Essential Elements; strontium.
**MONITORING EQUIPMENT:** AquaController (pH, Temp. ORP 390-450).
**DOSING EQUIPMENT USED:** Continuous drip Kalkwasser.
**MAINTENANCE SCHEDULE:** About 15-45 minutes per week. Almost everything, including water additions, is automated.

## LIVESTOCK

**FISHES:** Total 43, including 8 Yellow Tangs, 2 Sailfin Tangs, 1 Purple Tang, 1 Blue Tang, 1 Powderblue Tang, 1 Yelloweye Tang, 1 Naso Tang, 1 Orangeshoulder Tang, 3 unidentified tangs, 3 triggerfishes, 7 wrasses, 10 small Blue Green Chromis, 2 Percula Clowns, misc. gobies and damsels.
**STONY CORALS:** 60+ and various fragments.
**SOFT CORALS:** 20+.
**OTHER LIVESTOCK:** 1 rose anemone, 1 purple long-tentacle anemone, 8 *Tridacna* clams, several hundred snails, various starfishes.
**SPAWNING EVENTS:** The clowns have produced three batches of eggs.

## FEEDING

**REGIMEN FOR FISHES:** Twice per day. Several different brands of flake, frozen, fresh seafoods, fresh macroalgae (from sumps), and dried nori and various seaweeds using clips. Selcon and vitamins are also added to food every 3 days. Garlic powder is added to various foods and fed once a week.
**REGIMEN FOR CORALS/INVERTS:** Once a week using a homemade coral ration modeled after Eric Borneman's recipe from *Aquarium Corals* consisting of fresh seafoods, frozen foods, nori, and macroalgae, flake foods, and vitamins.

## NOTES

**THINGS THE OWNER WOULD LIKE TO CHANGE:**
1. Consider placing the overflow on the ends rather than the center.
2. If it fit through the door, I would have made the tank at least 36 inches wide rather than 30 inches.

**SPECIAL ABOUT THIS SYSTEM:**
1. The system mechanics are all outside of the house with a unique overflow resulting in an extremely quiet tank.
2. The 675-gallon sump system will allow for some coral farming.
3. The electric ball valve creates excellent surge throughout the display tank with no unsightly additional powerheads.
4. I am able to maintain a very stable, clean system, in part due to the volume of water and the ease of operation such as water changes (I can do a 165-gallon water change in less than 5 minutes).

**FAVORITE COMMENTS BY OTHERS:**
1. "Dude, that tank is totally Richter!" (As in earthquake ratings.)
2. "Mommy! Mommy! Look! It's SeaWorld!"
3. "I hope that thing never leaks."

dominated by many tangs and surgeonfishes representing different genera and species. By having so many tangs, Drew feels that any aggression is spread throughout this diverse group of potentially territorial fishes, and there is little aggression toward any one fish. Drew also keeps three triggerfish, and despite their reputation, he has not seen any aggression between them, or against the other fishes or even toward the snails or clams. There is no arguing that the presence of the many large, colorful fishes adds to the overall impact of this atypical reef display.

By avoiding all of the usual startup mistakes and by automating much of the technology, Drew has been able to keep this tank at its peak while spending less than 30 minutes per week on maintenance. He has also been able to reduce noise—one of the less desirable aspects of some large systems—by having most of the mechanics located outside of the house. This sense of quiet and peacefulness dramatically improves the serenity one feels when looking at this tank. There is none of the buzzing or droning of pumps and skimmers or fans that one encounters when viewing many large tanks. Despite its relative youth, this reef system shows that with good planning, the right equipment, and proper execution of known techniques, it is possible to have a beautiful and stable reef up and running in a relatively short period of time. Awestruck neighbors are already calling it "the Newport Aquarium."

# British Dream Reef

*Seasoned aquarists use superlatives to describe the dazzling 1,500-gallon reef that greets visitors to David Saxby's London flat.*

## AQUARIUM PROFILE

**OWNER & DESIGNER:** David Saxby
www.d-daquariumsolutions.com.
**LOCATION:** London, England.
**DATE ESTABLISHED:** 1995; current
configuration, September 1999.
**DATE PHOTOGRAPHED:** October 2000.

### TANK

**CONFIGURATION:** Somewhat L-shaped, with
sides being 3 m, 1.5 m, and 2 m
respectively and a height of 1.2 m.
**DISPLAY TANK VOLUME:** 1,500 gallons
(2,000 UK gallons), glass.
**SUMP VOLUME:** 1,500 gallons (2,000 UK
gallons).
**LOCATION:** Entry and living rooms.
**CABINETRY/ARCHITECTURAL DETAILS:**
Custom cabinetry.

### CIRCULATION

**MAIN SYSTEM PUMPS:** Eight 3,200 gph
pumps (9,000 L each) for circulation,
plus 3,000 gph moved through filtration.
**WATER RETURNS:** Movement is created by
the above pumps through a closed loop

To quote author Alf Nilsen, only one word adequately describes this aquarium: "magical." How else to describe a tank that almost literally draws you into a life-size portion of coral reef? Upon entering the beautifully decorated flat of David Saxby in London, England, even well-traveled, seasoned reef aquarists are struck with a sense of awe. Every point in the room offers something of visual interest, but it is the wall of bright light that immediately draws your attention. After being greeted by your jovial host, you really cannot believe what you are seeing. You sense that you have dived into a brilliantly lit portion of reef, but you are not getting wet. The thought that this may be the ultimate home marine aquarium is inescapable.

The tank itself contains approximately 1,500 gallons of water, connected to a sump of equal size. There are more than 90 colonies of magnificently hued and healthy stony corals, some 70 soft corals, as well as some 200-plus coral reef fishes. Even hard-to-keep sponges and gorgonians thrive in this tank. Once the visitor has recovered from the first impact of the sheer size and spectacle of the tank, closer inspection starts to reveal the true beauty of the system.

First, the technology behind a system of this size in a home may be unparalleled. A very elaborate IKS computer running two programs controls all pumps, lights, chillers, electronic ball valves, dosers, and other equipment. This computer allows for virtually every aspect of the tank to be monitored and controlled on a very precise basis. A tank this large and this heavily stocked with treasured corals and fishes will not tolerate a dramatic change in a crucial parameter, as this could trigger serious consequences.

There are separate systems for monitoring and controlling heat (4 chillers) and an ECO cooler, reactors to eliminate nitrite and phosphate, reactors to add calcium, and sophisticated controllers to maintain ever-changing water currents within the tank. The design of this system allows for an incredibly large and diverse group of both corals and fishes to be maintained in a tank that is virtually free of algae. Despite the large bioload, phosphates are virtually zero when read on a Merck professional test kit and nitrate ($NO_3$) is below 5 ppm, resulting in a tank that shows no traces of algae, even in its overflow boxes. Aggressive protein skimming no doubt plays a role, but David is also using a new phosphate-removing compound that has kept troublesome phosphate from acting as a fertilizer for algae, despite the heavy fish load and large amount of food introduced into the system three times daily.

David, who designed the system himself, has taken the concepts of good protein skimming, strong water movement and bright lighting to a new level. A converted Sander's Helgaland skimmer sits in an alcove beside the tank and, along with the two Deltec skimmers that sit next to the sump in a separate room 150 feet away, removes much of the nutrients before they have a chance to break down. To keep detritus and other waste products in suspension so that they can be removed, a multitude of pumps and powerheads move over 15,000 gallons of water every hour. Lastly, in an attempt to mimic the amount of light striking a reef, 5,000 watts of metal halide light, produced mostly by 1,000-watt metal halide lamps, illuminate the tank. This light is so intense that despite a water depth of 47 inches, the corals and other invertebrates at the bottom still receive enough light to grow as well as the corals at the surface.

The corals, sponges, and other invertebrates produce only part of the allure of this system. Schools of anthias and fairy wrasses also produce a more dramatic effect than is seen in most tanks. Literally hundreds of them move about the tank in unison behaving as they would on a reef face in any tropical sea. To keep them as fat and colorful as they are in the wild, David feeds them live river shrimp as well as frozen *Mysis* and copepods on a daily basis. The quantity of live river shrimp alone would foul most tanks, but is essential in keeping these high-energy planktivores alive and well.

Three mated pairs of clownfishes—Maroons, Saddlebacks, and Perculas—also live in the tank, with the Saddles laying eggs constantly. Each pair has its own territory. Similarly, several pairs of *Pseudochromis* sp. also live together throughout the tank. All of these showy fishes fill the tank with color and activity, but careful scrutiny also lets one discover tiny fish filling small niches within the tank. These include small pipefish, gobies, pseudochromids, and a pair of mandarinfish that dart about in small territories within the large reef structure.

These little biotopes within the tank make it virtually impossible to take in everything on a single visit. Depending on the time of day, different fishes and animals will either be out in the open or hiding. This further enhances the perception of observing a section of wild reef. The health and success of the plethora of corals and other inverts as well as the small fishes reveal just how magical a reef tank can be when meticulous attention to detail and patience are applied, as is the case with David Saxby.

system through holes in the bottom of the aquarium. Direction of flow is changed at intervals by the use of electronic ball valves so that 3 are on and 3 are off at any one time.

**ADDITIONAL PUMPS:** Three IKS pumps, 910 gph (3,500 L) with wave motion controlled by IKS computer.

**CONTROLLERS:** IKS computer.

**TEMPERATURE CONTROLS:** IKS computer.

**CHILLER(S):** 2 outdoor chillers, 2 under floor in courtyard, and a large Deltec Eco Cooler.

## FILTRATION

**SKIMMER:** Sander's Helgaland and Deltec. All heads self-cleaning with a Deltec skimmer cleaning system.

**OZONE:** Ozone used once a month for 12 hours. Redox never goes below 450.

**BIOLOGICAL FILTER:** Live rock; also run wet dry filter with sprinkler head to speed up oxidization and reduce $NO_2$.

**REFUGIUM:** Small 40-gallon refugium with *Caulerpa* in separate room attached to filtration system.

**LIVE ROCK IN DISPLAY TANK:** Approx. 1 ton of Red Sea live rock placed in tank within 24 hours of being removed from the sea (custom collected and imported by Saxby).

**SAND/SUBSTRATE IN DISPLAY:** Rowalith to a depth of 3-4 inches.

**SAND/SUBSTRATE IN SUMP/REFUGIUM:** Sugar sand 1 inch deep.

## LIGHTING

**METAL HALIDE BULBS:** Three 1,000-watt 10,000 K bulbs, one 1,000-watt 20,000 K, and one double 400-watt with 5,000 K and 20,000 K bulbs next to each other using a single reflector.

**PHOTOPERIOD:** Three 10,000 K bulbs on 8 hours; 20,000 K and double fixture on 10 hours.

**HOW OFTEN REPLACED:** Once every nine months.

**HEIGHT ABOVE WATER SURFACE:** 24 inches.

**LIGHTING CONTROLLER(S):** IKS computer.

## SYSTEM PARAMETERS & CHEMISTRY:

**WATER TEMPERATURE:** 76 to 78°F.

**SPECIFIC GRAVITY:** 1.26.

**PH:** 8.1-8.4.

**ALKALINITY:** 7.8.

**CALCIUM:** 470-480, using a fluidized calcium reactor. Also a calcium hydroxide stirrer is used and hydroxide is added five hours after the lights are switched off controlled by the IKS computer with a 7 minutes on and 3 minutes off drip via a float switch using RO water.

**NITRATE:** 5-10.

**NITRITE:** 0.02.

**PHOSPHATE:** Below 0.015. Phosphate remover is used on a constant basis to maintain phosphate levels below 0.015. 36 L of Rowaphos is replaced every 10-12 weeks to maintain this regime.

**OTHER READINGS:** Magnesium 1,100 mg/L. No denitrification used any longer.

*Built with a ton of Red Sea live rock that David had custom-collected and shipped immediately to London, no expense has been spared to give viewers a realistic encounter with a thriving, densely populated patch of Indo-Pacific coral reef.*

**WATER SOURCE:** Municipal Water Supply.
**REVERSE OSMOSIS:** Yes.
**DEIONIZATION:** No.
**SALT USED:** Instant Ocean initially, now Reef Crystals for make-up.
**WATER CHANGE SCHEDULE:** 10% every 4 weeks.
**ADDITIVES OR SUPPLEMENTS USED:** None.
**MONITORING EQUIPMENT:** IKS computer.
**DOSING EQUIPMENT:** Deltec hydroxide stirrer and Deltec calcium reactor and peristaltic dosing pump.
**MAINTENANCE SCHEDULE:** Glass cleaned every 2 days and daily maintenance of approximately 1 hour per day, including feeding fish and checking equipment.

## LIVESTOCK:

**FISHES:** 200.
**STONY CORALS:** 90.
**SOFT CORALS:** 70.
**NOTEWORTHY SPECIMENS:** Schools of anthias and fairy wrasses, 3 different mated pairs of clownfishes, each with its own anemone.
**SPAWNING EVENTS:** Yes, among corals and fishes.

## FEEDING:

**REGIMEN FOR FISHES:** 2-3 times per day, including live river shrimp, frozen Cyclops, brine shrimp, *Mysis*, romaine, and dry shrimp.
**REGIMEN FOR CORALS/INVERTS:** Marine Deluxe fed every few hours daily.

Product is kept cold via picnic cooler, stirred hourly, and dripped in hourly day and night.

## NOTES:

**PROBLEMS OVERCOME WITH THIS SYSTEM:**
1. Keeping the structure open enough to prevent dead spots (without water circulation) but with enough space to attach corals was difficult. To overcome this, *Acropora palmata* skeletons were used and attached to the live rock via ABS or PVC dowel rods.
2. A large amount of current flow was required and this demanded a large amount of overflow water. This could have produced a lot of noise, but the system relies on a siphoning approach where only small amounts of water flow over a few pipes, making the system almost silent.
3. The depth of the tank has made it difficult to place corals. To overcome this, the owner has designed several pieces of custom equipment that allow him to work in a tank of this depth and he glues all rocks and corals when placing them in the tank.

**THINGS THE OWNER WOULD LIKE TO CHANGE:** Make the tank even deeper.

**WHAT IS SPECIAL ABOUT THIS SYSTEM:**
1. Despite its large size it is still relatively easy to maintain.
2. You can watch the tank for hours and always find something new going on

somewhere in the tank.
3. The fishes and corals have maintained the vibrancy and health shown when they were first added to the tank.

**FAVORITE COMMENTS BY OTHERS ABOUT THIS AQUARIUM:**
1. "You could spend all day looking at it and never grow tired or bored."
2. "This is the tank I want to have when I grow up."
3. "It is like having an actual reef in your house."

**OVERALL POSITIVES:**
1. There is virtually no hair or microalgae anywhere in this tank including the overflows. Even though it is obviously thriving, David is always tinkering to make it even better.
2. The polyps on the SPS corals are virtually always expanded fully as are the soft coral colonies.
3. The anthias and fairy wrasses exhibit natural shoaling behavior that is quite impressive.

**OVERALL NEGATIVES (OR THINGS TO DO DIFFERENTLY NEXT TIME):**
1. Probably would add fewer coral specimens as the growth has been phenomenal and cutting and pruning have been necessary.
2. Fewer species and more specimens might have made the tank easier to care for long term.

The tank's 1.2 meter (47-inch) depth provides room for corals, such as the purple gorgonian that dominates this section of the aquascape, to develop into stately specimens. Lighting consists of four 1,000-watt and two 400-watt metal halide bulbs.

*Fishes, including numerous Blue Green Chromis and anthias of various species, display the same fascinating social behaviors seen in the wild. They are fed two or three times each day with a variety of live, frozen, and dry foods and romaine lettuce.*

*Numerous tangs of various species graze the reef, acting as one of many biocontrols of algal growth in the system.*

*Fishes and corals benefit from constant, powerful currents produced by eight dedicated 3,200 gph circulation pumps.*

*Festooned with a diversity of reef organisms, David's reef provides endless hours of viewing experiences for observers.*

*To control phosphate, a potent foe of corals, David uses a new German adsorbent medium called Rowaphos.*

# Other Microcosm/TFH Series Titles

**THE NEW MARINE AQUARIUM**
by Michael S. Paletta
*Step-by-Step Setup & Stocking Guide*

**NATURAL REEF AQUARIUMS**
by John H. Tullock
*Simplified Approaches to Creating Living Saltwater Microcosms*

**THE CONSCIENTIOUS MARINE AQUARIST**
by Robert M. Fenner
*A Commonsense Handbook for Successful Saltwater Hobbyists*

**CLOWNFISHES**
by Joyce D. Wilkerson
*A Guide to Their Captive Care, Breeding & Natural History*

**REEF FISHES, VOLUME 1**
by Scott W. Michael
*A Guide to Their Identification, Behavior, and Captive Care*

**POCKETEXPERT GUIDE: MARINE FISHES**
by Scott W. Michael
*500+ Essential-to-Know Aquarium Species*

**CORALS**
by Eric H. Borneman
*Selection, Husbandry, and Natural History*

**AQUARIUM SHARKS & RAYS**
by Scott W. Michael
*An Essential Guide to Their Selection, Keeping, and Natural History*

**REEF LIFE**
by Denise Nielsen Tackett & Larry Tackett
*Natural History and Behaviors of Marine Fishes and Invertebrates*

**REEF SECRETS**
by Alf Jacob Nilsen & Svein A. Fosså
*Starting Right, Selecting Fishes & Invertebrates, Advanced Biotope Techniques*

# Index of Tanks, Owners & Designers

# About the Author

**M**ICHAEL S. PALETTA is the author of *The New Marine Aquarium* (Microcosm/TFH) and one of North America's leading amateur saltwater aquarists. He has been involved in the design and setup of more than 60 marine aquariums, including the 4,500-gallon reef exhibit at the National Aquarium in Baltimore and a number of reef systems at the Pittsburgh Zoo Aquarium. He has a degree in biology, psychology, and chemistry from Dickinson College and holds a master's degree in psycho-pharmacology from Yale University. He works in the field of biotechnology and lives with his family near Pittsburgh, Pennsylvania, where he has several marine systems, including a 550-gallon reef aquarium and a 300-gallon coral-propagation tank (see page 8).